FASHION IN LATE OTTOMAN ISTANBUL

Dress cultures

Series Editors: Reina Lewis & Elizabeth Wilson

Advisory Board: Christopher Breward, Hazel Clark, Joanne Entwistle, Caroline Evans, Susan Kaiser, Angela McRobbie, Hiroshi Narumi, Peter McNeil, Özlem Sandikci, Arti Sandhu, Simona Segre Reinach

Dress Cultures aims to foster innovative theoretical and methodological frameworks to understand how and why we dress, exploring the connections between clothing, commerce and creativity in global contexts.

Published:

Delft Blue to Denim Blue: Contemporary Dutch Fashion
Edited by Anneke Smelik

Dressing for Austerity: Aspiration, Leisure and Fashion in Postwar Britain
By Geraldine Biddle-Perry

Experimental Fashion: Performance Art, Carnival and the Grotesque Body
By Francesca Granata

Fashion in European Art: Dress and Identity, Politics and the Body, 1775–1925
Edited by Justine De Young

Fashion in Multiple Chinas: Chinese Styles in the Transglobal Landscape
Edited by Wessie Ling and Simona Segre Reinach

Modest Fashion: Styling Bodies, Mediating Faith
Edited by Reina Lewis

Niche Fashion Magazines: Changing the Shape of Fashion
By Ane Lynge-Jorlen

Styling South Asian Youth Cultures: Fashion, Media and Society
Edited by Lipi Begum, Rohit K. Dasgupta and Reina Lewis

Thinking Through Fashion: A Guide to Key Theorists
Edited by Agnès Rocamora and Anneke Smelik

Veiling in Fashion: Space and the Hijab in Minority Communities
By Anna-Mari Almila

Wearing the Cheongsam: Dress and Culture in a Chinese Diaspora
By Cheryl Sim

Fashioning Indie: Popular Fashion, Music and Gender in the Twenty-First Century
By Rachel Lifter

Revisiting the Gaze: The Fashioned Body and the Politics of Looking
Edited by Morna Laing and Jacki Willson

Reading Marie Al-Khazen's Photographs: Gender, Photography, Mandate Lebanon
By Yasmine Nachabe Taan

Wearing the Niqab: Muslim Women in the UK and the US
By Anna Piela

Fashioning the Modern Middle East: Gender, Body, and Nation
Edited by Reina Lewis and Yasmine Nachabe Taan

Fashion, Performance, & Performativity: The Complex Spaces of Fashion
Edited by Andrea Kollnitz and Marco Pecorari

Silhouettes of the Soul: Meditations on Fashion, Religion, and Subjectivity
Edited by Otto von Busch and Jeanine Viau

Fashion in Altermodern China
By Feng Jie

Fashioning the Afropolis: Histories, Materialities and Aesthetic Practices
Edited by Kerstin Pinther, Kristin Kastner and Basile Ndjio

Jews in Suits: Men's Dress in Vienna, 1890–1938
By Jonathan C. Kaplan-Wajselbaum

Fashion Before Plus-Size: Bodies, Bias, and the Birth of an Industry
By Lauren Downing Peters

The Women of 'Little Paris': Women's Fashion in Interwar Bucharest
By Sonia-Doris Andraș

Dress in Auschwitz: Clothing and Survival in the Holocaust
By Sofia Pantouvaki

Fashion in Late Ottoman Istanbul: Photography and Identity in a Global City
By Nancy Micklewright

Reina Lewis: Reina.Lewis@fashion.arts.ac.uk
Elizabeth Wilson: Elizabethwilson.auth@gmail.com

FASHION IN LATE OTTOMAN ISTANBUL

PHOTOGRAPHY AND IDENTITY IN A GLOBAL CITY

Nancy Micklewright

BLOOMSBURY VISUAL ARTS
LONDON • NEW YORK • OXFORD • NEW DELHI • SYDNEY

BLOOMSBURY VISUAL ARTS
Bloomsbury Publishing Plc, 50 Bedford Square, London, WC1B 3DP, UK
Bloomsbury Publishing Inc, 1359 Broadway, New York, NY 10018, USA
Bloomsbury Publishing Ireland, 29 Earlsfort Terrace, Dublin 2, D02 AY28, Ireland

BLOOMSBURY, BLOOMSBURY VISUAL ARTS and the Diana logo are
trademarks of Bloomsbury Publishing Plc

First published in Great Britain 2026

Cover image: Untitled, Ali Sami, *c.* 1906. Los Angeles, Pierre de Gigord
collection of photographs of the Ottoman Empire and the Republic of Turkey.
Getty Research Institute, 96.R.14 (CD_002)

A catalogue record for this book is available from the British Library.

A catalog record for this book is available from the Library of Congress.

ISBN: HB: 978-1-3504-5485-9
         PB: 978-1-3504-5484-2
         ePDF: 978-1-3504-5486-6
         eBook: 978-1-3504-5487-3

Typeset by Integra Software Services Pvt.Ltd.
Printed and bound in India

For product-safety–related questions, contact productsafety@bloomsbury.com.

To find out more about our authors and books, visit www.bloomsbury.com
and sign up for our newsletters.

To Nurhan Atasoy and Renata Holod
with heartfelt thanks for your encouragement
and inspiration over the years

CONTENTS

ACKNOWLEDGMENTS

I am beginning these acknowledgments in Istanbul almost exactly forty years after I arrived in the city with a Fulbright grant to conduct dissertation research on women's dress in Ottoman Istanbul. That dissertation was completed in 1986, when gender studies in Middle East studies and Islamic art history was in its infancy, dress history was at a low ebb, the photo history of the Middle East was just developing, and we were decades away from the material turn in art history. Returning to the subject now, a wealth of new scholarship provides a context for my original research, and I bring my own work in Ottoman photo history over the past decades to bear on the project. This book is thus a very different undertaking than the dissertation, and it has been an exciting project during and post-pandemic.

The list of people and institutions to whom I am indebted for help along the way on a project that has encompassed nearly my entire professional career could be a book in its own right; some names inevitably will be omitted. As I was starting out, I was incredibly fortunate to have a stellar group of strong, accomplished women as mentors who shaped my thinking in important ways: Nurhan Atasoy, Esin Atıl, Patricia Baker, Renata Holod, Louise Mackie, Yedida Stillman, and Irene Winter. Renata Holod and Nurhan Atasoy especially have been lifelong advisers and supporters of this work. I dedicate the book to them.

My research has been supported by a variety of institutions and fellowships over the years, all critically important to advancing a project of extended humanities research. Without such funding this kind of work would be impossible. The University of Pennsylvania, University of Michigan, University of Victoria, American Research Institute in Turkey (ARIT), Institute of Turkish Studies, the Metropolitan Museum of Art, the National Gallery of Art, the Pasold Research Trust, the Social Science Research Council, the Social Science and Humanities Research Council of Canada, and the Turkish-American Fulbright Commission have all provided research support. In addition, innumerable smaller travel grants to participate in international conferences and seminars have helped advance my work, but it is impossible to list them all here.

A great deal of the research for this project was completed while I was Andrew W. Mellon Research Fellow in the Islamic Art Department of the Metropolitan Museum of Art. The fellowship took place during the pandemic but despite the challenges of those times, my time at the Met was exceptionally positive and productive. The Academic and Professional Programs team at that time (Marcie Karp, senior managing educator; William Gassaway, associate educator; and Zamara Choudhary, program coordinator) did everything possible to mitigate the limitations that the pandemic imposed. The staff of Watson Library was heroic in providing books and obtaining interlibrary loan material, despite working offsite and with the library closed for much of the fellowship year. I am especially indebted to Jessica Ranne Cardona and Robyn Fleming, who managed offsite book delivery and ILL requests respectively. This book would not have happened without their help. Navina Najat Haidar, Nasser Sabah al-Ahmad al-Sabah Curator in Charge of Islamic Art; and Maryam Ekhtiar, Patti Cadby Birch Curator, my hosts in the Islamic Art department, made me feel at home and facilitated my research. The opportunity to study the Ottoman costume collection with Deniz Beyazit, associate curator in the Islamic art department, has enhanced this project in innumerable ways. I am so grateful for her skilled examination and insights into the material, as well as her careful reading of chapter drafts.

The Ottoman costume collection is housed in the Antonio Ratti Textile Study Center in the Metropolitan Museum. Eva Labson, general manager of collections; Eva DeAngelis-Glasser, assistant administrator; and Elena Kanagy-Loux, former collections specialist, facilitated more virtual and in-person viewings than I had ever expected, allowing me the luxury of examining key objects repeatedly. The conversations in our viewing sessions, whether online or in person, with Elena Deniz and Julia Carlson, associate conservator in Textile Conservation, created a very rich collaborative learning experience. I thank them all for their time and willingness to think with me about the objects we saw together. The magnificent collections of the Metropolitan Museum's Costume Institute hold many garments relevant to this project, and I appreciate the opportunity to have examined some of them with Marci Morimoto.

Chapter 7 was researched and mostly written while I was Paul Mellon Visiting Senior Fellow at the Center for Advanced Study in the Visual Arts at the National Gallery of Art in Washington, D.C. I thank Dean Steven Nelson and Associate Dean Peter Lukehart for making my stay at the Center possible and all the Center staff for their kind assistance. Salima Appiah-Duffell, resource sharing librarian, did a stellar job of acquiring an enormous number of interlibrary loan titles, for which I am extremely appreciative. Smithsonian colleagues at the National Museum of African American History and Culture graciously shared their knowledge of the costume collection with me and facilitated access to the collection. I am deeply indebted to Elaine Nichols, Mary Elliott, and Candace Oubre.

In support of research for Chapter 8, I was fortunate to receive a grant from the Pasold Research Trust, which funded collection visits to Killerton House, Blaise House, the National Museums of Scotland, and the British Library. I am grateful to the curators of those fascinating institutions, Shelley Tobin, Catherine Littlejohns, Friedericke Voigt, and Michael Erdman, respectively, for their kind assistance during my visits. The Pasold also generously provided funds for image acquisition, for which I am very thankful.

Turkish colleagues and institutions have been welcoming and supportive of my work. The spectacular costume collection at the Sadberk Hanım Museum is foundational for this project, and it was a rare treat to spend time in the beautiful buildings and gardens of the museum. Sevgi Gönül, Sadberk Hanım's daughter and chair of the Museum Executive Committee until her death in 2003, welcomed me to the museum in 1982, just two years after it opened. More recently, senior curator Lâle Görünür, whose scholarship is so important for this topic, has generously shared her knowledge and insights into the collection. Her superb team (Samed Ercan, Havva Furat Ay, Elif Kıran, and Büşra Balçık) endured hours of costume viewing, random observations, and meandering but extremely valuable discussions over the course of my visits. Makbule Merve Uca has been a stimulating interlocutor for many aspects of this work. Museum director Hülya Bilgi was gracious and welcoming. My visits there have been a highlight of this project.

I was fortunate to be able to study the Esat Uluumay Costume Collection in the 1980s, an opportunity facilitated by Nurhan Atasoy, and to revisit the collection in the Uluumay Osmanlı Halk Kıyafetleri ve Takılar Müzesi in Bursa more recently. The Yapı Kredi collection is also an important resource, and I thank former director Nihat Tekdemir and Derya Sayın for providing access to their collection. Hülya Tezcan, former textile curator at the Topkapı Saray Museum, now professor at Nişantaşı University, was extremely helpful in my initial research, and her numerous publications have been essential. The ANAMED Library has been an outstanding research haven, and I am grateful for the hospitality I received there over the years. Similarly, the Istanbul Research Institute includes an impressive library. I thank Furkan Sevim, head librarian at the Istanbul Research Institute; and Scott Redford, formerly director at ANAMED, now Nasser D. Khalili Professor of Islamic Art and Archaeology at SOAS, University of London, for their help in facilitating my research at their respective institutions. Barış Kıbrıs has been very generous in providing access to works in the Pera Museum collections, for which I am most appreciative.

My initial research on Ottoman women's dress took me into the emerging field of Middle East photo history, a subject area that has occupied me for some years. I was very fortunate to work adjacent to one of the great research collections of historical photographs, the Special Collections of the Getty Research Institute (GRI), while I was at the Getty Foundation. Deborah Marrow, the late director of the Getty Foundation;

and Joan Weinstein, current director, kindly supported my research into the Pierre de Gigord Collection of Photographs of the Ottoman Empire and Republican Turkey. The GRI Special Collections staff, too many to name individually, have been extraordinarily helpful and responsive over the years, and I am in their debt.

Foundational work for this project took place during the nearly ten years I spent at the Smithsonian's Freer and Sackler Galleries (now the National Museum of Asian Art). Julian Raby, the museum director for most of that time (now director emeritus), was a generous supporter of my research and a stimulating interlocutor. My immediate team (Louise Caldi, Wen Li, Sana Mirza, Zeynep Simavi, Lizzie Stein, and Kailin Weng) were wonderful colleagues. We were lucky to do meaningful work together and to learn so much from each other.

The friends and colleagues I have found over the years have shaped my work in so many ways. With apologies to those I have no doubt left off this list, a million thanks to Özge Calafato, Ashley Dimmig, Elizabeth Frierson, Luke Gartlan, Christiane Gruber, Esther Juhasz, Reina Lewis, Mika Natif, Erin Hyde Nolan, Therese O'Malley, Amanda Phillips, Mary Roberts, D. Fairchild Ruggles, Ünver Rüstem, Joan Schwartz, Mira Schwerda, Jonathan Square, Susan Taylor, Fran Terpak, and Sandra Williams. My fellow participants in the 2009–2010 Orientalist photography workshop at the Getty Research Institute, Esra Akcan, Sussan Babaie, Ali Behdad, Hanna Feldman, Anne Lacoste, Rob Linrothe, and Mary Roberts, were inspiring. Likewise, I thank Kaitlin Booher, Alexandra Chiriac, Kaelyn Garcia, Marina Kliger, Louisa Raitt, Alexis Romano, and Courtney Wilder, members of the 2020–2021 fashion study group of Met fellows, for their insights, stimulating conversation, and occasional in-person meetings over the course of our pandemic fellowship year.

I am very grateful to Reina Lewis and Elizabeth Wilson, coeditors of the series Dress Cultures, for including the book in their series. Frances Arnold, Martin Thompson, and other members of the Bloomsbury team have been a real pleasure to work with, and I appreciate their expert guidance. Colleagues in Türkiye, Great Britain, and the United States, too many to thank individually, have helped with image acquisition, greatly easing what is often a difficult process. The project has benefited immeasurably from the comments of the anonymous peer reviewers and the generous readers who have reviewed all or part of the manuscript along the way.

My husband, Stephen Berer, and I each visited Istanbul in the early 1970s. Our first trip together was in 1977, and we have visited many times since, first when I was a student and later with our two sons, Josh and Caleb Berer, who have each established their own relationship with the city and its culture. Istanbul holds an important place in our family's collective memories, all the more so now that Rachael Strecher and Maddie and Jonah Becker have joined our travels.

On those early summer trips to Istanbul, Lee and Ute Striker were unfailingly kind and welcoming to indigent and slightly confused student travelers. Tony Greenwood, former director of ARIT, was always helpful, as has been his successor, Zeynep Simavi. Closer to home, but crucially important, Avinoam Shalem and Elisabeth Rochau-Shalem offered us their beautiful New York apartment, which was the site of much of the writing of this book. It is impossible to imagine a more serene and hospitable place to work.

Finally, my family have lived with the photographs and clothing of Ottoman women for decades. I thank them for their patience and for their help with so many aspects of the production of this book.

CHAPTER 1
SETTING THE STAGE

In the second half of the nineteenth century the women of Istanbul transformed their appearance, adopting European dress and new modes of self-fashioning, including photographs. I want to understand this dramatic sartorial change, embraced by women across ethnic, religious, and class boundaries, because it provides new insights into women's lives in a period of fast-paced social and political upheaval. Insisting on including a wider demographic than the elite women who are typically the focus of fashion histories means looking beyond or looking differently at the sources that can be deployed for the project. It requires asking different questions of the objects on which fashion histories are generally based and looking further afield to find examples of clothing worn by women who have been overlooked. While not ignoring the important information provided by traditional archival sources, primacy must be given to material more intimately connected with the women themselves, especially their clothing, as well as sources where their voices come through more directly. And when there is virtually nothing to go on, in this case concerning the dress of enslaved women in Ottoman Istanbul, I will need to look elsewhere for methodologies and examples.

In the following pages I lay out the questions that have shaped my project: my methodological concerns, how I understand fashion, and the place of photography in this endeavor. Then I introduce two complex aspects of nineteenth-century Istanbul essential for understanding its fashion history: its diverse population and the linked social institutions of enslavement and the harem. The last section of this chapter lays out the structure of the book.

Ottoman dress has received a certain amount of attention from different sets of scholars. For historians, dress is important as an indicator of state ideas about civic identity and control of expensive commodities such as fur and gold thread. Fashion historians are interested in individual garments, particularly those associated with the court and royal elite. The few, and crucially important, book-length studies of Ottoman dress focus on specific museum collections, as in the work of Nurhan Atasoy, Lale Görüner, and Hülya Tezcan; present a survey of costume across the Middle East (Jennifer Scarce); examine the impact of Ottoman dress on European fashion (Charlotte Jirousek, Adam Geczy); or consider dress for its economic and political importance (Suraiya Faroqhi and Christoph Neuman).[1]

I take a different approach. Setting out to examine a striking transformation in women's dress and in their lives, the project rests on the detailed analysis of a corpus of surviving garments. I tell the stories of the garment's production and later lives by bringing a maker's perspective to the study of the garments, and aspects of the garments themselves—tailoring, fabric choice, embroidery style, and alterations. I use close readings of the photographic record—that is, how women presented themselves for the camera and the clothing they chose for those sittings—to reveal the way they used both photography and dress to fashion new identities. The insights that I glean from this primary source material—the dresses and photographs—are examined together with a range of written sources, including those by Ottoman women. Although some aspects of this fashion transformation are relatively well-known, this project presents the first comprehensive account of Istanbul's fashion economy and of the process by which new styles were adopted. As part of my commitment to foreground fashion histories often marginalized or un-noted, I insert enslaved and working women back into the fashion history of Ottoman Istanbul.

The question of sources and methodology is central: how can the disparate kinds of information that remain be used to create a coherent narrative of dress history? And what about the impact of absence, whether of garment or voice? Reconstructing the dress practices of women who do not appear regularly in most sources demands different research methods. Unpicking, to use a sewing term, the complex process of fashion change through close attention to garments and fashion production can identify how women of different classes, religions, races, and ethnicities used dress and photography to fashion their identities in times of social change and political conflict. This book adds to a body of work that gives voice to Ottoman women in ways not possible in earlier times and demonstrates what can be learned through training a decentering lens on fashion history.

Decentering Fashion History

What does it mean to decenter or decolonize fashion history? In 2020 the editors of the journal *October* sent out a query, "What does the term *decolonize* mean to you in your work in activism, criticism, art, and/or scholarship?". The fall 2020 issue of the journal devoted 122 pages to the replies they received from thirty-eight academics, curators, writers, and others. A full account of their replies is beyond what I can undertake here, but I do want to highlight one sentence from Steven Nelson's essay. His pithy one-page list of seventeen statements all began, "To decolonize means" and included this: "To decolonize means analyzing Dakar in ways that don't center Paris" (Nelson 2020: 89).

This statement caught my eye because in the realm of fashion history, Paris has always been at the center. Fashion history, or costume studies, as the discipline was known in earlier times, grew up in Europe and generally concerned itself with the dress of the elite in the fashion centers of Europe and America. The clothing worn by people living in the rest of the world was understood to be "traditional" and unchanging or perhaps changing at a very slow pace. The study of such dress was most often the purview of anthropologists and ethnographers or researchers who wished to study the dress histories of their own cultures. However, over the past few decades, the dress of people from regions outside Europe and the United States has drawn more scholarly attention. The boundaries separating the ways in which dress practices in different parts of the world are studied have themselves been the focus of conversation and have begun to break down. Collaborative projects such as the Fashion and Race Database, founded in 2017, and the international Research Collective for Decoloniality and Fashion based in the Netherlands, as well as the work of individual researchers, are changing the parameters of the discipline.

Dress, costume, clothing, fashion: these are all words that can be used to describe what people wear. For some they might all mean essentially the same thing; others may understand them to have close but different meanings. Here, I am generally using them as defined in the 2015 edited volume *Dress History, New Directions in Theory and Practice*, drawing on earlier foundational work by Susan Kaiser and Joanne Eicher:

> "dress" is an inclusive term, encompassing all adornment and modification of the body. "Clothing" refers to the objects that are worn. "Costume" commonly applies to dress worn for specific events, although this word is also used to describe clothing associated with a particular group of people or historical period.... 'Fashion implies change in dress over time, as well as the "dynamic social *process*" by which this change occurs.'
>
> *(Nicklas and Pollen 2015: 2)*

Similarly, dress history and fashion history or fashion studies are close in meaning but can refer to slightly different things. Dress history is a term that has come into use in recent decades, although "history" suggests a reliance on archival materials (documents) that is not necessarily an accurate reflection of the primary sources that are often at the center of dress histories. Fashion history and fashion studies suggest a focus on change in dress practices. In this project, because I am looking at a period in the dress history of Ottoman women in which fashion was an emerging concern, I use dress history and fashion history interchangeably.

In their 2021 book *Rethinking Fashion Globalization*, editors Cheang, de Greef, and Takagi describe the project to decolonize fashion studies like this:

> The need for decolonial fashion publications, platforms and projects is urgent. These forums aim to critique the denial and erasure of other fashion systems, recover genealogies and trajectories of clothing and fashion without automatically tracing back to Western fashion systems and histories, and contribute to decolonizing fashion media and fashion curricula.
>
> *(Cheang, de Greef, and Takagi 2021: 6)*

In this project, I have placed the women of Ottoman Istanbul at the center of the conversation. They are not a monolithic group, but one that is multiethnic, multi-confessional (meaning following different religious traditions), and highly varied in economic status. But despite this diversity, in the period this book covers they were all confronting a rapidly changing political, economic, and social landscape that affected them in myriad ways, both small and large. Dress was one way of exploring change and finding their places in the evolving society in which they lived.

Although not discounting the importance of Paris or London in influencing some fashion choices made in Istanbul, I am more interested in understanding the extent to which those influences were shaped by local dress traditions, by cultural norms, and by individual choices. Fashion histories tend to privilege the clothing of the elite—and in the Ottoman case, the Muslim elite—but here I am also looking beyond the wealthy women of the city at the dress practices of working women, enslaved and formerly enslaved women. To the extent that the sources allow, I want to tease out the distinctions between how Ottoman Muslim, Greek, Armenian, and Jewish women engaged with the new fashions and the degree to which their fashion conversations overlapped.

Fashion

For most of Ottoman history, women are understood through the legal documents that marked their lives: inheritance registers, wills, and deeds of charitable foundations, as well as through their images. Virtually none of these were created by the women themselves.[2] Moving beyond documents, the material objects that shaped their daily lives provide other impressions of Ottoman women; and of these, clothing is the most personal and ubiquitous. Dress is practical and performative at the same time, signaling economic status, ethnic or religious identity, and personal taste, to name only the most obvious of these signifiers. Looks, to use a contemporary fashion term, can be ephemeral (such as a bridal outfit), aspirational, can serve as a disguise, or can be imposed by others. Untangling the individual fashion choices that women made is complex and often speculative, but if done thoughtfully it can provide insights into the subjectivity of the women we encounter in other sources.

Figure 1.1 *Bindallı* dress, full-length view and neck detail, late nineteenth century. Büyükdere, Courtesy of the Vehbi Koç Foundation, Sadberk Hanım Museum, SHM 2599-K.17a.

Using individual garments to reconstruct aspects of women's lives places a heavy burden of interpretation on pieces of clothing that may have had more quotidian roles in their own day. But often the garment tells its own story, if it is examined closely and carefully: what I call bringing a maker's perspective to the study of a piece.[3]

The *bindallı* dress illustrated in Figure.1.1 provides an instructive case in point. Associated with weddings and worn by women from different ethnic and religious groups across the Ottoman empire beginning in the mid-nineteenth century, *bindallı* dresses are discussed in detail in Chapter 4. My initial survey of the dress focused on its physical characteristics: construction, fabric, trim, embroidery, and so on. A closer look reveals important details (gathers at each side, addition of new trim, evidence of wear, and amateur repairs), telling us that the dress, made at a very high standard, was treasured enough to be passed down, altered, retrimmed, and mended, albeit with a certain lack of skill, until it entered the collection of a museum.[4]

Can the dress tell us anything about the woman for whom it was originally made? The dress has a matching jacket, also beautifully embroidered and well made. The hip-length jacket was a wardrobe component of traditional Ottoman dress and continued to be worn as European fashions were adopted, often by older or more conservative dressers (Görünür 2010: 53). Yet the owner of the dress, either the original owner or one shortly thereafter, was interested in exploring new fashion modes and added the waist gathers to the dress, suggesting an interest in contemporary fashion perhaps at odds with the dress/jacket ensemble.

Through their sartorial choices women could express multiple, even conflicting identities. Clothing can disclose a great deal about the women who wore it, if it is studied carefully. It asks us to think about the everyday lives of people who are far removed from our own day-to-day realities and to consider their fashion selections to understand how they saw themselves and how they wanted others to see them.

Photography

Like fashion, photography, invented in 1839, is a means of self-representation, of presenting an identity, experimental, aspirational, or familiar, through an image. For Ottoman women, photography allowed them to establish their own subjectivity and begin to control their representations. Two distinct photographic processes, Fox Talbot's calotype and Daguerre's daguerreotype, were announced simultaneously in England and Paris; the new medium found a ready home in Istanbul. The invention was announced in the official Ottoman newspaper, *Takvim I Vekayi*, in October 1839, and Daguerre's instruction manual was translated into Turkish in 1841 (Öztuncay 2015: 69). European daguerreotypists were working in Istanbul by the 1840s, and while some made their photographs and returned home, others remained in the city and opened studios. One of the best known of these was the Naya studio in Beyoğlu, operated by two Italian brothers beginning in 1845 (ibid.: 72). From there, the number of photographic studios in the city increased, run at first by foreigners, but as the technology changed and became more widely available, local residents began opening studios as well. Although photography is sometimes regarded as a foreign technology imported into the Ottoman empire, I find this an inaccurate way of understanding photo history globally. Photography was a new invention in Europe, and it spread around the globe very quickly, moving throughout Europe and to the eastern cities of the United States and Canada in 1839–1840, but also reaching Iran, Japan, Brazil, and Mexico in the 1840s, for example. New photographic technologies and modifications were developed everywhere and communicated internationally through scientific journals and photographic competitions. The photographers based in Istanbul were part of this international community of practitioners, and residents of the city became accustomed to the new image economy along with photographic consumers elsewhere.[5]

By the last decades of the nineteenth century, Istanbul had dozens of photographic studios (Öztuncay 2003). Many were concentrated in areas frequented by foreigners, but they could be found in neighborhoods across the city. The studios addressed multiple audiences: tourists, foreign residents in the city, locals, and the court, for both official projects and portrait photography. "Harem women" were a popular subject for commercial images directed at tourists,[6] but local women also visited the photographers' studios to have their portraits made. As early as 1847 a French couple who had a studio in Beyoğlu advertised that Muslim women could have their photos taken by Madam Loran Astras (Öztuncay 2015: 72). Decades later, two advertisements in the women's magazine *Kadınlar Dünyası* indicate the extent to which women could engage with the new medium. In 1913, Mademoiselle Servanis advertised her women-only photo studio, mentioning also that her staff could take photographs in their client's home if desired (Başcı 2004: 48). The next year, two German ladies placed an ad for their photography lessons, as well as notifying readers that they were seeking an investment partner for their business, preferably a woman, Muslim or non-Muslim (ibid.: 41). As photography became easier to do, and more people learned the technology (it was taught in the Imperial School of Engineering beginning in the 1860s), amateur photographers began turning their cameras on their own families, providing another means by which women could perform their identities in a photograph.

Most historic photographs survive with incomplete information concerning the circumstances in which they were made. Subject, date, photographer, and purpose of the image are rarely all in place for a single image. For photographs of Ottoman women in particular, distinguishing between the portrait of an individual and a type ("*Femme Turque*" being among the most popular) complicates the utility of these images for understanding fashion and women's self-representation.

The two photographs in Figure 1.2 demonstrate the challenges involved. They share similarities in composition and general subject, but the identity of the woman in the image on the left and the circumstances of the photograph are unknown, whereas both the subject and the photographer of the right image have been identified. More subjective interpretation, based primarily on details of the composition and comparison with other photographs, is required to decide whether the photograph on the left might have been a portrait of a specific person or a type and thus assess its utility as a source of fashion information. It is impossible to know the exact circumstances of the photograph on the right, which is an image of his wife, Refia Hanım, by the photographer Ali Sami—perhaps the photographer wanted to try out a new piece of equipment, perhaps a birthday or other special occasion, or perhaps to document a new dress. In any case, it is a fine record of a dress worn by someone whose social circumstances are well known, a relatively rare and very useful visual document.

Ottoman photo history has been a serious area of study for about forty years; and in that time, the corpus of available images has grown beyond what the early researchers could have imagined. New research centers, founded in Türkiye and elsewhere, have assembled important collections of photographs, many of which are completely digitized. Private collections have been amassed, well published in some cases. Institutional collections in universities, museums, and governments have been pulled together from photographs scattered across departments, which have then been rehoused and often digitized. Some of these collections reflect the particular interest of their owners or the institutional priorities of the collecting organization, whereas others are more disparate, even random in their contents. The exact size of the Ottoman photo corpus is unknowable, and it is impossible for any single person to see everything. As is the case with much humanities research, the task of the researcher thus becomes one of combing through as many different collections, websites, publications, and photo archives as possible to understand the universe of images that are relevant for the topic at hand.

For this project, the thirty-five photographs included in the book come from eighteen different collections (research centers, museums, government institutions, private collections), but dozens more collections were

Figure 1.2a *Femme turque*, Pascal Sébah date unknown. Los Angeles, Pierre de Gigord collection of photographs of the Ottoman Empire and the Republic of Turkey. Series III. Loose and mounted photographs, Getty Research Institute Special Collections, 96.R.14 (PF.B3.076)

Figure 1.2b *Refia Hanım*, Ali Sami Aközer, 1890s. Istanbul, Salt Research Center, Engin Özendes Collection, EOZH0078.

consulted. Choosing the photos to be illustrated involved a certain amount of "cherry-picking," to use Edhem Eldem's term (Eldem 2017: 47), a process that is inevitable given the practical limits of illustrations and page numbers, a challenge I have discussed elsewhere (Micklewright 2011). Over the next chapters, I look further into the ways in which fashion and photography were each a part of how the Ottoman women of Istanbul shaped new, modern identities in the late nineteenth and early twentieth centuries.

Who Lived in Ottoman Istanbul

Ottoman Istanbul, the capital of the empire for 470 years, is generally described, in its own time and today, as having been an international city, a melting pot, a multiethnic and multi-confessional society, a chaotic mix of people and languages, to name only a few descriptors. These adjectives may have been more or less accurate, but they don't necessarily help in understanding what was certainly a complex city whose inhabitants may have claimed membership in multiple subgroups within Ottoman society. Given that a key function of dress is signaling identity with specific groups, it is important to spend some time untangling the very complex strands of affiliation that Ottoman women may have claimed in the long nineteenth century, a period stretching from the late eighteenth century through the first two decades of the twentieth.

In the Ottoman context, subjects of the empire could be classified in a number of different categories, each of which had significant social, economic, and legal consequences for its members—for example, Muslim versus non-Muslim, women versus men, and enslaved versus free.[7] Considering the descriptive social terms more familiar to us today, the Ottoman divisions mirror but also crisscross religion, ethnicity, class, and gender. In the period I consider here, ethnicity, class, and religious identities operated somewhat differently than they do today; in general, religious identity was the primary determinant in women's dress decisions. Ottoman subjects were Muslims, Christians, and Jews, but these large designations encompassed a very wide range of practice and doctrinal distinction; within each of these three religious groups, individuals were organized around their own mosques, churches, and synagogues. In terms of ethnicity (sharing a common ancestry, language, or culture), Arabs, Turks, Armenians, Kurds, people from the Caucasus, Greeks, Albanians, Roma, people from the Balkans, and more were all part of the Empire, and many found their way to Istanbul.

A fourth important population category, specific to the Ottomans, was *askeri* versus *reaya*. The *askeri* were the men, overwhelmingly Muslim, who were the officials of the court, and the military and religious institutions, along with their dependents. *Reaya*, on the other hand, worked in a variety of nongovernmental arenas, as farmers, long-distance traders, merchants, craftsmen, manufacturers, and others. *Askeri* received significant social and economic benefits (particularly tax exemptions and higher social status), but the *reaya* could also accumulate substantial wealth, employ servants, and acquire other trappings of high economic status. A certain amount of fluidity existed between these two groups.

The *askeri* were Muslim but could be of different ethnicities: from the Balkans, the Arab lands, or Turkish Anatolia. *Reaya* varied in their ethnicity and religion (Muslim, Christian, or Jewish). *Askeri* and *reaya* alike could have been wealthy, struggling to make ends meet, or anything in between. The enslaved were not initially Muslim, were of many ethnicities, and were found at all points of the economic scale. Gender, of course, cuts across all the previous categories and is a key determinant of life experience.[8]

Threading through all these and often connecting people across those larger categories were language and occupation.[9] Many people living in Istanbul (*İstanbullus*), men and women, spoke more than one language, or at least understood more than one. Turkish, French, and Armenian were the most commonly spoken, but the fact that Istanbul newspapers were published in at least nine languages in the last decades of the nineteenth century indicates the richness of the linguistic community (Yanatma 2015: 30). Likewise, people from different ethnic and religious groups shared occupations, workplaces, and in some cases worked for each other.

Population numbers from Istanbul in the nineteenth century provide a clear idea of the diversity of the city's residents in terms of religion, ethnicity, occupation, and place of residence.[10] Over the course of the century, the Ottoman government collected census figures, which have been preserved in various archives and were published in contemporary publications. Collecting and recording practices were not without their issues, but nonetheless, the data is important.[11] The figures concerning religion and ethnicity are of particular interest here because those were the most important from the point of view of fashion choices. A key source is the 1885 census, which shows that the population of Istanbul was 44.06 percent Muslim, 17.48 Greek Orthodox, 17.12 percent Armenian Gregorian, 5.08 percent Jewish, 1.88 percent other Christians, and 14.74 foreigners (Shaw 1979: 266–67). Counted among the foreigners were the Levantines, people of European origin who had settled in Istanbul and other coastal cities for trading purposes. Many of them were descendants of people who had been living in Istanbul for decades, if not centuries, complicating the idea of "foreign." The overall population of greater Istanbul at this time was about 874,000, a number that rose to more than a million at the turn of the century (Duben and Behar 1991: 25). At mid-century, the population had been about 430,000 (Shaw 1977: 241), so the increase in the size of the city in the second half of the century was significant.

Over these years, both the size of the population and its makeup were affected by various political and economic circumstances. Large numbers of Europeans traveled through Istanbul during the Crimean War (1853–1856); some lived in the city only for those years and others remained permanently, starting businesses of different kinds. Following the Crimean War, enhanced business opportunities and increases in diplomatic contacts resulted in a growth in the numbers of foreigners in the city. According to Çelik, about 100,000 foreigners arrived between 1840 and 1900 to take advantage of business opportunities (1986: 38). Both the Russo-Turkish war of 1877–1878 and the Balkan Wars of 1912–1913 led to large numbers of Muslim refugees in the city, some of whom became permanent residents. At the same time, the numbers of Armenians in Istanbul declined following the massacres of Armenians in Anatolia in the mid-1890s, part of an overall decline in the percentage of non-Muslims in Istanbul from the period 1885 to 1914 (Duben and Behar ibid.; Bastermajian 2017: 186, 257).

These statistics provide important information for understanding the social dynamics of the city and the impact on fashion. For one thing, for most of the century the Muslim population of the city was in the minority. All the women of the city were constrained by imperial policy in how they dressed while in public view, but women of the various Christian communities, Jewish women, and foreign women would have been self-fashioning within different social and cultural regimes than their Muslim counterparts. They would have interacted differently with new fashion trends as they became aware of them.

Second, although people tended to live in neighborhoods largely organized by religion, centered around a place of worship (Duben and Behar ibid.: 28–31), their work, education, shopping, recreational activities, and more brought them into contact with *İstanbullus* of different religious and ethnic groups. As social actors, residents of Istanbul belonged to many overlapping communities; the boundaries between those communities were not rigid. Finally, the constant influx of people into the city brought new ideas, new technologies and products, and new social expectations. Many came as refugees or as enterprising businessmen/women from Europe, adding to the push in Istanbul toward adopting the goods and social customs of Europe. To cite one example, Duben and Behar write,

> Though they were a minority in numbers, the character of turn-of-the-century Istanbul was very much set by those originating in the European, especially the Balkan provinces, and also by many coming from Russia. These people were trendsetters in westernization, in politics and in family life-styles. Many of them came from the middle social strata in the provinces, and they moved quickly into the Hamidian bureaucratic cadres that had expanded very rapidly from the 1880s on, into the newly established professional schools, and for the first time into commercial enterprises that had traditionally been the province of non-Muslims.
>
> *(24–25)*

Untangling the specific impact the population of Istanbul—it's rapid expansion in the second half of the century, the complex, intersecting communal identities, and influx of foreigners—had on women's dress practices is challenging but key to understanding the fashion transformations that took place.

Istanbul as a Global City

The constant flux in size and makeup of the city's population and increasing numbers of foreign residents over the course of the nineteenth century were one important component of the far-reaching changes that took place in Istanbul. From the beginning of the Tanzimat period of reform and modernization in 1839 through the end of the nineteenth century, the population, architecture, transportation infrastructure, and commercial institutions changed dramatically. In these decades, Istanbul was an imperial capital, but it was also a port city, a commercial city, and most relevant to this project, a cosmopolitan city.

In this context, cosmopolitanism describes an organic mixing through interaction of the diverse, heterogeneous populations of the city, as opposed to a defining of boundaries among different groups, equating difference with mutual exclusion (paraphrased from Keydar 2019: 26). In her 2015 book, *Istanbul Exchanges. Ottomans, Orientalists, and Nineteenth Century Visual Culture*, Mary Roberts says this about such mixing:

> The exchanges and alliances that Muslim and non-Muslim Ottomans formed with European artists
> and patrons in this context are significant, I argue, precisely because of the diversity of cultural
> backgrounds and motivations that coalesced during this period. In a context where rigid distinctions
> between East and West were defied, identity became multivalent.

(4)

Roberts is speaking specifically about the art world of nineteenth-century Istanbul, but similar claims can be made about fashion. Women of different nationalities, ethnicities, classes, and religions came together around dress and fashion, sharing expertise, resources, and beliefs. Their sharing was intimate: clothes were fitted on the body, tried on in each other's company, and passed from one to another. Moreover, in a time of complex, ongoing social change, dress was perhaps the easiest and most obvious way to claim an identity or to experiment with a new one. The fashion transformations I uncover in this book could only have happened in the cosmopolitan, global city that was late Ottoman Istanbul.

Enslavement and the Harem

Enslavement was a part of the economic, social, and political culture of Islamic empires (such as the Mamluks in Egypt and the Safavid Empire in Iran), including the Ottoman Empire, for many centuries. Although it shared some characteristics with the better-known Atlantic slavery, enslavement in the Ottoman Empire differed in some significant ways.[12] For one thing, the Ottoman sultan himself was regarded as the slave, or *kul*, of God, and all Ottoman subjects were slaves, or servants, of the sultan (Zilfi 2010: 15). He could, for example, exile them to distant places or seize all their property and wealth, as he chose. That said, specific legal provisions surrounded the enslaved regarding the rights of owners, rights of the enslaved, and so on, setting them apart from the free. Unlike Atlantic slavery, where the single term "slave" could accurately describe an entire population of men, women, and children working in fields, plantation big houses, and city residences, a multitude of words describe the different positions and responsibilities that enslaved people in the Ottoman context may have held, in imperial households, other households, villages, the military, industrial contexts, and more. The diverse vocabulary suggests the contingent nature of Ottoman enslavement, where the experiences of the individual enslaved varied significantly depending on the economic and social circumstances of their household, as well as the personalities of their owners. Here, my focus is on understanding, at least to some extent, the enslavement of women in Istanbul during the long nineteenth century and their role in the households in which they lived.

Historically, slaves were most often acquired through capture in war, kidnapping, and raiding; as gifts to the sultan; through the sale of children (often by their families); and self-enslavement by desperate people hoping for better circumstances (Toledano 1982). A robust slave trade also brought people captured in Africa, as well as from the Caucasus. In the nineteenth century, circumstances changed. After the 1828–1829 war with Russia, the enslavement of war captives became illegal; the practice was considered kidnapping, and captives had to be returned. In 1847, the African slave-trading network was abolished, and the public slave markets in Istanbul closed; ten years later, the importation of new African slaves was banned (Toledano ibid.; Zilfi 2010). Although this did not end the trade in African slaves or the sale of enslaved people in the city, it did reduce the number of people coming from Africa. Trade in Circassian women continued through the nineteenth century, although again, numbers were reduced. Slavery was officially abolished in 1924.

In the nineteenth century, most enslaved people coming to Istanbul were from Africa and the Caucasus. Previously, with slave acquisition a part of military action and raiding, the makeup of the enslaved population had been much more diverse, bringing people from the Balkans, other parts of Europe, and the Crimea as well as Africa and the Caucasus. No legal distinction was made between Black and White slaves, although darker-skinned women tended to have the more physically demanding work of the household: laundry, cooking, and so on (Zilfi ibid.; Toledano ibid.). However, they were also nursemaids to children and maids in the harem. Lighter-skinned women were preferred as concubines, but so were Ethiopian women. Female slaves from Africa created their own social networks, practiced traditional medicine, continued some of their spiritual practices including divination, and had an annual celebration.[13]

The imperial harem was home to hundreds of women, most of them enslaved. During the reign of Mahmud II (1808–1839), the number of enslaved women in the harem was about 470 (Argit 2020a: 41). Over the course of the century, the imperial harem moved from the Topkapı Palace to the newly built Dolmabahçe Palace in 1856, then to Yildiz in 1878. Consorts and other members of the harems of deceased sultans remained in the Topkapı Palace; and after Sultan Murat V was deposed in 1876, he lived together with his household in the Çırağan Palace until his death in 1904.

The imperial harem was a highly organized institution whose inhabitants included the female members of the sultan's family and the female servants, enslaved and free, who performed all the duties of the harem.[14] Girls and women entered the harem through purchase and gift (and in earlier centuries as war captives). They were trained in specific kinds of duties, including as potential consorts of the sultan. Becoming a favorite of the sultan, and potentially a mother to his children, was a highly desirable path, but most women in the harem were trained for other work. Custom dictated that sexual partners of the sultan (or indeed of private heads of households) were entitled to their own apartments, a suite of servants and other economic benefits, which in practice limited the number of consorts who could be supported, even in the imperial harem.

The highest-ranking woman in the harem administration was the *kethuda kadın*, or *haznedar usta*, who oversaw all the work of the harem, including other high-ranking women who supervised specific areas (treasury, laundry, table service, bath, toilette services, and so on). These women all had assistants and enslaved women assigned to them. Everyone in the harem was paid for their work in both money and food allowances, as well as receiving clothing or fabric for clothing at regular intervals and gifts from time to time. High-ranking palace women could accumulate substantial wealth during their service; the *haznedar usta*, for example, was paid more than the sultan's mother or children (ibid.).

Enslaved women who were the personal maids to female members of the sultan's family, and others responsible for their clothing and jewelry, would have acquired a detailed understanding of current fashions and would have been familiar with the dressmakers and others who provided harem fashions. During the period of Mahmud II, for example, consorts of the ruler had between three and thirteen slaves assigned to them, and the daughters of the sultan in this period, between five and fourteen (ibid.). The sisters and daughters of the sultan who married would also have had large numbers of enslaved women in their elaborate households. All these women, royal and enslaved, would have been fashion tastemakers in their own circles, a subject discussed at length later in the book.

The imperial harem had the largest number of enslaved women, but wealthy Istanbul households also included enslaved women. Owning slaves was a mark of both social and economic status, which was demonstrated openly when enslaved women accompanied their mistresses in public (see Figure 7.7 for an example). Conversely, appearing in public without a retinue of slaves or servants compromised elite women's respectability (Peirce 2021: 13). As was the case in the imperial harem, enslaved women in domestic contexts had a variety of duties, from the heavy work of laundry and cooking to taking care of children and acting as maids to the mistresses of the household. Masters of the household were legally entitled to have sexual relationships (without marriage) with the enslaved women in their household, with the economic considerations described above; the children of these encounters were free and raised in the household. The experiences of enslaved women in Istanbul households were contingent on a range of factors: the economic standing of the family, the size of the household, and the personalities of the women and men to whom they were subservient, to name the most obvious. Numerous accounts describe enslaved women in the harem as members of the family, treated kindly and well taken care of, but other sources describe different circumstances.

Enslavement in the Ottoman context was generally time limited. Enslaved women in domestic settings could be manumitted after about seven to ten years, although this was not necessarily a consistent practice. Slaves could request to be sold to a new mistress if they were unhappy in their situation; equally, some who had the option to be freed elected to remain with their mistresses or remained in their household as freed servants. When women were manumitted, depending on the circumstances, their owners would arrange a marriage with a suitable man and help the new couple set up their household. The relationship between an enslaved woman and the household of her owners did not end with manumission; an ongoing legal tie remained between them, including an inheritance relationship (Argit 2020b: 189–209). The owners continued to be a source of social and economic stability for the manumitted woman; in turn, she carried something of her status as a "palace woman" into her new life and her new neighborhood. The relationship between manumitted women from the imperial harem and their former owners was even stronger because it was institutionalized. The sultan had a right to a share of the inheritance of a manumitted palace woman, so the court, through the office of the chief Black eunuch, took an ongoing interest in the financial affairs of manumitted women as indicated by the extensive correspondence and other archival material that survives (ibid.).

I may never know as much as I would like about the personal stories and life histories of enslaved women in Ottoman Istanbul, but as more work is done in this area, perhaps these women will come into sharper focus. Their dress practices and role in the fashion economy are investigated in detail later in the book.

What's In, What's Not

Ottoman fashion history is a rich, diverse topic, and there is more to it than I could include here. To begin with an obvious exclusion: this book is concerned with women's dress but not that of men. Why exclude men's clothing? The reasons are complex, some historically contingent, some practical. Men's dress in Istanbul was the first to become Europeanized, beginning with the 1829 edict of Mahmud II requiring government officials to wear trousers and frock coats, a change that drew wide attention among visitors and in the press. But the very fact of the change being the result of government rule removes the aspect of individual choice, at least to a large degree, and from a fashion history point of view, is thus less interesting. For reasons that I consider later in the book, women's dress was caught up in complex ways with the identity of the Empire, with religion, and wide-ranging conversations about women's roles, traditionally and going forward. Men's dress did not occupy such a central place in public discourse. And on a practical level, apart from the costumes of the sultans and princes in the collection of the Topkapı Palace Museum, men's dress is found in significantly fewer numbers in museum collections.

Just as men's dress in Ottoman Istanbul was regulated by government decree, so was the outdoor dress of Ottoman women. Their public appearance was cause for great concern on the part of government bureaucrats and the leaders of different religious communities, as indicated by the number of edicts issued repeatedly to address lapses in taste and propriety. But as with the dress of men, the very fact of externally imposed norms (even though they were often ignored) reduces the aspect of individual choice in how women presented themselves in public. Similarly, relatively few examples of the outdoor garments that women wore are part of museum collections, so although this important aspect of women's dress will be considered here, my examination of outdoor dress, including veiling practices, takes second place to understanding how women dressed at home, for themselves and their social circles.

Jewelry was an important component of women's dress. Precious stones, bracelets, rings, brooches, and more all appeared on the ensembles of women from different levels of Istanbul society. Likewise, head covering of one kind or another was an aspect of all women's toilettes, whether dressing for indoors or outdoors. Details varied according to ethnicity, class, and role, but head covering of some kind was ubiquitous. Other accessories included belts and sashes, gloves, parasols, stockings, and shoes. Although not minimizing the significance of these aspects of dress, they could not be explored here in the detail they require to understand their significance for different social groups and the way they changed over the time.

Last but certainly not least, much as I have wanted to reconstruct, at least partially, the dress practices of all the women of Istanbul, it has not been possible. Museum collections and secondary scholarship cannot yet support an investigation into the dress of all Istanbul communities. Armenian, Jewish, and Greek women, in addition to Ottoman Muslims, are included here, but unfortunately the minority communities from the Balkans, the Roma, and others do not make an appearance.

The Book's Structure

Casting an unusually wide net in terms of sources, this project examines the relationship between fashion and photography in the Ottoman context and interrogates the evidence for Ottoman women's fashion, the fashion economy, and how women engaged with dress. The three primary modes of evidence for dress (visual, written, and the objects themselves) are each incomplete in various ways, yet make essential contributions to writing a history of Ottoman women's dress. In Chapter 2, "Picturing Fashion and Understanding Dress: The Sources," I assess the challenges presented by each body of material. I begin with visual sources (book illustration, painting) and then the photographic archive before moving on to the written sources by foreigners and Ottoman women themselves. Last, the histories and collecting practices of the main repositories of Ottoman costume in Türkiye and abroad are examined, because these have shaped the collections available to us for study.

Surviving garments, along with written and visual sources from the mid-eighteenth century into the first decades of the nineteenth century, form the core of Chapter 3, "The Garments: Tailoring, Construction, and

Transformation." Setting the stage for the fashion changes soon to follow, the chapter presents an overview of the tailoring and construction of eighteenth-century Ottoman women's clothing through an examination of key surviving garments as well as their textiles and decorative finishes. The focus then moves to the fashion changes of the first half of the nineteenth century, in which I trace the beginnings of the dramatic transformation in women's dress that soon followed.

In Chapter 4, "Acceleration of Change: The Dress, the Photograph, and Ottoman Weddings," the fashion narrative is complicated in a number of ways. I begin by focusing on a single type of garment, the *bindallı* dress, which began to be worn for weddings in many regions of the Ottoman Empire in the mid-nineteenth century. The dress itself is a key element in the move from Ottoman to Euro-American fashion because it is the first example of a dress, put on over the head, to be worn in the Ottoman context. The chapter looks at the garment's structure and ornamentation, as well as its many variations over the decades of its use, but also at the impact that European wedding dress styles had as Ottoman women were drawn more closely into a global fashion system. This chapter deploys historic photographs as evidence of dress—in this case images of women wearing the *bindallı* dress and other wedding photographs—opening a discussion of the intertwined relationship between fashion and photography in self-fashioning. I take advantage of the relative abundance of surviving wedding garments to look beyond Ottoman Muslim women to consider the wedding traditions and sartorial practices of Ottoman women from different religious and economic groups.

The changes in dress practices that I trace in Chapters 3 and 4 did not occur in a vacuum. At a minimum, they required an awareness of current European fashion, specialized knowledge of garment design and construction, and access to new fabrics, trimmings, and other materials. In Chapter 5, "The Fashion Economy in Istanbul," I focus in detail on how the women of Ottoman Istanbul learned about new fashions and the changes in fashion media, sales, and production that enabled the fashion transformations that took place in the last decades of the nineteenth century. My reconstruction of the fashion economy is informed by examining the fashion media available to Ottoman women, the new shopping opportunities, and accounts of the social interaction of Istanbul women in a time of changing social dynamics.

"Fashion influencer" is a term that gained currency in the twenty-first century with the growth of social media, but the knowledge that certain people or groups (tastemakers) had a significant influence on dress trends has a very long history in fashion. In Chapter 6, my attention turns to the fashion tastemakers in the Ottoman context, women of the court and other elite women. Their clothing is well documented by surviving examples of actual garments and extensive photography, particularly in the last decades of the nineteenth century and pre–World War I years. I look at this evidence to understand what these women wore and how they engaged with the fashion economy to stay abreast of current fashions and acquire their wardrobes.

The dress practices of fashion influencers are easier to trace than those of the women who are more typically overlooked in fashion history. Yet elite women were only one segment of the Ottoman population. In Chapter 7, "The Elusive Fashion Stories of Enslaved Women and Domestic Servants," I set out to examine the clothing of this often-overlooked segment of Istanbul women. Because this is uncharted territory, I draw on scholarship addressing a similar challenge in the American context: the fashion history of enslaved African American women. Guided by that example, I turn to a variety of visual and written sources to augment the scanty evidence provided by surviving garments and reach some preliminary conclusions.

Moving to another group of women who are generally left out of fashion history, in Chapter 8, "Dressing for Work," I consider the changing role of women in the public work world in the last decades of the nineteenth century and how this affected their clothing choices. Because they were the first to begin working outside the home, I am better informed about the dress practices of minority women, who receive more attention in this chapter. Few, if any, actual garments survive, so other evidence needs to be brought into the conversation. Photographs, paintings, and clothing worn by other working women in this period are employed in reconstructing the wardrobes of Ottoman working women.

In the tumultuous years of the early twentieth century, the Ottoman Empire faced serious challenges both inside and outside the Empire. The political and social changes that followed the Balkan wars, World War I, the Turkish war of independence, and the founding of the Republic in 1923 were substantial and far-reaching; fashion changes that had been underway in previous decades continued apace, with clothing being deployed as a signifier of Türkiye's new identity, particularly in the first decade of the new republic. This project concludes with an epilogue that considers the cultural significance of two intriguing examples of the long afterlife of Ottoman costume—the *bindallı* dress and the bridal fashion that evokes a romanticized version of an Ottoman past made popular in the twenty-first century on *The Magnificent Century* and other Turkish television programs.

CHAPTER 2
PICTURING FASHION AND UNDERSTANDING DRESS: THE SOURCES

For the most part, the lived history of Ottoman women lies outside of the archival record, by which I mean official documents such as inheritance registers, wills, endowment deeds, and other court records resulting from various kinds of legal actions. Since the 1990s, a determined and quite successful effort has mined the archives to bring women as political actors, patrons, consumers, and individuals into Ottoman history.[1] However, given the somewhat limited contexts in which women appear in the archival record, my project gives priority to other kinds of evidence: the material objects that provide a different way of understanding women's lives. In doing so, I am looking to recent work by Kate Strasdin, *Inside the Royal Wardrobe, A Dress History of Queen Alexandra*; and Serena Dyer, *Material Lives: Women Makers and Consumer Culture in the 18th Century*, among others. Described by Ann Smart Martin in 1993 as "complex symbolic bundles of social, cultural and individual meanings fused in something we can touch, see and own" (Martin 1993: 141), the material objects of Ottoman women—their clothing, their photographs, and to a lesser extent, their writing— are at the center of this project. Objects, whether garments, paintings, or photographs, present their own challenges of legibility and interpretation. They require the same detailed attention to the circumstances of their creation, their author (in this case, their maker), and their history that is generally given to written documents. In the next pages, I review the categories of evidence brought together for this project, beginning with visual sources, and the challenges of interpretation they present.

Visual Sources: Painting and Book Illustration

Painted representations of Ottoman women occur in a variety of contexts: costume manuscripts and books, Ottoman manuscript illustrations and album pages, travel literature about the Ottoman Empire, and the work of European artists resident in Istanbul, to name only the most obvious. For this project, the most important works are those in which representations of women's dress are of particular interest to the artist, specifically the work of the Ottoman and European painters discussed below. Other categories of images (e.g., illustrated costume books, Ottoman manuscript illustration, and travel literature), although important for different areas of inquiry, are not central to my project. However, I do look briefly at one example of the illustrated books that were a mainstay of travel information in the eighteenth and nineteenth centuries, because these books and their illustrations shaped the perceptions of later artists and visitors to Istanbul.

The two books illustrated by Thomas Allom (1804–1872); *Constantinople and the Scenery of the Seven Churches of Asia Minor* by Robert Walsh, published in 1838; and *Costume and Character in Turkey and Italy*, which appeared in nine editions between 1839 and 1845, were extremely popular in their own time. Allom, an English architect and artist known primarily for his topographical illustrations, arrived in Istanbul in 1837 at the behest of the publisher Fisher, Son & Co., and traveled through Anatolia, Syria, and Palestine for ten months, producing an extensive series of sketches. Allom's sketches continued to be included by Fisher in other publications related to the Ottoman Empire; and in 1850 Allom used them to produce a public exhibition, *Panorama of Constantinople and the Dardanelles*, shown in London in 1850 and again in 1854

(Wilson 2006: xi–xii). Of the eighty-seven sketches that Allom made for the 1838 book, eleven illustrate women in Istanbul, mostly in the outdoor scenes often found in such books. Two images present harem women, "The Favorite Odalique" (Figure 2.1) and "Interior of a Harem," both of which were also included in the later book and have been reproduced many times since then. Despite their questionable accuracy and highly romanticized depiction of a scene that Allom was unlikely to have witnessed in person, they remain standard images of an Ottoman domestic interior.

The English artist William Bartlett also produced views of Istanbul that were extremely popular, illustrating *The Beauties of the Bosphorus* by Julia Pardoe, published originally in 1838 by George Virtue and reprinted many times throughout the nineteenth century. Like the work of Thomas Allom, Bartlett's views of Istanbul are still in circulation today, but because women appear in just a few images, and only outdoors, I do not illustrate them here.

The work of the nineteenth-century illustrators such as Allom is to some extent dependent on the images produced by the eighteenth-century artists who left a rich collection of paintings and prints depicting the people and life of Istanbul. I focus here on the work of Jean-Baptiste Vanmour and Jean Etienne Liotard,

Figure 2.1 *The Favorite Odalique,* Thomas Allom, 1838, *Constantinople and the Scenery of the Seven Churches of Asia Minor.*

two artists who spent a considerable amount of time in the city during the eighteenth century. Although they are not the only European artists who visited Istanbul over the course of the century, each took a particular interest in depicting the dress of their subjects, and thus their work is especially valuable for this project.

Jean-Baptiste Vanmour, the Flemish-French artist, arrived in Istanbul around the turn of the eighteenth century and remained there until his death in 1737. Initially employed by the Marquis de Ferriol, French ambassador to the Ottoman court from 1698 until 1711, Vanmour also received commissions from many of the European ambassadors in Istanbul and produced a substantial body of work, more than fifty-five paintings (Nefedova 2009: 103), during the more than thirty years in which he resided in Istanbul. Most of his work is now in the collection of the Rijksmuseum in Amsterdam, with a second small group in the Suna and İnan Kıraç Foundation Orientalist Painting Collection in Istanbul. Vanmour is known particularly for his records of the reception ceremonies for foreign ambassadors at the Ottoman court, as well as other ceremonies and celebrations. Of particular importance for this project are approximately eleven paintings he did of specific moments in women's lives, such as weddings, outdoor excursions, and social visits (Figure 2.2).[2]

However, Vanmour was best known in his day for the depictions of Istanbul residents commissioned by the Marquis de Ferriol, which formed the basis for the engravings in *Recueil de cent estampes représentant différentes nations du Levant, tirées sur les Tableaux peints d'après Nature, en 1707 et 1708, par les Ordres de M. de Ferriol Ambassadeur du Roi à la Porte,* [*Collection of one hundred prints representing different nations of the Levant, taken from Paintings done from Nature, in 1707 and 1708, by the orders of Mr. de Ferriol, King's Ambassador to the Porte*], first published in 1712–1713. The project was extremely successful and reprinted a number of times. None of the original paintings done by Vanmour and his studio assistants on which the engravings were based survive, but a few single figure paintings give some idea of the original paintings for the project, among them two of women: *Woman at her Embroidery Frame* and *Jewish Woman.*[3]

The *Recueil* engravings, with their wide dispersal and specificity of detail, were copied in later works and established a certain image of the Ottoman Empire and its inhabitants. Seventeen of the illustrations in the *Recueil* show the Ottoman women of Istanbul, identified as Turkish, Greek, Jewish, or Armenian, mostly in ordinary occupations such as spinning or playing music, but also as brides or in ceremonial dress. Given his long residence in Istanbul and his familiarity with court circles as well as the foreign community, Vanmour would have had more access than many male artists to the homes of Istanbul residents, although most likely not the harems of Muslim households. It is reasonable to assume that much of the detail regarding dress and interior spaces in his work comes from his own observation, with the dress of Greek and Armenian women also appearing on the Muslim women in his paintings. Vanmour was also commissioned to paint portraits of specific individuals, three of which depict women.

The work by Vanmour illustrated here is a representative example of his paintings illustrating various social events among Ottoman women. The small oil painting (45 cm. x 58.5 cm.) in Figure 2.2 is a complex composition, with fourteen women arrayed across the horizontal picture plane in an indoor setting that resembles the others that the painter used for his harem paintings. Seven women are seated around a round table laden with food, attended by five servants. Two other women are off to the left, one of whom is nursing an infant.

Figure 2.2 *Meal of Distinguished Turkish women*, Jean-Baptiste Vanmour, *ca.* 1720–1737. Amsterdam, Rijksmuseum, SK-A-2004, 47.

I find this painting of interest because of Vanmour's attention to the clothing of the various figures: the distinction is clear between the dress of the servants and the women at the table, some of whom are wearing fur-trimmed robes over their *entaris*. The fabric of the servants' clothing is plainer, and several of them wear aprons tucked into their waists. Two of the servants are African, and most likely all of them are enslaved, but it is possible that some of the women at the table are also enslaved members of their households.

A second important eighteenth-century artist for this project is the Genevan artist Jean Etienne Liotard. He spent five years in the Ottoman Empire, much of it in Istanbul, arriving in 1738. Liotard was hired by a party of Englishmen to document their travels, including "to draw the dresses of every country they should go into" (Fehlman 2015: 65); examples of his costume sketches, generally done in black and red chalk, can be found in the Louvre and other collections. Once in Istanbul and after his employers had traveled on, Liotard remained there at the invitation of the British ambassador, Sir Everard Fawkener.

Comfortably embedded in the foreign community of Pera, Liotard made numerous portraits of both foreign and local residents, including high-ranking members of the Ottoman court. His foreign subjects were nearly all wearing local dress. Liotard's position within the Pera community would have ensured his awareness of the work of local artists such as Vanmour (who had died in Istanbul the year before Liotard's arrival), Abdulcelil Levni, and Abdullah Boukhari, all of whom produced works illustrating contemporary dress.[4] In general, Liotard and his oeuvre has a great deal to tell us about cultural interaction and communication between Europe and Istanbul in the eighteenth century, but his import in the context of this project is as an observer of dress. Liotard's portraits, both in Istanbul and later, were characterized by a meticulous level of finish and attention to details of fabric, color, texture, and other aspects of dress. In his own time Liotard was known (and often disparaged by his artist contemporaries) for his truthful depictions of his sitters, including details of dress (Ribeiro 2015: 41).

Eighteenth-century Ottoman painters also turned their attention to the depiction of women and their dress. Two whose work is particularly significant for this project are Levni Abdülcelil Çelebi (d. 1732), the court painter of Sultan Ahmed III (r. 1703–1730); and Abdullah Boukhari, who worked under Mahmud 1 (r. 1730–1754). Levni, one of the most important court artists of his time, left a substantial body of work. It included portraits of the sultans; the lively and detailed illustrations in the *Surname-I Vehbi* of the festivities marking the circumcisions of the sons of the sultan; and in an album in the Topkapı Sarayı Museum, Hazine 2164, forty-two images of single figures, including a number of women, discussed in Chapter 3.

Like Levni, Abdullah Boukhari also produced single-figure studies. Boukhari's life and oeuvre have been much less studied than his more famous contemporary,[5] but his paintings of women are important sources for the study of eighteenth-century dress. Many of these are found in an album (T.9364) in the Rare Book Library of Istanbul University (Compagnon 2023: 7). In *Lady in Brown* (Figure 2.3), Boukhari paints a woman standing

Figure 2.3 *Lady in Brown*, Abdullah Boukhari, 1745. Istanbul, Istanbul University Nadir Eserleri Library, T.9364, fol. 9a.

in an empty space, wearing a multilayered outfit consisting of a luxurious short-sleeved blue robe, lined and trimmed in a dark fur, a brown *entari* whose sleeves extend from beneath the fur robe, a second shorter robe in an orange striped fabric, and pink flowered *şalvar*, or trousers. Her yellow leather slippers are just visible beneath the *şalvar*. A turban, necklace, and narrow metal belt complete her outfit. This color palette and indeed some of these favorite striped and flowered fabrics appear in other Boukhari figure paintings worn by both men and women.

Compagnon makes the point in her consideration of Levni and Boukhari's paintings that their interest in fabric pattern was driven by design aesthetics, not a desire to reproduce the actual fabrics they may have seen around them, writing, "rather than imitating the patterns of textiles at the time, they signify a certain textile aesthetic" (ibid.: 171). It is a convincing argument, which means from a fashion history viewpoint these paintings are more important for understanding the general shapes of garments and the way in which multiple layers were combined than as a photo-realistic presentation of eighteenth-century dress and fabric.

The work of the nineteenth-century painters, both Ottoman and European, is a key visual source for following fashion trends in women's dress. As the numbers of foreigners, including artists, in the city increased, and Ottoman artists began experimenting with Western art media, and in some cases traveling to Paris for training, the interchanges in Istanbul among painters, illustrators, and others created a vibrant, fluid international community, as described in Chapter 1. The artists whose work is especially important in understanding women's dress are introduced here.

The works of Amadeo Preziosi, a Maltese artist who spent most of his life in Istanbul (*ca.* 1842–1882); and Fausto Zonaro (1854–1929), an Italian who lived in Istanbul 1891–1910, are particularly well known. Preziosi's career and his work, *La tasse de café*, circa 1858 (Figure 7.8), are discussed at length in Chapter 6; here, I consider briefly the careers of Zonaro, and his wife, Elisa, a professional photographer and artist in her own right. Zonaro had studied art in his native Italy and Paris before arriving in Istanbul; Elisa on the other hand, returned to Paris in 1893–1894 to study photography, opening a studio, "Atelier Elsa Constantinople," in their home upon her return (Berberoğlu 2023: 85–87).

They collaborated closely to build successful careers in Istanbul. With the support of his patrons in the diplomatic community, Fausto Zonaro became court painter to Abdülhamid in 1896, a position that paid him a salary of forty liras and required his presence in the palace for four days a week. Elisa was also recognized by the court, receiving two medals from Abdülhamid for her work (Berberoğlu 2021: 267). The full story of their artistic collaboration has been uncovered by Berberoğlu (2023); for my purposes, the fact that Elisa's photography encompassed portraiture of women is of particular interest. Her work would have informed her husband's representations of women in his painting, but it also speaks to the engagement of Ottoman women with photography, a subject I take up in Chapter 5.

In the second half of the nineteenth century, Ottoman and European women began to have a place in the artistic community of Istanbul. Artists such as Mary Adelaide Walker, Henriette Browne, and Elisabeth Jerichau-Baumann visited the city, gaining access to Ottoman harems and creating portraits of elite and royal women. Mary Adelaide Walker, who arrived in Istanbul in the late 1850s and remained there for about thirty years, is a particularly intriguing figure. Sister of the British chaplain in Istanbul, she was not a particularly well-known artist in her native England, but she became an important figure in the Istanbul art world during her time there, commissioned to paint a portrait of Fatma Sultan, a daughter of Abdülmecid, shortly after she took up residence in Istanbul. This prestigious commission led to others, and eventually she began offering classes for ladies in drawing, showing her work at her studio in Pera, participating in local exhibitions, and teaching at the Women's Teacher Training College of Istanbul (Roberts 2007: 110–27; 2015: 221–48).

None of Walker's painted portraits of elite Ottoman women have come to light, but she writes extensively about them in her 1886 book, *Eastern Life and Scenery: With Excursions in Asia Minor, Mytilene, Crete, and Roumania.* Fully understanding the importance of elite commissions, Walker nonetheless regretted the uncompromising demands that her subjects made in terms of their self-fashioning. Although she would have preferred to paint them in the exotic silk *entaris* and *şalvar* of the recent past, they wished to be shown in the most current Parisian fashions. Here is one passage from her memoir (Zeïneb Sultana was the pseudonym she used for Fatma Sultan):

> Zeïneb Sultana stamped her foot, said I did not care to please her, and that the portrait must be done according to her wishes, or—not at all. I could not risk the "not at all," and, with many an inward groan and rebellious struggle, submitted, with less difficulty than might otherwise have been the case, because the picture when finished would rarely, if ever, be seen by persons competent to judge the merits of a painting.

(Walker: 17)

In her account of this commission, Walker presents Fatma Sultan more as a spoiled child than as a person with a legitimate desire to control her own representation. But at the end of the day, it was Fatma Sultan's vision of herself, taller, slimmer, and dressed in her interpretation of the most current fashion, that prevailed.

These complex commissions were in contrast, in both subject matter and the agency of the subjects, to the illustrations she created for Emelia Hornby's 1863 book, *Constantinople during the Crimean War* (Figure 2.4). These more informal works show harem genre scenes with subjects dressed in traditional clothing sitting at home, washing hands, preparing to go out, and so on. Walker would have witnessed such

Figure 2.4 [Untitled], Mary Adelaide Walker, late 1850s, published in Emelia B. M. Hornby, *Constantinople during the Crimean War*, 1863, p. 244.

23

activities while working on her portrait projects in elite Istanbul harems, although her choices of dress and setting for these works reflect her own ideas and fantasies of Ottoman harems.

The Ottoman women who aspired to be artists in the late years of the nineteenth century and early twentieth century received their training in the newly established vocational and teacher training schools for girls, from private tutors, and after 1914, at the Academy of Fine Arts for Women (Shaw 2011b: 138–39). Some traveled to Europe to study and work, but for the most part women artists in this period were constrained by gender-based social expectations. They were able to exhibit their work in the Istanbul salons and exhibitions, teach in girls' schools, and pursue their art as their family obligations permitted. Portraits of other women and self-portraits comprised much of their work, providing a rich body of visual information about how the women who sat for these portraits fashioned themselves and the importance of dress as a mark of social identity for both artists and subjects.

Mihri Hanım (1885–1954) was the daughter of a prominent Istanbul physician, encouraged to pursue her interest in painting as a young woman. She studied with the Italian artist Fausto Zonaro for two years, leaving Istanbul in the early years of the twentieth century for Rome and Paris. She returned in 1914 to teach at the newly established Academy of Fine Arts for Women, becoming the director shortly after her arrival (ibid.: 139). She left Istanbul again in 1922, eventually settling in New York. Through both her painting and her position at the school, she had a significant impact on other women artists in Istanbul, but until recently her work and the details of her life have been largely overlooked. She was the subject of an exhibition, *Mihri: A Nomadic Painter of Modern Times,* at Istanbul's Salt Gallery in 2019, and the Türkiye İş Bankası Painting and Sculpture Museum in Istanbul now holds one of her paintings (Figure 2.5).

Mihri Hanım's self-portrait is a bold representation, in both its imposing size, 140 cm. x 70 cm. (4 ft. 7 in. x 2 ft. 3 in.) and the full-length depiction of the figure, standing with one hand on her hip and one leg thrust forward. The painting's background is a collection of loose strokes in pastel, drawing the attention of the viewer to the figure, whose full-length dark blue *ferace* (coat) and transparent black veil mostly obscure the outlines of her body. In contrast to the open, almost unfinished background, the artist has created a skillful composition with the figure, taking the eye of the viewer from the tassel hanging on the left, to the gold tip of her parasol, the light reflecting on her stylish pointed shoe, her exposed hand with its prominent green ring, and finally her neck and face, with the pearl button of her *ferace*, pearl necklace and earrings framing her face, only slightly concealed by the veil. I read this painting as an embrace of fashion and modernity: by focusing on the stylish details of her appearance (parasol, shoes, jewelry, makeup), the effect of the thin veil, as well as the pose of the figure and the size of the work, the artist is both performing and demonstrating an identity that does not compromise social expectations (the full-length *ferace*) but certainly pushes those boundaries.

In comparison to the work of Mihri Hanım and other female painters, the work of male Ottoman painters from the late nineteenth century is much better known. These artists, trained in the Ottoman military academies and often in the Paris studios of French painters, worked in a variety of genres, including portraiture. Osman Hamdi Bey (1842–1910), well-known in his own time and the subject of a great deal of recent scholarship, is particularly useful for this project. The son of a high-ranking Ottoman official, Osman Hamdi studied painting in the Paris studios of Jean-Leon Gerome and Gustave Boulanger. Returning to Istanbul in 1869, he served in various administrative posts, becoming the director of the Imperial Museum in 1881, as well as working in archaeology and continuing his painting. Osman Hamdi's painting oeuvre is rich and diverse; for my purposes, two groups of his works are particularly useful—the harem scenes from the 1880s and the portraits he painted of friends and family (Figure 2.6).[6]

Paintings from each of these groups, different as they may be in subject matter, audience, and subsequent reception, provide detailed information about how women were dressing and specific garments. In some cases, figures in his paintings are wearing garments for which close matches can be found in museum collections. For example, a yellow *entari* in the Sadberk Hanım Museum closely resembles that worn by the central figure

Figure 2.5 *Self-portrait*, Mihri Hanım, *ca.* 1909–1912. Istanbul, İşbank Art Collection

Figure 2.6 *Mimozalı* Kadın, Osman Hamdi Bey, 1906. Istanbul, Istanbul Painting and Sculpture Museum.

in several Osman Hamdi works. His portraits, as in the 1906 example here of his second wife, Naile Hanım, in *Mimosalı Kadın*, present meticulously depicted fashions that would have been worn by elite Ottoman women in the years he was producing the portraits. Shown against a deep red background, Naile Hanım is seated with her black *çarşaf* (outdoor garment) thrown back to reveal an elaborately trimmed dress with a newly fashionable high boned collar, extensive use of lace, and ruffled edges to the sleeves.

Halil Paşa (1852–1939), a slightly younger contemporary of Osman Hamdi, learned to draw as part of his military training. Like Hamdi, he studied painting in Paris, exhibiting work there and returning to Istanbul to teach art. He served as director of the School of Fine Arts, exhibited at the Istanbul salons and at the Galatasaray Exhibitions (Kaya 2019: 100–103), becoming a major figure in the burgeoning contemporary art scene in Istanbul. Although many of the Ottoman artists who received their training at military schools focused on landscapes and still life, Halil Paşa took a particular interest in portraiture (Figure 7.9), which makes his work of particular relevance for my project.

Visual Sources: Photography

With the advent of photography in 1839, the corpus of images of the dressed bodies of Ottoman women expanded exponentially. There are thousands of photographs that I might draw upon to understand the fashion choices that Ottoman women were making, but not all are of equal value for this work. These photographs could be organized in innumerable ways, but for my purposes, they can be divided into four main categories, discussed below. These categories are based on the original circumstances of the image in terms of audience, circulation, relationship between photographer and subject, among other factors. Given the size of the photographic archive, organizing the images conceptually is helpful, but at the same time, it is essential to remember that even when these images were made, there was slippage among categories, and all the more so as photographs moved across time, geographies, and institutional settings.

A portrait that may have been taken at the behest of an individual could have been incorporated into the catalog of images available for purchase in a photographer's studio, or over time, become separated from the family to whom the portrait originally belonged and may now be found in a museum collection, archive, or antique store. At the same time, considering photographs as belonging to categories of images does not determine what they may reveal about the people or dress practices in the image: reading the photographs with my own questions in mind is a key part of mining this particular archive.

Perhaps the most familiar of these images are the commercial photographs, typically albumen prints, of harem women that were a mainstay of photographs intended for the tourist market in Istanbul and Cairo beginning in the 1850s and continuing through the nineteenth century (Figure 2.7). This extensive body of work has received a great deal of scholarly attention, which I will not rehearse here.[7] For this project, I need to assess their value as reliable sources of information regarding dress. Using this one example as indicative of

Figure 2.7 [Robed woman reclining on Cushions], No. 678, Sébah & Joaillier, *ca.* 1880s. Los Angeles, Pierre de Gigord collection of photographs of the Ottoman Empire and the Republic of Turkey. Series III. Loose and mounted photographs, GRI Special Collections, 96.R.14 (F3.041).

the category more generally,[8] what is there to see? On the one hand, the image is immediately identifiable as the product of a commercial studio—it is signed by the studio in the lower right corner and given an inventory number in the lower left. Moreover, the carpet, backdrop, and props (water pipe, octagonal table, coffee pot and cups, and cushions) familiar from other works by this studio, are intended to evoke the harem in the space of the photographer's studio. The reclining figure who is the focus of the image appears in other harem scenes by Sébah and Joiallier. On the other hand, this woman is wearing actual clothes that did exist at the time the photograph was taken, so surely that is useful. And indeed, it is possible to make out details of the cut and fabric of the *entari* (robe) and *şalvar* (baggy trousers) the model is wearing, including the *oya* (needle lace) that trims the *entari* and the *gömlek* (chemise) beneath the *entari*. The challenges that this category of image present as documents of fashion history arise from the fact that the photographer was creating these photographs to conform to a certain idea of harem women, derived from Orientalist fantasies and targeted at a specific audience. So, although these photographs show actual garments, it is impossible to know whether they were still being worn outside the photographer's studio at the time that the photograph was made, in what circumstances, and by whom.

A second category of photographs is the studio portraits taken by commercial photographers. Unlike the harem images examined above, these were taken at the behest of the sitter for circulation among family and friends. In many cases they no longer have any identifying information about the sitters, resulting in

Figure 2.8 Wedding photo of Serpouhi Mendilian Encababian and Karekin Encababian. Sepastia, Encababian Frères, 1909. Watertown, MA, Project Save Photograph Archive, K2005.041.029.

a significant amount of slippage between these categories of private portraits and commercial images of types. Whenever possible, in this project I am working with portraits for which I have a certain amount of information about the circumstances of the image. And because of their focus on dress, wedding portraits, discussed in detail in Chapter 4, are particularly important.

For example, in Figure 2.8 the couple pictured here, Serpouhi Mendilian Encababian and Karekin Encababian, were married in Sepastia (Sivas) in February 1909. Karaken Encababian was a photographer working in the family business, Encababian Frères, founded in 1898. Surviving images from Encababian Frères are held in the Project Save Photographic Archive in Watertown, Massachusetts,[9] and include three other wedding portraits of the couple as well as a portrait of the bride. As members of a family of photographers, the couple would have been very comfortable in front of the camera and would have had the luxury of taking multiple views to document the event. Figure 2.8 shows an untrimmed print against a plain backdrop. The couple's pose is informal, almost intimate. The bride looks directly at the camera, and the details of her elaborate two-piece bridal outfit are easily visible (in other views she is also wearing the floor length veil that was part of her ensemble).

As cameras became easier to use, and photographic training more widespread, people began recording their own families, their houses, and their daily lives. Although many of these images are unmoored from their original contexts, they are still important documents. Here I examine two by Ali Sami, a military photographer during the reign of Abdulhamid II (Figures 2.9, 2.10).[10] The photographs are not dated, but they were taken at about the same time, based on the people who appear in them. Each shows a family group at home, engaged in reading, playing backgammon, and perhaps conversation. The photographs are carefully staged with participants acting as directed by the photographer (looking at the camera or not, sitting without moving, holding newspapers so that their titles are visible, and so on). The photographs are informative on several levels, demonstrating everyday family activities for the *askeri* class as well as domestic interiors of a family of this social standing, and most important for my purposes, revealing what people wore at home. In the first image (Figure 2.9), the family members whose clothes are visible are dressed informally, the boy and two men in quilted kaftans and loosely cut trousers, and the female figure in the foreground, in a loose-fitting robe with high neck and long sleeves. In the second photograph (Figure 2.10), the women are all wearing European-style clothing, skirts and blouses in three cases; a dress, in the fourth case. Apart from details of specific garments, this pair of photographs is an important reminder that clothing choices were highly variable and situational; that is, the same people could wear very different styles of clothing depending on circumstances.

A fourth category of photographs of women is organized by subject, not photographer. Images of women working, at leisure, in school settings, and elsewhere were taken by professional and amateur photographers for commercial, personal, and institutional purposes. As is the case with the photograph of girls and women working in a Bursa silk factory illustrated here (Figure 2.11), these photographs most often show more than one person. Although they are carefully composed, the women or girls are wearing their own clothes, not costumes that may have been provided by the photographer. These images, particularly ones like this showing nonelite women of different religious and ethnic groups, are critically important sources for the dress practices of the working women often omitted from fashion history.

The relationship between fashion and photography is complex. Today it is impossible to imagine fashion without photography, but in the late nineteenth century that relationship was just forming. Photographs of dressed bodies, whether of the self or others, highlighted details of clothing, of gesture, of self-fashioning, and invited speculation about the sensorial effect of clothing. Image consumers could see how others dressed via photos shared among friends, illustrations in newspapers, window displays in photographic studios, and

Figure 2.9 [Family Spending Leisure Time at Home], Ali Sami, 1890–1915. Los Angeles, Pierre de Gigord collection of photographs of the Ottoman Empire and the Republic of Turkey. Series III. Loose and mounted photographs, GRI Special Collections, 96.R.14 (CD1.060).

Figure 2.10 [The photographer's family at home]. Ali Sami, 1908. From the Engin Özendes collection.

Figure 2.11 *Filature de soie à Brousse*, Sébah & Joaillier, 1875. Los Angeles, Pierre de Gigord collection of photographs of the Ottoman Empire and the Republic of Turkey. Series III. Loose and mounted photographs, GRI Special Collections, 96.R.14 (C3.24a).

elsewhere. Through their exposure to these images, over time Ottoman women developed a fashion gaze: an awareness of subtle differences in style; of new fabrics, trims, colors; of accessories, and pose, but also a sense of "fashion ideals as a guiding principle in identity formation" (Arnold 2019: 18). In the period of this project, photographic formats changed continuously. Albumen prints, cartes de visite, cabinet cards, snapshots, postcards, and photographic images in the press were all in play. (How) did the photographic format alter the relationship between the image, the subject, and fashion? (How) did the photographs change how women saw their bodies, their clothing, and their public selves? These questions may be unanswerable, but they are worth considering as I investigate the changing dress practices of Ottoman women.

Written Sources

Written sources describing dress present different kinds of information than the visual representations considered above. These take a variety of forms and were penned by Ottomans and foreigners alike. Visitors came to the Ottoman Empire for a variety of purposes: diplomatic, business, employment, and travel being only the most obvious, and many of these recorded their experiences. Their writings must be used carefully, but despite the challenges involved in using this body of material, it can provide crucial information not available elsewhere. Surviving works incorporate a range of voices, including in rare and very useful cases the servants and companions who accompanied their employers on their travels. Two examples of these include the Hon. Mrs. William Gray's book, *Journal of a Visit to Egypt, Constantinople, The Crimea, Greece, Etc.,* recounting the trip of the Prince and Princess of Wales in 1869; and Emmeline Lott's 1865 account of her experiences as a governess in the household of the Egyptian khedive, or ruler.[11] Writing from very different positionalities, Mrs. Gray as the companion to the Princess of Wales, and Lott as the paid governess, the extreme disparities in two authors' descriptions of their encounters with Ottoman women are important reminders of the impact of personal opinion and experience on the information conveyed in print.

As observers of dress, women are generally more useful. Although many of the men who visited Istanbul carefully recorded what they saw, their interests were in archaeological sites, Ottoman politics, economic matters, and the military. They did not have many opportunities to meet Ottoman women and would not necessarily have had the interest or experience to enable them to describe accurately what the women wore. Because the idea of the harem was endlessly fascinating to American and European readers, nearly everyone included a chapter on the institution and its functioning, but few would have had any firsthand knowledge, and their reports are not reliable. They are on firmer ground when describing the social life of the European community of the city or their visits to the bazaar, and their reports can be very helpful in some ways. An exception among the male writers is Charles White, whose 1845 book, *Three Years in Constantinople*, is a virtual encyclopedia of facts concerning every aspect of life in Istanbul in the mid-nineteenth century.

The voluminous writings by foreign women about the Ottoman Empire can be divided into three groups: travel accounts, memoirs written following a longer stay in the Empire, and works written specifically on the subject of Turkish women based on their own observation.

Books falling into the first category are perhaps the most numerous. They are not as reliable or as detailed in their information as memoirs, but nonetheless the authors often carefully describe what they saw and are interested in Turkish women and what they look like. Apparently, a trip to Istanbul was not complete without a visit to a harem, for every foreign visitor somehow manages to get herself invited to visit a Turkish lady at home, and the accounts of these visits are full of crucial details about at-home dress and manners.

Memoirs are less numerous but much more valuable sources for information about social customs and dress. They vary in their usefulness, depending on the position, powers of observation, and personality of the author. For documenting women's dress in the late-eighteenth and early-nineteenth century three women especially were very astute witnesses: Lady Mary Wortley Montagu, Lady Elizabeth Craven, and Julia Pardoe. Their observations, discussed in the next chapter, provide important details about the dress habits of the Ottoman women they encountered. For the later nineteenth century, Emilia Hornby, Carolyn Paine, and Lady Enid Layard are especially valuable.

Books written about Turkish women, a category of publication that did not begin until late in the nineteenth century, moved beyond an accounting of a single writer's experience with Ottoman women to a broader investigation of the traditions of different ethnic and religious groups or the current state of Ottoman women in terms of their legal positions, social constraints, political roles, and so on. Given the appeal that this topic had among European and American feminists, it is not surprising that there is a rich body of work in this area. For my project, Lucy Garnett's *The Women of Turkey and their Folk-Lore* and the work of Grace Ellison have been the most useful. Each of these European and American authors brought their own perspectives, positionalities, and experiences to their presentations of Ottoman women; reading with and through their attitudes is a crucial aspect of using their writing.

Ottoman women themselves are fundamental sources of information about dress and social life more generally. With the emergence of women's periodicals in Istanbul in the last decades of the nineteenth century, Ottoman women had the opportunity to engage in ongoing conversations through the periodicals about subjects of concern to them, including fashion. The second half of the nineteenth century also saw the emergence of Ottoman women novelists and poets, whose work provides important insights into the daily life and intellectual concerns of their subjects, including discussions of changing dress practices. Their novels and poetry, important though they are, fall outside the scope of this project.

The memoirs written by Ottoman women in this same period are also invaluable sources for this project. *The Imperial Harem of the Sultans. Daily Life at the Çırağan Palace during the 19th Century* by Leyla Saz Hanımefendi is particularly important, but hers is not the only account of late Ottoman harem life. Ayşe Osmanoğlu (1887–1960), a daughter of Abdülhamid, wrote a memoir about her father, originally published in the late 1950s (Osmanoglu 1994). Other late Ottoman women have been the subject of biographies, both scholarly and popular.[12] Although dress is not necessarily a central concern in the books written by Ottoman and foreign women about changing circumstances for Ottoman women (e.g., Zeyneb Hanoum and Demetra Vaka Brown), their observations about women's lives, including their clothing, are important. For the twentieth century, the memoirs of Emine Foat Tugay and Halide Edib Adıvar are crucial. Further important sources for late Ottoman fashion history are diverse media such as newspaper ads and articles in both the foreign and Ottoman press, fashion periodicals, commercial directories, and the record books of tailors and seamstresses.

The Garments: Museum Collections of Ottoman Women's Dress

Surviving garments provide the most reliable and tangible evidence for what women in Istanbul were wearing. Examined in conjunction with the visual and written sources described above, they allow a reasonably accurate reconstruction of a trajectory of fashion change. Before examining actual garments, though, I want to introduce the histories of the most significant collections of Ottoman women's dress to understand the impact their institutional histories, missions, and collecting practices have had on the material available to study. It is also useful to put the Ottoman example in the context of fashion collections more broadly.

For the most part, the examples discussed here are drawn from three significant collections of Ottoman women's dress: the Topkapı Sarayı Museum in Istanbul; the Sadberk Hanım Museum in Büyükdere, north of Istanbul along the Bosporus; and the Metropolitan Museum of Art in New York. Other important collections in Türkiye include the Ethnography Museum in Ankara and the Uluumay Collection of Ottoman Folk Costumes and Jewelry in Bursa, among others. Collections of dress are also found across Türkiye in smaller provincial museums and private collections. Outside of Türkiye, there are substantial collections of Ottoman women's dress in the Victoria and Albert Museum in London, the National Museum of Scotland in Edinburgh, the Israel Museum in Jerusalem, and the Museum of Fine Arts, Boston, to mention just a few.[13]

Each of the museums mentioned here has a unique collecting history, the circumstances of which have had a direct influence on the shape and content of the collection available to visitors and researchers. In Türkiye the development of the museum sector generally has been the subject of important research over the past two decades,[14] but here I focus on the museums that are particularly relevant for this project. Present-day Türkiye has a robust museum sector, which began to take shape in the mid-nineteenth century. The display of dress dates from this early period, with the presentation of the uniforms of the Janissaries (the elite Ottoman military corps abolished in 1826) in the military museum set up in the Byzantine church of Hagia Irene and moved to its own site in the Ibrahim Paşa Palace on the Hippodrome, the Elbise-I Atika [Ancient Clothes]

Museum. The collection, displayed on about 140 wooden mannequins, was moved several times over the next decades, eventually returning to the Askeri Müze, or Military Museum in Hagia Irene.

In 1856 Abdülmecid and his court moved to the newly completed Dolmabahçe Palace, a grand building along the Bosporus built in the Western style of palatial architecture. Although the Topkapı Palace continued to be the site of specific royal ceremonies, it no longer served as the center of court life. Even before the move to the Dolmabahçe Palace, foreign visitors had been given permission to tour the Topkapı grounds; but with the transition of the sultan and his court to the modern palace, the Topkapı gradually took on a new identity as a museum. By the late nineteenth century, it had become a popular site for visitors to Istanbul, the carefully orchestrated visit described in numerous travelogues and memoirs (Özlü 2015, 2022).

The Imperial Treasury, a multiroom display of jewels, porcelains, weapons, and coins, "a maze of objects rare and perfect make to gratify every extravagant whim," as described by the American writer and educator Edwin Grosvenor in his 1900 book *Constantinople* (quoted in ibid. 2015: 178), was the highlight of the tour. A particularly impressive component of the Imperial Treasury display was the collection of twenty-three costumes of the Ottoman sultans, displayed in chronological order, each in its own glass case (Figure 2.12). In opening the Topkapı Palace and its treasures to visitors, the Ottomans were participating in a display practice taking place across Europe as other royal dynasties set up carefully curated public viewing of imperial treasuries, crown jewels, and other paraphernalia (ibid. 2022: 166). Fully aware of the Orientalist attractions

Figure 2.12 *The royal costumes of the Ottoman Sultans kept in the Imperial Topkapı Sarayı*, Abdullah Frères, *ca.* 1880–1890. Abdul Hamid II Collection, Library of Congress Prints and Photographs Division Washington, D.C., LC-USZ62-81450.

of the Topkapı Palace, the Ottomans staged the palace in a manner that would satisfy the curiosity of foreign visitors (Ottoman subjects could not visit the palace until the early years of the twentieth century), displaying the magnificence of the Ottoman past but also demonstrating their engagement with modern museum practices.

The clothing and personal belongings of the Ottoman sultans and some members of the royal families were carefully saved in the Topkapı, labeled and wrapped in muslin. Unfortunately, over the centuries, the labels have sometimes become detached from their garments, so it is no longer always possible to identify the original owner of the garments. Most of these objects belonged to the sultans and princes, but the collection also includes some garments that were worn by the consorts and daughters of the sultans. In her inventory of the costume collection, Hülya Tezcan lists fifteen garments belonging to women and seventy children's kaftans out of a collection of 1,550 pieces (Baker, Tezcan, and Wearden 1996: 10–30). As the Topkapı Sarayı evolved into a fully professionalized museum over the course of the twentieth century, the museum collections, including costume, have been the focus of a great deal of serious scholarship.[15]

The Sadberk Hanım Museum is the oldest private museum in Türkiye and holds the most important collection of Ottoman dress outside of the Topkapı Sarayı. The museum is named after Sadberk Koç (1908–1973), who marshaled her own interest in Türkiye's cultural heritage, particularly costume and textiles, and Koç family resources to form a groundbreaking collection, which was then made available to the public with the founding of the museum in 1980, decades before other private museums took shape in Istanbul. The costume collections focus on the dress and jewelry of elite women and, to a lesser extent, children. The beautifully designed and maintained galleries in the museum's historic house display the permanent collection; and over the years, the museum has mounted important temporary exhibitions showcasing specific aspects of the collection, generally accompanied by significant publications.[16] The museum continues to expand its collection through purchase and donation, and it is fortunate in being able to link many of the garments in its collection to specific women, based on information provided by descendants of the garments' original owners.

A third important collection of Ottoman dress (of men, women, and children) is located in Bursa, the Uluumay Osmanlı Halk Kiyafetleri ve Takılar Müzesi (Uluumay Ottoman Folk Clothing and Jewelry Museum), which opened in 2004.[17] Assembled by Esat Uluumay (1939–2018), a Bursa businessman with a strong interest in Turkish folklore (he was an accomplished folk dancer), the collection includes urban, rural, and tribal dress from all over the former Ottoman Empire. The Uluumay collection, which has not been extensively published, is more diverse in both geographic scope and quality than the collections of the Sadberk Hanım Museum or the Topkapı Palace, providing an opportunity for researchers to see material not readily available elsewhere. Pieces from his collection were exhibited publicly from time to time beginning in the 1980s, but not until the 2004 opening of the museum in the Şair Ahmet Paşa Medrese was the collection regularly accessible to visitors. Now approximately half the collection is on view.[18] The dress collections of the Uluumay Museum, along with the Sadberk Hanım Museum, the Topkapı Palace, and others not discussed here, each with a distinct collecting history, document the rich history of dress in the Ottoman Empire. The Istanbul collections, as could be expected, are particularly important for documenting the clothing of the diverse population of the Empire's capital and of the court.

In Britain, despite the long history of the monarchy, the royal wardrobe was not systematically preserved or collected (Strasdin 2017: 137–48). Although royal wardrobes were extensive and often saved in the palace, items that were no longer worn were frequently given as gifts to palace staff. They were free to use them or sell them (without attribution to their royal owners). Even the most magnificent of garments could end up in the auction house, as when the velvet and ermine coronation robes of George IV (r. 1820–1830) were purchased at auction by Madame Tussaud in 1831 and displayed publicly until the 1860s (ibid.). More recently, in 2020 a collection of clothing and boots belonging to Queen Victoria came to auction, having been saved for more than a century by the family of a royal photographer to the queen, who perhaps received the items from palace staff in return for taking their photographs.[19]

At the 2020 auction of Queen Victoria's clothing, several of the objects were purchased by the Royal Ceremonial Dress Collection, the national collection of royal and court dress. The collection was organized in the early 1980s, and in 1989 it came under the supervision of the Historic Royal Palaces. Today the collection is housed at Hampton Court Palace and Kensington Palace,[20] where it may be studied. At the beginning of the twentieth century, the London Museum, founded in 1912, included a significant exhibition of costume, donated by the royal family and others.[21] That collection became part of the Museum of London in 1975.[22]

For the most part, collections of royal clothing are often held in institutions specifically devoted to preserving the history and traditions of the royal family or the court, such as the Topkapı Palace Museum in Istanbul or the Royal Ceremonial Dress Collection in London. The inclusion of dress in more general museums follows a different trajectory, although individual pieces originally belonging to members of a royal family may end up in those more general collections. For example, the costume collection at the Victoria and Albert Museum contains several garments and accessories that belonged to Queen Mary (1867–1953).[23]

Displaced or exiled royalty were sometimes left with few resources apart from their personal possessions and once in exile, sold their clothing for income (Ekıncı 2015). It seems likely, for example, that a number of Ottoman garments reached collections in Europe and America following the abrupt exile of the Ottoman royal family in March 1924 when their valuable clothing would have been one of their few financial assets. Auctions were often held after the death of the clothing's owner, but in some cases, clothing belonging to royalty was auctioned for charity, as in 1997 when Princess Diana donated seventy-nine evening gowns to an auction to raise money for two specific foundations.[24]

In the United States, the core of the costume collection at the Metropolitan Museum of Art was formed in the first decades of the twentieth century by Irene Lewisohn, a wealthy New York philanthropist. Lewisohn founded the Museum of Costume Art in 1937 to house the collection of costume she had acquired in the course of her travels, intended to be used in the plays produced in the theater companies that she and her sister supported (Lewisohn 1937). Following Lewisohn's death in 1944, the Museum of Costume Art merged with the Metropolitan Museum of Art in 1946 to become the Costume Institute. The collection of costume from the Middle East continued to grow through gift and purchase (in part via the Lewisohn Bequest), and in 2018 as part of a collections' reorganization was transferred to the Department of Islamic Art. It is now housed in the Antonio Ratti Textile Center and Reference Library. Most of the Ottoman costume that is addressed here entered the collection between 1940 and 1986, although much of that had been collected earlier in the region by the donors who eventually gave their pieces to the museum.

The museum collections mentioned so far have focused primarily on the dress of the elite and generally, members of the dominant culture. These collecting priorities mirror the interest in the fashion world, and until relatively recently, fashion scholarship, in the clothing of the elite. However, understanding what is saved and what is left out of museums (as well as archives and libraries) is crucial in assessing the impact those decisions have on shaping a broader understanding of history and culture. Without specific, concerted, and funded efforts to counteract the collecting practices established over decades (centuries?) of privileging dominant social and political narratives, it is impossible to rewrite/retell stories of the past to include more diverse voices.

One particularly telling example of building more inclusive museum collections comes from the American context. For Black American fashion history, long overlooked in mainstream museums, two institutions were and continue to be key resources: the Black Fashion Museum and the National Museum of African American History and Culture (NMAAHC) at the Smithsonian. Founded at different times and under very different circumstances, these two institutions both demonstrate the impact a single institution can have in enhancing research and public awareness. The Black Fashion Museum was the result of the passion and energy of a single individual, Lois K. Alexander-Lane (1916–2007), an extraordinary woman who turned a lifelong interest in fashion into the establishment of the Harlem Institute of Fashion and the Black Fashion Museum. With a $20,000 grant from the National Endowment for the Arts in 1977 to found the Black Fashion Museum, Alexander Lane, drawing upon her extensive network of influential Black women across the United States, assembled a donated collection of historic and contemporary Black fashion. The Black Fashion Museum opened in Harlem in October 1979, and in 2007 the collection, which consisted by then of several thousand pieces, was donated to the National Museum of African American History and Culture (NMAAHC), where it forms the core of its extensive fashion collection.

In the book he wrote about the creation of NMAAHC, founding director Lonnie G. Bunch III describes the process by which the collection of the new museum was built, which included foundational donations such as that of the Black Fashion Museum. He wrote,

> When I became director of the museum, I had many concerns … Nothing … caused me greater concern than the challenge of building a national collection. If there was one axiom that shaped the museum careers of curators of color [in the United States], it was the belief in the paucity of objects that illustrate African American history and culture.

(Bunch 2019: 90)

He goes on to recount an earlier experience involving finding exhibition material in unexpected places, concluding by saying, "I came to believe that all of the twentieth century, most of the nineteenth century and a bit of the eighteenth century still existed in the basements, trunks and attics in people's homes. What we [the NMAAHC staff] needed was a strategy to help us access these collections" (ibid.: 91).

The museum developed an initiative, Save Our African American Treasures,[25] that raised the profile of the not-yet-open museum in communities across the country, helped the museum staff to identify potential collection objects, and resulted in significant gifts to the museum. After a decade, the museum had built a collection of more than thirty-five thousand objects, "70 percent of … [which] … came from the basements, garages, and attics, from the homes of a diverse array of Americans." (ibid.: 96). Welcoming more than three million visitors in its first year (2016),[26] NMAAHC has made visible and accessible an aspect of American history and culture that has been overlooked and often unseen. The Black Fashion Museum and the National Museum of African American History and Culture are examples of the way in which significant gaps in the collecting priorities of mainstream museums can be addressed.

In the case of Ottoman fashion history, attempting a more inclusive account of what the women of Istanbul wore presents substantial challenges. Existing museum collections have so far focused primarily on the clothing of the elite, most often the Muslim elite. The clothing of working women, enslaved women, and Greek, Armenian, and Jewish women is much more difficult to document. Costume collections tend to be ethnically or religiously separate; thus Armenian women's dress can be found in museums devoted to Armenian history and culture,[27] the clothing of members of the Greek Ottoman community is mostly held in Greek museums, and the clothing belonging to the Jewish women of Türkiye is held primarily in The Quincentennial Foundation Museum of Turkish Jews in Istanbul and the Israel Museum in Jerusalem. For the clothing of nonelite women, remembering Lonnie Bunch's words, I believe examples are still to be found in the trunks and boxes of Turkish families and in the collections of provincial museums across Türkiye, which often depend on local donations for their collection and thus may hold material from local, nonelite families.

Bringing clothing worn by Ottoman women of different ethnicities, religions, and economic classes together in one museum or one collection is a dream project, one that is most likely impossible given the realities of institutional structures and limited resources. In the meantime, I will do that virtually over the next chapters, as I examine a range of images, written descriptions, and garments worn by the diverse population of the Ottoman women of Istanbul. I begin in the next chapter by looking at a sample of surviving garments to understand their construction, tailoring, fabric and embellishment as Ottoman women began experimenting with aspects of Euro-American fashion.

CHAPTER 3
THE GARMENTS: TAILORING, CONSTRUCTION, AND TRANSFORMATION

In the previous Chapter I considered the sources available for a study of Ottoman women's dress and the challenges presented by factors such as institutional collecting histories, accidents of time, and accessibility of those sources. Now I want to deepen the investigation into the dress practices of Istanbul women in the decades leading up to the dramatic fashion changes that began in the mid-nineteenth century. In this chapter, I examine a sample of surviving garments, considering aspects of their tailoring, construction, fabrics, and the ways in which they were modified to reflect changing styles. Even at this early stage of fashion transformation, the women of Istanbul were self-fashioning in ways that reflected their identities, both personal and in terms of their broader social, ethnic, and religious identities.

Elite Women's Dress in Eighteenth-Century Istanbul: Tailoring and Construction

Ottoman women's dress, and Ottoman clothing generally, incorporated a variety of forms and fabric types, but in terms of tailoring it can be described by a few general characteristics. The sizes of the pieces out of which a garment was constructed were determined by the width of the loom on which the cloth was woven. Because weaving cloth by hand or even using early mechanized looms was a time-consuming process, garments were assembled with a minimum of waste. Pieces were rectangular in shape or cut along straight lines so that the entire loom width of fabric was used with no scraps left over. The boxy, loose-fitting clothes that resulted from such construction were held on the body by means of drawstring gathering or sashes. Buttons could be used to close the neck of an undergarment or the bodice of a robe. The visual impact of these outfits depended on the lavish (but not wasteful) use of rich materials and the vibrancy that resulted from the combination of colors, textures, and patterns assembled in a single outfit. The elaborate tailoring that characterized European garments was not found in traditional Ottoman dress, but simple tailoring should not be confused with careless construction. Although the traditional clothes are assembled from only a few pieces, many of the garments show meticulous attention to details of lining, pockets, trim, and other finishing.

A women's costume consisted of three essential components, to which other elements were added. The *gömlek*, or undershirt, *şalvar* (baggy trousers), and *entari*, or robe, formed the basic outfit, supplemented by vests, overdresses, jackets, sashes, shawls, and other accessories. (Loose-fitting underdrawers, or *dizlik*, were worn under the *şalvar*, but these rarely appear in museum collections and will not be discussed further.)

The undershirts that have survived generally all show the same construction, although there are variations in fabric and finishing details. The fabric used for these undergarments ranged from a coarse cotton plain weave to a fine silk and cotton material (Figure 3.1). The undyed cotton plain weave was often creped—during the weaving process, the yarn is twisted so tightly that it retwists itself when no longer under tension, producing a puckered, slightly elastic effect. The cotton *gömleks*, with creping for part of their length and typically with colored selvage stripes, were generally purchased ready-made with the neck uncut, to be finished at home. *Gömleks* as in Figure 3.1 were made of *bürümcük*, a lightweight crepe woven of silk or a silk/cotton mix that often had decorative warp stripes of varying widths woven in.

Figure 3.1 *Gömlek*, nineteenth century. New York, Metropolitan Museum of Art, Purchase, Martin and Caryl Horwitz Gift, 1991 (1991.217.2) Image copyright © The Metropolitan Museum of Art. Image source: Art Resource, NY.

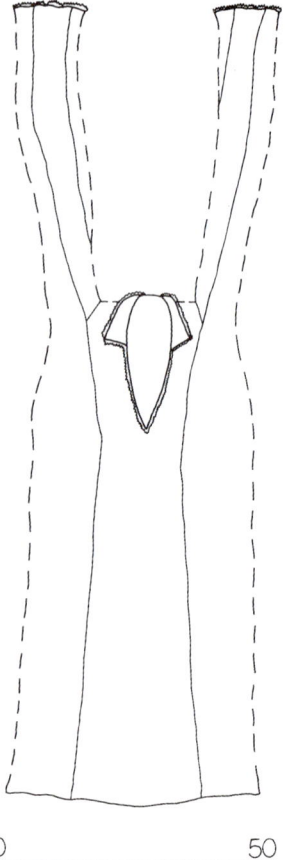

nm
UL bg 122

0   50

Figure 3.2 *Gömlek*, date unknown, private collection, drawing by the author.

Five pieces were used in the construction of the *gömlek* (Figure 3.2). The body of the garment was a single loom width of fabric with no seam at the shoulder. An additional width of fabric was added to each side, running the length of the garment and sleeve. The sleeve was completed by a half-width of fabric, joined at the shoulder. If creped fabric was used, the creping would be positioned at the upper bodice and sleeve, allowing a closer fit. An opening was cut for the neck, and the front could be closed either by a tie or a button. A collar was sometimes added, and the sleeves were occasionally gathered into cuffs. In many cases, the neck, front opening, and sleeve ends were finished with needle lace (*oya*), often in two colors. Other decoration was provided by the stripes that ran the length of the garment and decorative stitching that sometimes appeared at the shoulder seams. The bottom of the *gömlek* was finished with a narrow rolled hem.

Şalvar could have a variety of shapes: the example illustrated here is of a kind worn by women in Istanbul (Figure 3.3). It is composed of two large, rectangular pieces of fabric joined at center front and back to which elongated diamond-shaped gussets were added. Extra fabric, typically a plain white cotton plain weave, was often added at the waist and bottom of each leg, perhaps because the silk used in the garment was too delicate for gathering, and to economize on the use of expensive fabric. At both waist and leg hem, fabric was turned to the inside to form a placket for the ties, *uçkur*, which gathered the garment and held it on the body. The white cotton at the bottom of each leg would not have been visible when the *şalvar* was worn because they were tied just below the knee so the fabric would fall in graceful, billowing folds to the floor.

The *entari* was modified in a number of ways over time, but its basic form consisted of a long robe, often open down the front (in some examples, buttons indicate that the bodice of the *entari* would have been closed), with a slightly flared skirt and long, wide sleeves. A single loom-width of fabric made up the body of the robe, with no shoulder seam. Extra width was given to the skirt by the addition of long triangular pieces (*peş* in

Figure 3.3 *Şalvar*, mid-nineteenth century. Istanbul, Topkapı Sarayı Museum, 13/1974, drawing by the author.

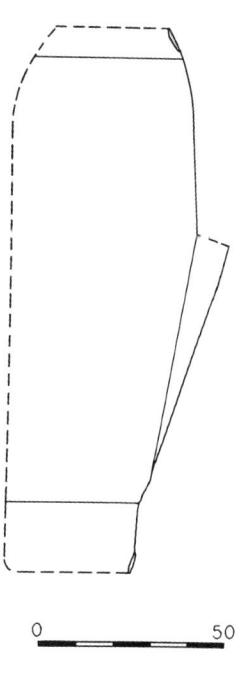

0   50

NM

TKS 13/1974

Turkish) at each side, front and back, and similar-shaped pieces were attached to each side of the center front, allowing the front pieces of the *entari* to overlap. The sides of the garment could be open to the knee, in which case the *entari* was called *üç etek*, or three skirts (two in front and one in back). If pockets were included, they could be in the skirt sides, as in the example illustrated here, or in the upper bodice. The sleeve was formed by a large rectangular piece of fabric with a seam under the arm and a small underarm gusset. The sleeve seam often extended only to the elbow, with the sleeve open from there. The neckline was either left plain or finished by the addition of a small stand-up collar of the same fabric as the rest of the garment. The *entari* was fully lined, often in an undyed cotton plain weave, which sometimes was starched to provide more stiffness for the garment. The inside areas that would have been visible, around the side and front skirt openings and the sleeves, were sometimes lined with a contrasting material. Decorative trim, frequently of several kinds, was sewn around all the garment edges and could be used to cover the seams as well. The *entari* described and shown here is a simple one; more elaborate examples could have different proportions, distinctive shaping of the sleeve ends, or scalloped skirt edges, but the basic construction would be the same (Figure 3.4).

The Ottoman painter Levni Abdülcelil Çelebi (d. 1732), mentioned in the previous chapter, created single-page paintings of men and women, Ottoman and foreign, many of which are saved in *Hazine* (Album) 2164 in the Topkapı Palace. With a certain amount of variation among the paintings of Ottoman women, each single page displays a woman and her sartorial choices. These images, done with Levni's characteristic attention to detail and interest in fabric, costume, and hairstyle, provide a clear idea of how court women in the early eighteenth century combined the basic components of their dress (*gömlek*, *şalvar*, and *entari*) with sashes, jewelry, headdress, and other accessories into striking and elegant outfits. In Figure 3.5, the extravagantly dressed woman wears a full-length purple *entari* with close-fitting sleeves over a patterned hip-length jacket. The *entari* is partially buttoned and held closed by a belt of linked metal plaques with a metal clasp. Her striped *şalvar* with its embroidered tie and long, sheer *gömlek* are visible beneath the *entari*, which she holds open so the viewer can see her outfit more clearly. The swirls and folds of fabric, created in part by the movement of

Figure 3.4 *Entari*, first half nineteenth century. Istanbul, YapıKredi Kültür Sanat Yayıncılık, 1/104, drawing by the author.

Figure 3.5 *Lady in Purple Smelling a Carnation*, Levni Abdülcelil Çelebi, *ca.* 1707–1732. Istanbul, The Directorate of National Palaces, Topkapi Palace Manuscripts Collection, Inv. No. H.2164, fol.8b.

the figure as she holds open her long robe and lifts a carnation to her nose, invite the viewer to imagine the colors, textures, feel, and sound of the layers of fabric combined in this single outfit.[1]

The subjects in several works by the painter Jean Etienne Liotard, slightly later than those by Levni, wear a low-cut *entari* of a white silk or cotton embroidered with flowers, trimmed with narrow blue braid or *oya* (needle lace), and held in place by a cloth belt with circular metal clasps (Figure 3.6). In this example dated circa 1752, *Women in Turkish Dress*,[2] the long sleeves of the *entari* fall open to reveal their yellow lining. Her full-length *gömlek* or chemise is clearly visible in a depiction detailed enough to identify the *bürümcük* fabric from which it is made.

Elite Women's Dress in Eighteenth-Century Istanbul: The Textiles and the Garments

Ottoman seamstresses and tailors had a stunning array of textiles of different materials, weave structures, patterns, and colors from which to choose when they set out to clothe their patrons. Cotton, wool, and silk were all produced locally and woven into a variety of textiles, but textiles also came from both east (Iran and India) and west (England, Holland, Venice, Hungary, and France). Textiles had been produced in volume by the Turkish textile industry since the fifteenth century, but despite the robust domestic production, demand

Figure 3.6 *Woman in Turkish Dress, Seated on a Sofa*, Jean Etienne Liotard, *ca.* 1752. New York, Metropolitan Museum of Art 2019.141.16, Bequest of Mrs. Charles Wrightsman, 2019.

exceeded supply, thus the need to import cloth from outside the empire (Tezcan 1993: 20). Apart from providing basic necessities such as the wool broadcloth used for military uniforms, the import of textiles was also driven by fashion (Phillips 2021).

The variety of textiles produced or imported into the Ottoman Empire provided a wealth of colors and surface designs through their raw materials and weave structures. Another key element in the creation of the dress fabrics worn by the Ottoman women of Istanbul was embroidery, added to the woven fabric after it was taken off the loom. Embroidery had always been a highly valued aspect of Ottoman textile arts, but in the late-eighteenth and nineteenth centuries embroidery became more complex and exuberant. No longer content with using one or two stitches on a piece, embroiderers now brought a dazzling variety of stitches into the execution of a single object. Colors also became more varied, and metallic thread, which had long been employed in embroidery, was used in more diverse forms.

Entaris in the collections of the Sadberk Hanım Museum (Figure 3.7) and the Topkapı Sarayı Museum show close resemblances to the painted depictions in the work of Liotard and Levni illustrated above. Both garments have fabric similar to that of the *entari* appearing in Liotard's painting, which shows a small floral motif repeated against a plain background. These two *entaris* are both made of *sevai*, a fashionable fabric produced in Istanbul and Bursa, as well as Iran. *Sevai* is a lightweight silk often produced with a repeating pattern of small flowers arranged on the bias. The flowers are created from wire-wrapped yarn by hand during the weaving process while the fabric is still on the loom (Tezcan 1993: 36). According to Görünür, the fabric of the Sadberk Hanım Museum *entari* was most likely produced in Iran, while the Topkapı Sarayı Museum *entari* is made from Ottoman *sevai* (2010: 37). Both *entaris* have a deep neckline and narrow trim decorating all the garment edges. The garment proportions are restrained compared to the exaggerated length and fullness of the nineteenth-century garments that follow. The Sadberk Hanim *entari* in Figure 3.7 is constructed in the typical manner, with a few distinctive details. The slits in the sides of the skirt are short, very different from the high slits seen on some *entaris*, especially later ones. A layer of cotton wadding between the silk on the exterior

Figure 3.7 *Entari*, eighteenth century. Büyük dere, Courtesy of the Vehbi Koç Foundation, Sadberk Hanım Museum. 14150-K.808.

and the starched muslin lining would have added warmth (as is also the case with the Topkapı Sarayı Museum *entari*). Decorative elements, such as the flat metallic braid covering some of the seams on the skirt and edging the hem and sleeves, and the treatment of the sleeve ends are characteristic of eighteenth-century fashion.

Garments made from *sevai*, an expensive fabric, would have been treasured, perhaps passed down, and thus survive in a number of museum collections. The Victoria and Albert Museum holds a garment that entered the museum collection in 1958, and according to family tradition, belonged originally to Lady Mary Wortley Montagu.[3] Lady Montagu, who visited Istanbul in 1716–1718, described her Turkish clothing in detail, and numerous portraits survive, purporting to depict her in her Turkish garb. Her detailed description is worth quoting because it is such a clear account:

> The first part of my dress is a pair of drawers, very full that reach to my shoes, and conceal the legs more modestly than your petticoats. They are of a thin rose-coloured damask, brocaded with silver flowers. My shoes are of white kid leather, embroidered with gold. Over this hangs my smock, of a fine white silk gauze, edged with embroidery. This smock has wide sleeves hanging half way down the arm, and is closed at the neck with a diamond button; but the shape and colour of the bosom is very well to be distinguished through it.—The *antery* is a waistcoat, made close to the shape, of white and gold damask, with very long sleeves falling back, and fringed with deep gold fringe, and should have diamond or pearl buttons. My *caftan*, of the same stuff with my drawers, is a robe exactly fitted to my shape, and reaching to my feet, with very long strait falling sleeves. Over this is my girdle, of about four fingers broad, which, all that can afford it, have entirely of diamonds or other precious stones; those who will not be at that expence, have it of exquisite embroidery on sattin [*sic*]; but it must be fastened before with a clasp of diamonds.—The *curdee* is a loose robe they throw off, or put on, according to the weather, being of a rich brocade (mine is green and gold) either lined with ermine or sables; the sleeves reach very little below the shoulders.
>
> *(April 1, 1717, to her sister, Lady Mar)*

The Victoria and Albert *entari* is made of a pinkish *sevai* fabric with a series of gold stripes alternating with a pattern of ribbon and floral motifs, with scalloped edges at the neck, front opening, hem, and high side slits in the skirt, a narrow stand-up collar, and narrow gold trim at all edges. The design and proportions are similar to other eighteenth-century examples of *entaris* from Istanbul, and in terms of construction, the *entari* displays the traditional tailoring modes described above. The back view of the garment reveals that a long dart was taken up the central back at some point, perhaps to provide a more fitted silhouette for the wearer. It is impossible to know when in the long history of this garment the modification was made, but it is an important reminder of how garments could be altered over time to reflect changing tastes or the different identities that their wearers wished to perform. Such alterations, carried out for any number of reasons, are an enduring aspect of the fashion history explored in this project.

The shape and construction of the *entari* associated with Lady Mary Wortley Montagu is very similar to Figure 3.8, from the Metropolitan Museum of Art. Made from *sevai* and trimmed with narrow braid around the scalloped edges and stand-up collar, the entari is rather plain, allowing the elaborate woven pattern of the *sevai* to shine. This particular design, wide floral stripes in pink, red, black, white, and green, alternating with a herringbone stripe of lighter silk separated by a narrow line of tiny blue and white rectangles, is sometimes called Üsküdar *savai* because it was produced there (Tezcan 1993: 94–95). *Entaris* of similar fabrics may be seen in the collections of the Sadberk Hanim Museum and the Museum of Fine Arts, Boston,[4] and perhaps elsewhere as Üsküdar *savai* seems to have been very popular over a long period. In terms of construction, the sleeves of this *entari* have an extra piece of fabric at the shoulder to allow for a longer length and are partially

Figure 3.8 *Entari*, front view and sleeve detail, nineteenth century. New York, Metropolitan Museum of Art, Gift of Charles Collingwood, 1979.566.5.

lined with a more coarsely woven fabric that resembles the *sevai* in its use of floral bands and stripes, although in a different and less-subtle color palette. There is a pocket at hip level on each side of the garment, which has been relined at some point. There are no buttons at the bodice, but snaps have been added in modern times, perhaps when the *entari* was relined.

In addition to the Topkapı Sarayı *entari* discussed above, the museum holds a group of seven garments that belonged to Fatma Sultan (1764–1821), a daughter of Mustafa III (Tezcan 2006). Taken as a group, the garments provide an intriguing look at part of the wardrobe of a woman in the royal family, whose fashion choices would have certainly influenced the trends of elite women in Istanbul more generally. They include a child's *kaftan*, a fur-trimmed *kaftan*, and five *entaris*. The *entaris* are modestly proportioned with plain edges and very little trim. In four cases, they are made from extremely expensive fabric, silk with an all-over woven design of silver arabesques, *seraser* with embroidered floral motifs in colored silks, and *selimiye* with an all-over pattern of gold rosettes. A highly prized silk fabric whose extensive use of metal-wrapped thread produced a shimmering effect, *seraser* was used for imperial furnishings as well as garments. *Selimiye* was a silk brocade, typically with wide vertical stripes containing floral designs separated by narrow stripes made up of small squares, all created by the warp threads, a weaving technique likely imported from Europe, along with the looms on which the fabric was woven. The Jacquard looms, developed in France in 1804, were imported by Selim III and set up in workshops near the Selimiye Mosque in the Istanbul neighborhood of Üsküdar; hence the name of the fabric (Tezcan 1993: 28–36). The *entaris* made from these very exclusive fabrics would have been eye-catching and vibrant, the plain cut of the garments foregrounding the expensive and slightly stiff fabric, with no need for elaborate trim or exaggerated proportions.

Fatma Sultan's coat (Figure 3.9) is an example of a garment that figures frequently in written descriptions and images of women's dress from the eighteenth century (Figure 2.1) but is less commonly found in museum

Figure 3.9 Coat belonging to Fatma Sultan, eighteenth century. Istanbul, The Directorate of National Palaces, Topkapı Palace Sultans' Costumes Collection Inv. No. 13.814.

collections, a fur-trimmed or fur-lined *kaftan*, often with short sleeves. Fur was a highly desirable component of clothing, valued for its warmth but also because its use was regulated by the court and was thus an indicator of the status of its wearer (see Tezcan 2004 on the regulations and customs governing the use of fur in clothing). This example is small (63 cm. in length), so was perhaps made for Fatma Sultan when she was a child. The *kaftan*, with its luxurious use of fur, also had panels of embroidered silk with metal trim and would have been worn over the *gömlek*, *şalvar*, and *entari*.

Women's garments made of wool survive in fewer numbers than those of silk, but wool was a staple in the Ottoman fabric universe, produced locally but also imported from Europe as noted above. The very fine wools, *sof* and *çali* (challis), produced from the fleece of Angora (Ankara) goats, were in high demand both among Ottoman consumers and European markets (Tezcan 1993: 24–26). A peacock blue wool twill was used for the elaborately embroidered eighteenth-century *entari* illustrated in Figure 3.10, in the collection of the Metropolitan Museum of Art. The proportions and structure of the *entari* resemble those of other eighteenth-century examples, although the sleeves and skirt are already showing the more generous proportions that became popular at the end of the century and into the nineteenth. As is the case with many garments that have survived over the centuries, at some point in its history modifications were made to this *entari*. The straight seams joining the sleeves to the body of the garment have been altered to create a more rounded armscye, resembling the set-in sleeves of European construction, and the entire garment has been neatly relined with a dark salmon-colored silk. Whether these changes were within several decades of the *entari*'s construction to satisfy the fashion aspirations of a later owner or by a twentieth-century wearer is impossible to know.

Figure 3.10 *Entari*, eighteenth century. New York, Metropolitan Museum of Art, Gift of Harriet Marple, 52.204.

The embroidered fabric is known as *hüseyni* or *tepebaşı*, after the Istanbul neighborhood in which it was made. Wool twill, blue in this case, but often red, is covered with embroidery in polychrome silks, using chain stitch, couched metal threads, and sequins to create an exuberant all-over design of large clover-like flowers, smaller blossoms, leaves, and bows. The embroidery was carried out before the garment was assembled, with passementerie in the same shades as the floral embroidery and small sequins edging the sleeves, front opening, and skirts added to this example once the *entari* had been constructed.

The garments discussed here and others that have survived, along with the descriptions of dress left by the intrepid eighteenth-century travelers whose writings I have examined and the visual representations created by the European and Ottoman artists, together provide a reasonably clear view of what elite women in Istanbul were wearing over the course of the century. The painting styles of the various artists whose work is illustrated here and in the previous chapter (Levni, Liotard, Abdullah Boukhari, Vanmour) differ sharply in the depiction of the body, the use of light and shadow, painting medium, and so on. However, the representation of dress in many of the works of these artists show a remarkable correspondence in details of fabric, garment shapes, layering of garments, and other aspects of dress practice over the years in which they were active. The paintings show the *gömlek* worn over the *şalvar* (not tucked in), often reaching almost to the feet. *Entaris* of this period were shorter than those that followed in the next century, and the sleeves were long and narrow, in some cases with decoratively shaped ends. Skirts may have had short slits at the side. In many cases, the *entaris* had U-shaped necklines, something seen less frequently in the nineteenth century. Silk fabric was very popular, but there were also *entaris* made of wool. *Entaris* were often closed by wide shawls or sashes loosely tied around the waist and hips, and narrower belts closed with elaborately worked metal buckles were also worn.

Dress in the First Decades of the Nineteenth Century

The fabrics and trims of eighteenth-century fashion continued to be important in the nineteenth-century wardrobes of Ottoman women. The elaborately trimmed *entari* illustrated in Figure 3.11 is an example of what a wealthy woman in Istanbul wore in the first decades of the nineteenth century. The fabric used in this example is a *kutnu*, a sturdy fabric made with silk warps and wefts of cotton or cotton and silk mixed, used for women's garments and upholstery (Tezcan 1993: 28). *Kutnu* was imported from Iran and India but also produced in Bursa, as was this example (see Tezcan 2016:111 for a piece of the same fabric). *Kutnu* was often striped, as seen here, where vertical stripes of small green and white alternating squares edge a wider stripe with a red geometric design. The garment's proportions are generous, although not as exaggerated as some nineteenth-century examples, and the slits in the skirt are very high. The open front, side slits, and hem are all scalloped, and a slit in the center back reaches to the waist (this *entari* is thus an example of a *dört etek entari*, or a four-skirt *entari*). The sleeves are open for their entire length and end in a narrow band of the same fabric. The fabric at the end of the sleeves has been irregularly pieced, which suggests that the tailor or seamstress who made this garment was using every bit of available fabric to complete it.

Although the striped fabric is striking, the trim on the *entari* is the more remarkable feature of this garment. The scalloped edges and sleeve ends are neatly finished with a braided cord trim of green and pink to which an intricate floral passementerie of plied cord, also green and pink, has been tacked. The cord has been twisted and knotted to create flowers, leaves, and stems that extend several inches beyond the garment's edges. Unlike some costumes that are found in museum collections, this one shows signs of wear and was relined at some point after it was made, suggesting that this piece, with its carefully coordinated colors of fabric, trim, and ornate floral passementerie was a treasured part of someone's wardrobe.

Figure 3.11 *Entari*, front view and sleeve detail, nineteenth century. New York, Metropolitan Museum of Art, Gift of Julian Clarence Levi, C.I.66.21.15.

An Üsküdar *savai* fabric similar to that in Figure 3.8 was also chosen for the *entari* illustrated in Figure 3.12. Apart from its popular fabric, this *entari* displays a number of decidedly fashionable details: high slits in the long skirts, extremely long sleeves, watch pockets, and the decoratively cut edges of the front opening, skirts, and sleeves. Watch pockets were small, circular pockets generally placed on each side of the bodice, thought to have been used for the pocket watches that began to be imported into the Ottoman Empire in the late eighteenth century and were fashionable items in their own right (Yagou 2019). The treatment of the neck on this *entari* is a little unusual—it has no collar, perhaps to enable the carefully cut decorative edging to continue without interruption. The double scalloped design, rhythmic but not boringly so, changes shape as it rounds the corners of the garment, evidence that the design was measured to fit this *entari* exactly before a single cut was made in the fabric. The edges are all finished with a twisted gold cord. The decorative edging is made more dramatic by the sleeve treatment. Open to the elbow and lined with a contrasting deep red fabric, the sleeves would have been eye-catching when the garment was worn.

Transformations

The two *entaris* just considered are at the very pinnacle of fashion and expense; other women would have been wearing garments displaying the same basic elements, made of less costly fabric, more modest decoration, and more restrained dimensions, depending on their resources. The multi-garment outfit with exaggerated proportions, the lavish use of soft fabric that draped well, and the elaborate trim at all the edges of the outer garment already demonstrate the influence of French fabrics in their construction (and indeed Ottoman fashion had always been in conversation with European modes to some extent), but in the main, the Istanbul fashions of this period demonstrate a close connection to women's dress of the preceding century described previously. This is the backdrop against which fashion begins to change more rapidly. The transformation in

Figure 3.12 *Entari*, front view and sleeve detail, nineteenth century. New York, Metropolitan Museum of Art, Gift of Jessie Franklin Turner, C.I.42.56.1

the dress of the women of Istanbul that I have traced over the course of the nineteenth century did not happen overnight. Rather, it was the result of a series of gradual changes as women began experimenting with what they learned of European dress from fashion magazines and newspapers, the foreign women with whom they came in contact, and the foreign goods that were becoming available, discussed in detail in Chapter 5.

Women who had more contact with the foreign community, whether through their family's employment, schools, churches, or far-flung family, had greater opportunity to see what foreign women were wearing, and their dress practices reflected that. Greek and Armenian women in Istanbul began adopting European fashions earlier than their Muslim and Jewish counterparts, and their dress transformations were bolder. (Palace women were also important fashion influencers; their dress practices are the subject of Chapter 6.) Julia Pardoe, visiting Istanbul in 1836, reports on the women she saw when having dinner with a Greek family before going off to a ball:

> the elder matrons wore the dark headdress and unbecoming vest of by-gone years, half-concealed by the warm wrapping pelisse; the next in age had mingled the Greek and European costumes into one heterogeneous mass, each heightening and widening the absurdity of the other; and had overlaid the inconsistent medley with a profusion of diamonds absolutely dazzling; while the younger ladies presented precisely the same appearance as the belles of a third rate country town in England: their petticoats too short, their heads too high, their sleeves too elaborate, and their whole persons overdressed.

(154–55)

Exposure to the fashions worn by foreign women was an important factor in how Istanbul women made their dress decisions, but it was not the only one. Wealth and social standing were also key aspects affecting fashion choices, as was age and the extent to which a woman's family was traditional or more progressive. A wealthy Jewish woman might have been more fashion forward than a poor Greek woman, depending on her resources, personal taste, and family circumstances. For example, the *entari* illustrated Figure 3.13 belonged to a Jewish woman from Thrace. The Sadberk Hanım Museum collection records document the Jewish identity of the owner and the fact that the garment was worn for special occasions, but they may not reveal the whole story of this garment. It may not originally have been made for a Jewish owner but perhaps was purchased secondhand or received as a gift. Whatever the longer history of the *entari*, the fact that it was worn by a Jewish woman gives us useful information about how fashion trends crossed class, ethnic, and religious boundaries. Made of green satin, it is embellished with finely executed gold embroidery in the *dival* technique, in which metal-wrapped threads, sequins, and other metal embellishments are used to create large-scale, elaborate designs. With this technique, the embroidery was designed for specific parts of the garment (sleeves, bodice, hem, and so on), as opposed to an embroidery program that covers the entire surface of the fabric. In most cases, the embroidery was completed before the garment was assembled because it would have been easier to execute the complex embroidery before the garment was sewn. This *entari* is embroidered with small floral motifs scattered across the fabric, and a running floral scroll encircles the neckline, sleeve ends, and garment edges. Silver cord trimming finishes the garment edges. The structure and cut of the *entari* are traditional in some aspects (round neck, sleeve structure) but reveal an interest in current fashion. The exaggerated proportions of the skirt were often seen in the nineteenth century; but instead of the similarly exaggerated

Figure 3.13 *Entari*, nineteenth century. Büyükdere, Courtesy of the Vehbi Koç Foundation, Sadberk Hanım Museum, 15239-K.955.

sleeve length that might have been expected, this *entari* has shorter sleeves with no decorative shaping at the ends. Neatly sewn gathers at each side provide some definition of the waist, a fashion innovation discussed in more detail below.

The initial fashion experimentation with European fashion among Muslim women took a variety of forms and was quite subtle, as demonstrated by the surviving garments that reveal aspects of this fashion change. One example of such experimentation can be seen in a three-piece outfit in the Topkapı Sarayı collection. Made of a fine mauve wool twill, perhaps an imported fabric, the outfit consists of *şalvar* and *entari*, exaggerated in their dimensions as was the fashion, and constructed in the traditional mode (Figure 3.14). The third piece is a short jacket, or *cepken*, to be worn over the *entari*.

In the traditional Ottoman garment (the upper example in Figure 3.15) the main body of the jacket is made from a single piece of fabric folded over the shoulders with a round neck and long gussets added at the sides for fullness. The sleeves are each a single piece of fabric, seamed under the arms. It has no cuffs and no collar. The lower jacket in Figure 3.15 is from the Topkapı Sarayı outfit and is completely European in style. The jacket is now tailored, with very wide, set-in sleeves closed by cuffs with a single gold button. Small, pleated ruffles edge the cuffs, front opening, stand-up collar, shoulders, and the three flounces that decorate each side of the bodice. The details of cut (particularly the diamond-shaped construction of the back) and ornamentation are closely related to the short jacket known as a spencer, worn in Britain and France from the late eighteenth century into the 1820s (Figure 3.16).

Given the complexity of the garment, it seems likely that it was copied by an accomplished tailor from a fashion illustration or an imported original. Julia Pardoe, cited earlier, mentions garments imported from Paris, and certainly the complexity of this *cepken* suggests such an origin. However, the use of matching fabric for the entire ensemble argues for the involvement of a highly skilled tailor or seamstress, most likely trained

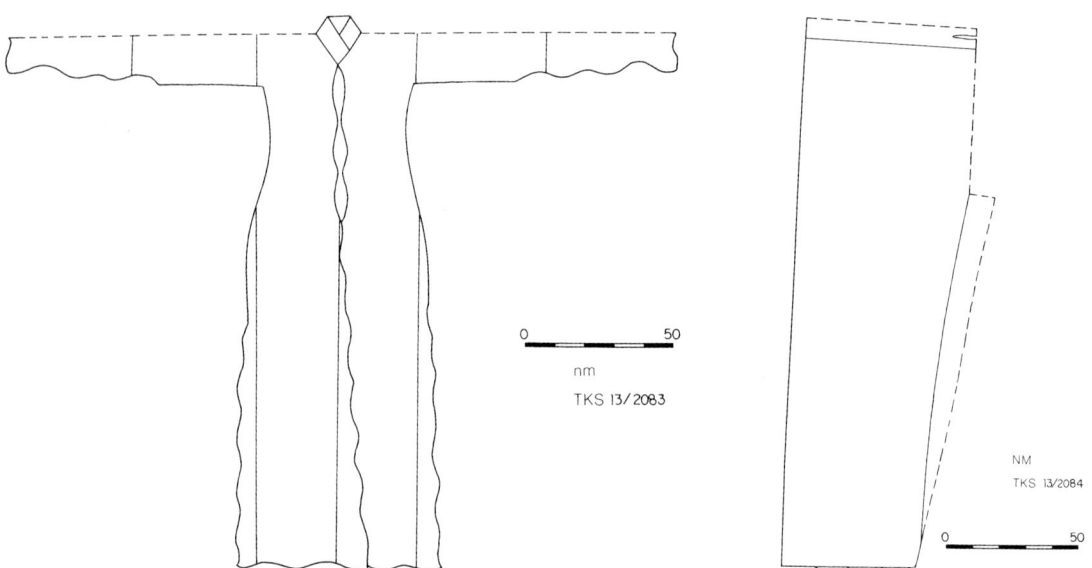

Figure 3.14 *Şalvar* and *entari, ca.* 1820s. Istanbul, Topkapı Sarayı Museum, Inv. No. 13/2084 and 13/2084, drawings by the author.

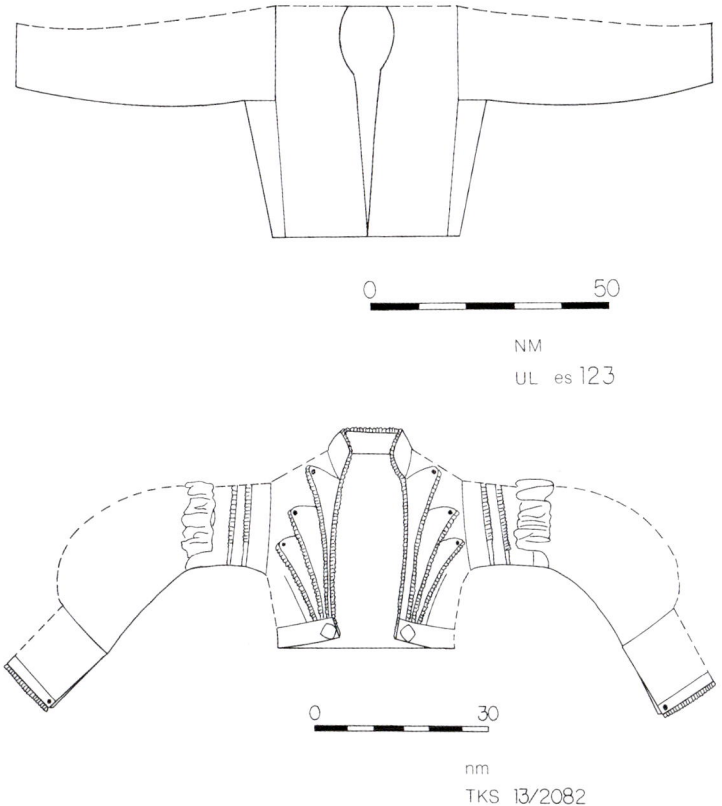

Figure 3.15 Upper: *Cepken*, nineteenth century. Private collection, drawing by the author. Lower: *Cepken*, *ca.* 1820s. Istanbul, Topkapı Sarayı, Inv. No.13/2082, drawing by the author.

Figure 3.16 Spencer, front and back views, *ca.* 1820. New York, Metropolitan Museum of Art, Purchase, Irene Lewisohn Bequest, 1987.237.2.

in Europe. In this example, the basic elements of the ensemble (*şalvar*, *entari*, *cepken*) are unchanged, but the details of one garment are completely different. It is a striking experiment but one that does not challenge norms of modesty or disrupt the overall structures of the typical ensemble.

An *entari* in the Met's collection provides an example of a different kind of sartorial experimentation (Figure 3.17) and is a stunning example of the decorative possibilities of embroidery for women's garments in this period. Made of a fine white muslin, the fabric was embroidered with an all-over design of small flowers, stems, and leaves, openwork baskets filled with delicate bouquets, and a thin blue ribbon that winds through the flowers. At least eight colors of silk are used in the embroidery as well as a virtuoso array of stitches. In addition to the embroidery, the border areas of the *entari* are trimmed with a running floral motif using colored silk cord in the laid cord technique and matching the embroidery in some of its details. An elaborate passementerie comprised of twisted blue cord alternating with small baskets holding flowers, repeating the embroidery motifs, edges the front opening, skirts, and sleeve ends of this high-fashion garment.[5] In such work the design would be drawn on the fabric by draftsmen and then embroidered before the fabric was cut and assembled into a garment. In some cases, as was likely in the embroidered wool *entari* discussed previously (Figure 3.10), the fabric might be cut into the required pieces and then embroidered before assembly. In this example, close examination shows where a seam interrupts the embroidery, a clear indication that the fabric was embroidered before the garment was assembled.

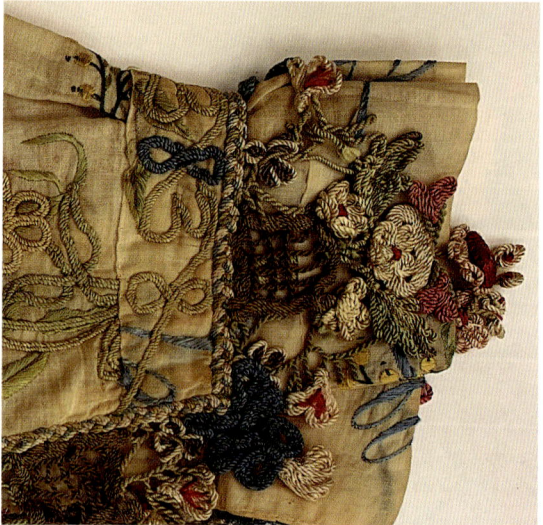

Figure 3.17 *Entari* and cuff detail, second half nineteenth century. New York, Metropolitan Museum of Art, Gift of Mrs. Robert Hewitt, 1939 (C.I.39.133) Entari Photo Credit: Image copyright © The Metropolitan Museum of Art. Image source: Art Resource, NY.

The beautifully embroidered fabric, the exaggerated dimensions (this gown would have trailed lavishly on the floor), and the elaborate trim all place this garment at the height of fashion, belonging to a wealthy woman with a well-developed fashion sense. But my particular interest here is the cuffs of the sleeve, another fashion innovation. Cuffs were a feature of European tailoring adopted early in the transition to European fashion. They could be incorporated into the traditional garment easily, signaling an interest in fashion experimentation without a radical change in appearance.

But what is revealed here and in other early examples of cuffs is intriguing. To appreciate why, looking into tailoring methods to see how cuffs were constructed in the European tailoring tradition is helpful: the sleeve end was gathered and sewn into a separate piece of fabric, the cuff, which is then folded to the inside and sewn to itself, creating a neat finish with the sleeve end completely hidden. If a ruffle was wanted, that would be attached separately to the bottom end of the cuff. The tailor or seamstress who made the cuffs for the Ottoman *entari* most likely did not have access to either a pattern or an example of a European-made cuff. His or her solution was to sew a band at the bottom of the sleeve on the outside of the fabric, gathering the sleeve fabric underneath the band on the inside of the sleeve. The sleeve fabric then extends beyond the cuff band to create a ruffle. The result resembles a cuff that might have been seen on a European dress, but the way that effect was achieved was completely different.

An *entari* in the collection of the YapıKredi Kültür Sanat Yayıncılık, no. 102, provides a very different example of fashion transition. Based on its dimensions, fabric choice, and construction details, this *entari* is a much more modest garment than those just discussed, providing important evidence of how fashion experimentation extended beyond the elite women who might have worn the Topkapı Sarayı or Metropolitan Museum outfits just discussed. The modifications made to this *entari* are small but telling: the sleeves now end in cuffs and were intended to conform to the actual length of the wearer's arms, and gathers were made on either side of the robe to add a shaped waist to the contours of the garment. The use of gathers or pleats to create the impression of a shaped garment, known as *çantalı entari*, can be seen in any number of examples (Görünür 2010: 52). Unlike the previous example, in this case, the sleeve has been neatly pleated into a narrow cuff, which has been constructed in the European manner.

These changes signal that the owner of this garment was watching European fashions and had realized a key difference between that mode and the traditional dress of Ottoman women, which is the fit of each individual element of an outfit. As outlined above, in the Ottoman context, the outfit is a loose-fitting series of garments, held on by ties and sashes. The impact of the outfit is in the lavish use of expensive fabric and the layering of different fabrics, colors, and patterns. European dress of the same period was completely different, depending on its impact in large part on precise tailoring to fit the body exactly, based on the specific measurements of the individual who would be wearing the garment. Waist, shoulders, wrists, and hem length were all carefully measured and visible. The *entari* in the Yapı Kredi collection is an attempt by a dressmaker or her patron to adapt what she was seeing of European fashion to the local dress.

Fashion-conscious Istanbul women could also alter their garments to make them conform more to European fashion trends, as this next example reveals (Figure 3.18). A two-piece outfit (*şalvar* and *entari*) of purple silk decorated with lavish gold embroidery in the collection of the Topkapı Palace Museum, the *entari* has a series of gathers at the waist on each side, a fashion innovation noted above. The sleeve of the *entari* is made of two pieces of fabric with offset seams, a construction feature that came into use in the middle of the century, replacing the older way of sleeve construction that involved a single piece of fabric, folded and sewn together, with the seam at the underarm. At some point after it was completed, the *entari* was modified by the addition of three long darts on each side of the bodice at the waist. The darts are uneven in size and sewn with large stitches. Their messy execution and uneven placement indicate that they were not done by a professional tailor or seamstress but by a less-experienced sewist, perhaps a junior member of the harem.

The National Museum of Scotland holds a second example of a traditional *entari* that was modified at a later date to reflect a European fashion aesthetic (Scarce 1987: 68–81; 1980: 144–67). The *entari* is part of a complete ensemble acquired by the museum, with *şalvar* and *entari* of a heavy green silk extensively embroidered in gold metal-wrapped thread. The construction of the *entari* follows the traditional mode, with the exaggerated proportions typical for *entari* and *şalvar* of the mid-nineteenth century. In this case, the modifications made to the original garment are more complex and ambitious than those in the Topkapı Sarayı entari just discussed. Two darts, symmetrically placed and of the same size, were taken in the back, to create a closer-fitting bodice. The sleeves and shoulder were recut, making shaped armholes and a sloping shoulder line. Finally, the front neckline was deepened by turning the original front edges of the garment to the inside. Given the extent and complexity of these changes, it seems likely that they were carried out by a professional tailor or dressmaker, not the garment's owner.

Apart from the tailoring changes that these examples illustrate, at this relatively early stage of transition other kinds of modifications would have been seen in accessories—stockings instead of socks, shoes imported from Europe, and the adoption of gloves and parasols (Figure 3.19). The new parasols are described in some detail in

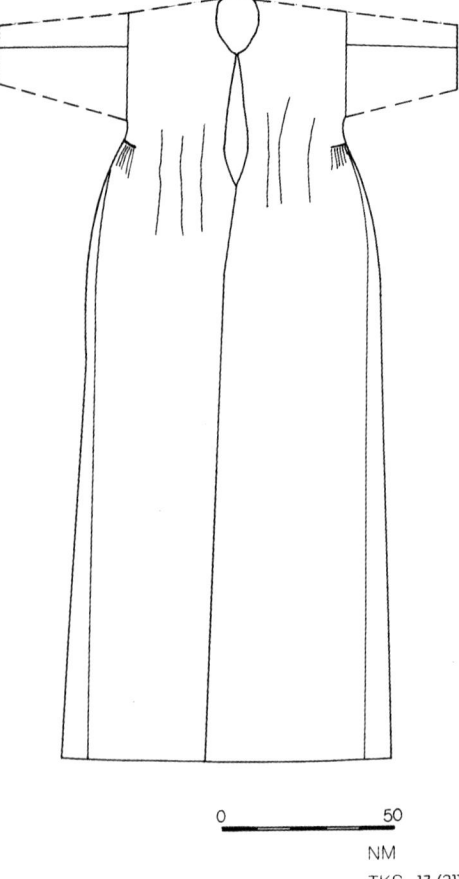

Figure 3.18 *Üçetek entari*, nineteenth century. Istanbul, Topkapı Sarayı Museum, Inv. No. 13/2112, drawing by the author.

0   50

NM

TKS 13/2112

Figure 3.19 *Turkish women walking*, Amadeo Preziosi,1858. *Stamboul. Recollections of Eastern Life.* Philadelphia, Kislak Center for Special Collections, Rare Books and Manuscripts, University of Pennsylvania.

the writings of the European travelers, although they are rarely seen in museum galleries, the 2023 *Elegance from Past to Future from the Sadberk Hanım Museum* exhibition being a welcome exception (Bilgi 2023: 214–21).

The first decades of the nineteenth century saw continuing changes in women's dress in Istanbul. The trends that began in the late eighteenth century, with softer fabric and more generous proportions of the *entari* and *şalvar*, continued with even more dramatic use of fabric and extensive trims. Women began adding foreign accessories to their wardrobe and modifying traditional garments with features borrowed from European fashion, such as cuffs and waists. Among some Istanbul communities, particularly the Greek and Armenian, the adoption of European fashion proceeded much more quickly. As the nineteenth century progressed, the costume changes became more pervasive and comprehensive. In the next chapter I consider one particularly pivotal garment, the wedding dress.

CHAPTER 4
ACCELERATION OF CHANGE: THE DRESS, THE PHOTOGRAPH, AND OTTOMAN WEDDINGS

In the middle of the nineteenth century, Istanbul brides wore a variety of wedding fashions, depending on their ethnicity and religion. At around the same time, bridal couples began to document the occasion of their marriages with photography. Wedding dresses and photographs together mark an important moment in Ottoman fashion history and the engagement with photography by Ottoman women; in this chapter I look at how these two significant aspects of visual culture, dress and photography, intersected.

In the previous chapter I demonstrated the ways in which fashion change in Istanbul began with small substitutions of elements from the Euro-American fashion tradition (stockings, shoes, a newly styled jacket) for those from the local tradition and minor design alterations such as cuffs to traditional garments. Moving forward, travelers' accounts, surviving garments, paintings, and photographs all indicate that by the middle of the nineteenth century, much more extensive modifications had taken place. A key change was the adoption of the dress, a one-piece garment designed to be put on over the head. Over time, as Istanbul consumers and seamstresses became more familiar with the dress as a wardrobe element, dresses began to follow European fashion more closely, with complex tailoring, elaborate trim, and other embellishments.

One such early dress was the *bindallı* dress (figure 4.1), typically worn for weddings, and, preserved in numerous museum collections and in the photographic record (Figure 4.2). Depending on its style, initially the *bindallı* dress was sometimes worn together with *gömlek* and *şalvar*, but it could also be worn without the *şalvar*. From its beginnings as a simple dress shape, closely related to the *entari* in design and construction, the *bindallı* dress evolved into highly fashionable European-style two-piece outfits. Within the same decades, some Istanbul brides adopted the white wedding dress made popular by Queen Victoria, a fashion development examined later in this chapter.

Wedding dresses and wedding photography across cultures are particularly fruitful areas for an investigation of fashion evolution and of the relationship between fashion and photography. With the possible exception of unique children's garments such as circumcision outfits, in many cultures around the world wedding dresses are the garments most likely to be saved and passed down. They could often be the single most expensive outfit a woman ever wore. Similarly, a wedding was the one occasion that could bring members of nearly all social classes to the photographer's studio. In Istanbul, and in the Ottoman Empire more generally, wedding fashions were shared across religious and ethnic boundaries.

Photographs: One Case Study

I purchased the photograph illustrated in Figure 4.2 at the Örtakoy flea market in Istanbul in the early 1980s. This photograph, together with the image of Fehime Sultan in Chapter 6 (Figure 6.2), are the visual signposts around which much of my thinking about this project has revolved. In each of these photographs, the subjects are performing very specific versions of themselves in front of the camera, versions in which their dress is key. In the next few pages, I use the photograph in Figure 4.2 as a case study to examine how I read photographs, the questions an image generates, and the tools I deploy in seeking answers.

Figure 4.1 *Bindallı* dress, late nineteenth century. Büyükdere, Courtesy of the Vehbi Koç Foundation, Sadberk Hanım Museum, SHM 2598-K.16.

Historic photographs are crucially important visual documents, but they also present significant challenges in their study and interpretation. This photograph embodies many of these challenges. It shows a closely cropped image of a woman wearing a *bindallı* dress, one hand at her metal belt, the other holding out her skirt to display the elaborate embroidery. The garment itself is a beautiful example of a *bindallı* dress, heavily embroidered, with lace trim at the sleeve ends and around the round neck and front opening. The woman wears a close-fitting necklace of gold coins around her neck and a white bridal veil with crocheted edging that

Figure 4.2 [*Bindallı* portrait], photographer, date unknown. Collection of the author.

frames her face. She is standing slightly angled away from the picture frame, apparently looking out of the frame at someone to her left.

This photograph provides a clear record of the dress and the other elements worn in this bridal outfit, but unfortunately virtually no other documentary evidence can be gleaned from the picture. The photograph was sold by Tuğrul Acar, who in those days had a shop in the Istanbul neighborhood of Erenköy, in addition to his Ortaköy flea market stall. It is a modern rephotographing of an older image, and much of the original detail has been lost. The close cropping has eliminated the backdrop and floor, which often can provide evidence of a photographer's studio. No studio signature is visible, but given that such information would have increased the value of even a modern reprint, it seems likely that the original was also lacking such information.

I looked at this image for many years, wondering about the circumstances in which it was made. I was intrigued by the contradiction the image seemed to present: a careful depiction of a historic garment and the relatively modern stance of the photograph's subject, a woman who was very comfortable in front of the camera. Thanks to the detective work of a colleague who found the photograph in a 1989 book, I can now piece together something of the photograph's history. The book, *Harem. The World behind the Veil*, is a lavishly illustrated account of the harem, part memoir and part [quasi]-historic overview, written by Alev Lytle Croutier. Croutier identifies the woman in the photograph as her aunt Ayhan, who was part of the extended family with whom the author grew up, from 1944 until she left for the United States in 1962. The caption to the photograph reads, "Ayhan, posing in a traditional wedding dress of red velvet embroidered with gold" (70), with no date or other details provided. According to the book's preface, the family, originally from Macedonia, had settled in Istanbul by 1906, eventually moving to Izmir and then to Ankara in 1950. The author also writes, "As a child, I played dress-up with embroidered clothes that the women from another era [previous occupants of the Izmir house] had left behind" (ibid.:10).

This story for the photograph answers some questions but raises others. I know the first name of the photograph's subject. Given the author's reference to "posing" in the image's caption, and her reference to playing dress-up, it seems clear that the photograph records an occasion when Ayhan was trying on a *bindallı* dress. Now I am left to wonder whether the dress was one of the embroidered garments left behind in the Izmir house in which the family lived, or if they had brought the dress with them from Macedonia, or if someone in the family had purchased it for their own wedding. I may never know the exact date for the image. A few other photographs in the book, which seem to have been taken at about the same time in a photographer's studio, show cousins and aunts dressed in various costumes—perhaps the *bindallı* image was part of that same excursion, and the garment belonged to the photographer, kept on hand for his clients to wear. Such a scenario would explain how the same photograph turned up at a flea market stall several decades later—when photographers closed their businesses, their stock was often purchased by their former competitors, who added it to their own holdings. Images could thus travel far from their original place of production.

This apparently straightforward picture of a woman wearing a dress opens up questions about the circumstances of the photograph, the source of the objects shown within it, the identity of the subject, the circulation of the image after its immediate reception, and so many more. The fact that many of the questions can never be answered is in some ways beside the point. The process itself: examining the photograph, looking beyond its surface to consider all the questions it poses and their possible answers, advances thinking about the project, suggesting new directions. Reading the layers of meaning embodied in historic photographs is complex, presents challenges of interpretation, and yields insights often not to be found elsewhere. I apply this same process of slow looking and thoughtful consideration of the questions raised by individual photographs to the wedding images throughout this chapter, and to the photographs deployed in subsequent chapters.

The *Bindallı* Dress and Changes over Time

Wedding dresses, often the most expensive and emotionally potent garment in a woman's wardrobe, were saved and perhaps passed down from one generation to the next. *Bindallı* dresses are among the most numerous surviving women's garments in museum collections across Türkiye,[1] are still regularly offered to museums, and still appear for sale regularly on various internet auction sites. Dress is an immensely important part of wedding celebrations, serving as a marker of social and religious identity and economic status at a pivotal life-cycle event for the bride and groom as well as their families. Wedding costume thus provides a unique window into dress practices of women of different ethnic and religious groups, as do weddings themselves. The decades from 1860 through 1920, the period roughly covered by the costumes considered in this chapter, were a time of significant change in the Ottoman Empire, socially, economically, and politically. *Bindallı* dresses and the other wedding fashions worn in these decades are key garments for understanding the way in which European styles were adopted and adapted to local use, as well as the changes in Ottoman women's self-fashioning and presentation.

The name of these early dresses, *bindallı,* means thousand branches and refers to the embroidered decoration that was generally an elaborate design of plant motifs, often growing out of vases or arranged in garlands, executed in a couched embroidery technique using gold- or silver-wrapped thread over cardboard. The dresses were worn by women of different ethnic and religious groups in Egypt, Syria, the Balkans, and across Anatolia for decades; over the long period of their use, they appeared in a range of fabrics and styles. One reason for their ubiquity across time and geography may be that they were sold ready-made from Istanbul. As described by Görünür, *bindallı* dresses "could be purchased ready made in boxes, and were also known as *kutu içi entari,* or *kutu entarisi*" [boxed entaris] (2010: 51). Maskareli, writing about Serbian wedding fashion, reports that *bindallı* dresses, high-status items often purchased as part of a dowry, were acquired ready-made in Istanbul (Maskareli 2017, 2020).

The term *bindallı* is used to refer both to embroidery designs (see more below) and to the garments decorated with that embroidery. The dresses appear in a variety of shapes over the decades in which they were worn, demonstrating clearly the changes in dress design and tailoring modes that characterized women's clothing in Istanbul. Although it is tempting to arrange the different *bindallı* variations in a simple chronology according to their evolution toward European style tailoring, my research demonstrates that it is more likely that multiple styles of the dresses existed simultaneously, responding to local tradition, economic circumstances of the wearer, and personal taste. The lack of documentation for many surviving garments and the fact that they could have been passed down in a family further complicate attempts to establish a strict design chronology.

In its simplest form, the basic structure of the garment is closely related to the *entari* and was, in fact, known as the *biretekli entari* or single-skirted *entari* (Görünür 2010: 51) (Figure 4.3). Constructed similarly to an entari from a single width of fabric, with extra fullness added to the skirt by a triangular side section on either side, the long central opening of the *entari* has here evolved into a round neck with a shorter front opening at the bodice. The side slits in the skirt have been eliminated (thus the name "single-skirted"), and the sleeves are shorter: the robe of traditional Ottoman women's attire has become a dress but not exactly a closely fitted garment. In many examples, gathers at each side mark the waist (*çantalı entari*), and the dresses were often worn belted, as in Figures 4.1 and 4.2. In some cases, the side slits in the skirt remained; in that case, the dress would be worn with matching *şalvar* (Figure 4.4).

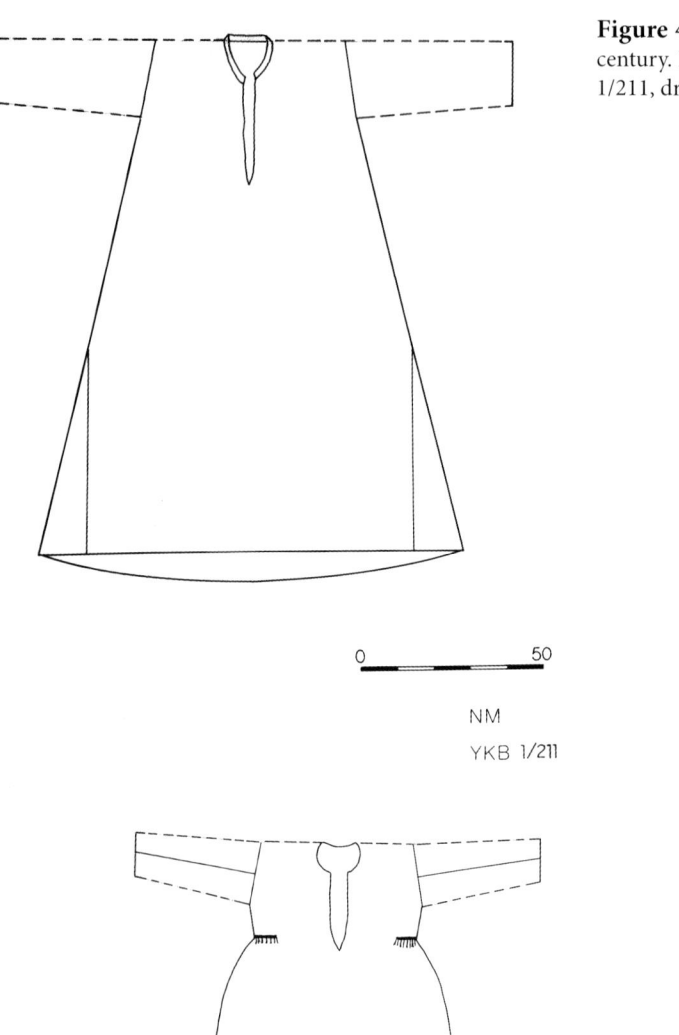

Figure 4.3 *Biretekli entari,* second half nineteenth century. Istanbul, YapıKredi Kültür Sanat Yayıncılık, 1/211, drawing by the author.

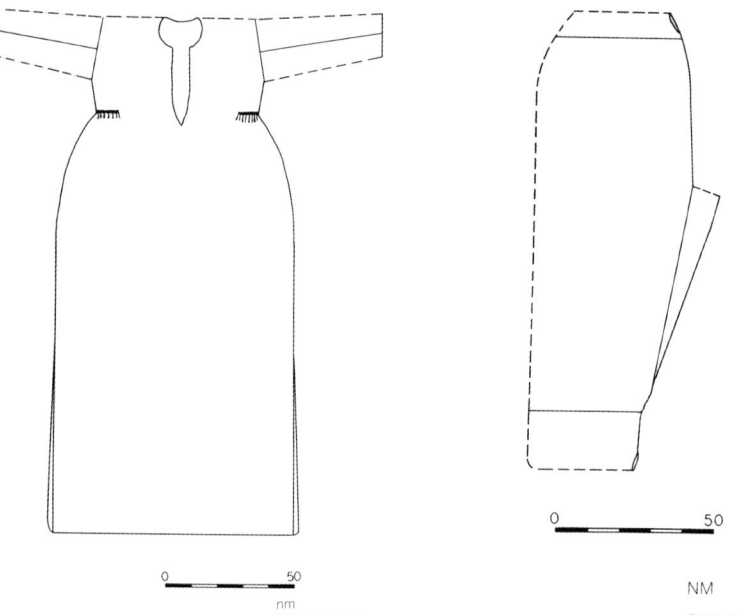

Figure 4.4 *Dress and matching şalvar,* second half nineteenth century. Istanbul, Topkapı Sarayı collection, 13/1974, drawings by the author.

The *bindalli* dress illustrated in Figure 4.3 is relatively modest in its form and embroidered decoration (not visible in the drawing); much more typical is the garment illustrated in Figure 4.5 with its longer train, lace trim around the neck, front opening, sleeve ends, and hem, and very lavish embroidery. Surviving *bindallı* dresses illustrate numerous other design variations: for example, a garment in the Sadberk Hanım Museum collection with a fitted collar and puffed sleeves on an otherwise standard dress (ibid.: 142–43). The dresses were typically made in dark-colored silk or cotton velvet, in maroon, purple, dark rose, or navy, although there are also surviving examples in silks in the same range of colors. Over time the one-piece *bindallı* dress became a two-piece outfit resembling European fashion much more closely in its construction and tailoring. Examples of such wedding outfits have survived in both the traditional dark velvets, but more commonly in pastel satins.

One such ensemble is illustrated in Figure 4.6. Constructed of a greenish satin, the outfit is comprised of a fitted overblouse and a flared skirt decorated with *bindallı* embroidery and beaded trim at the sleeve ends and hem of the top. The blouse closely resembles similar garments made in Europe at this period, with its high neck and sleeve shape. The blouse fit was achieved through darts and boning in the bodice and tailored specifically for the wearer, although perhaps not as closely fitted as a European counterpart may have been.

Figure 4.5 *Bindallı* dress, early twentieth century. Jerusalem, The Israel Museum, Jerusalem, Gift of Evelyne Mayorkas Hertzig, Dinah Mayorkas Pichot, Jacques Mayorkas, Paris, Alberte Mayorkas Wadler, New York, in memory of their mother, Colombe Papo, Photo © The Israel Museum, Jerusalem, by Mauro Magliani, B.84.0816.

Figure 4.6 Two-piece *bindallı* dress, early twentieth century. Büyükdere, Courtesy of the Vehbi Koç Foundation, Sadberk Hanım Museum, SHM 1293-K.211a, b.

The gored skirt has small gathers at the waistband and a long train. From such an ensemble, it was a short step to wedding outfits for the elite women of Istanbul that were indistinguishable from those worn by their peers in Europe at the same time, a development discussed in more detail below.

Bindallı Embroidery

The second half of the nineteenth century is sometimes described as a time of decline in Ottoman embroidery (Berker 1981). Yet the *bindallı* dresses that have survived in such large numbers from these same decades were distinguished by their highly proficient and expensive embroidery, a circumstance that speaks against the decline paradigm. Given this, it is worth exploring the embroidery form in some detail.

The *bindallı* embroidery that decorates the garments discussed in this chapter was carried out using a style called *dival* or less commonly, *maraş*, which is characterized by the use of metal-wrapped threads and couching.[2] Embroidery using metal-wrapped thread, especially gold, has a long history in Ottoman embroidery; and in the nineteenth century, *dival* work using gold-wrapped thread became particularly popular. Most *bindallı* designs are carried out exclusively with *dival* work, supplemented by the use of metal sequins, tiny coils of metal wire (*tırtıl* in Turkish), and pearls, the exception being the later examples of *bindallı* dresses made of satin fabric too thin to support the heavy *dival* stitches. In those examples, a range of embroidery stitches are used to execute the design.

Dival embroidery began with the pattern designs being drawn on paper and then cut out of cardboard. The cardboard pieces were pasted onto the dress fabric, with the fabric then clamped into a stand to hold the it taut and secure.

The metal-wrapped threads that comprise the embroidered design were drawn back and forth across the pattern pieces and held in place at the edges of the cardboard by cotton couching. The cotton thread used for couching is visible on the wrong side of the garment, but the metal-wrapped thread remains on the outer surface of the fabric (Figure 4.7). In some cases, additional texture for the design was created by using padding between the cardboard (the pink material visible in some parts of Figure 4.7) and metal-wrapped thread. The tiny *tırtıl* that outline the petals of the large flowers in this example add to the complexity of the overall design. Given the high cost of the materials and level of skill required for dival embroidery, most of it was carried out by professional embroiderers, working either in workshops or at home (Krody 2000: 40).

Embroidery designs on *bindallı* dresses fall into three general groups. In each of these design types, the embroidery uses the blank fabric of the dress differently, although the three types share many elements. On almost every dress, the front opening and the dress hem are articulated with some kind of linear design. Similarly, the sleeve ends are nearly always ornamented, with the ornament extending up the sleeve in a few different ways. In many examples, the bodice is decorated with a pattern designed to fit within that area of the dress, in some cases extending over the shoulders and ending in the center back.

The simplest of the three designs involves a long garland extending in two lines down the front of the dress on either side of the front opening and encircling the hem of the dress. The space between the double garland on the front of the dress may be filled with individual motifs such as bows or floral elements, often then scattered on the ground of the skirt as well. The sleeve ends generally have additional ornamentation, perhaps extended along the length of the sleeve. This design variation leaves much more of the dress fabric

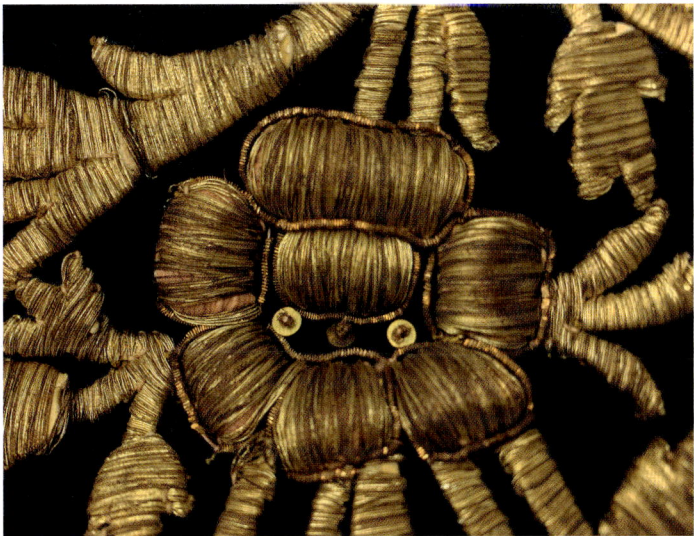

Figure 4.7 Embroidery detail (14x magnification). New York, Metropolitan Museum of Art, 2004.330.

exposed than others and requires a significantly smaller quantity of embroidery. Based on examples in published work and displayed online, this variation seems to be the least numerous of the three *bindallı* design types.

A second design type is characterized by registers of garlands arranged around the skirt of the dress, in anywhere from two to four rows (Figure 4.5). The garlands may be comprised of small bouquets or floral elements, with smaller related motifs scattered between the rows. This design almost always includes a medallion motif on the bodice of the dress that extends across the shoulders and back of the dress. The sleeves generally have an embroidered design at the bottom, with smaller motifs scattered on the rest of the sleeve. In some cases, the entire sleeve may be covered with an elaborate design. This design variation involves more embroidery than the garland example but significantly less than the all-over design, the third *bindallı* embroidery type.

The all-over *bindallı* presents a riot of embroidery, generally quite large in scale, that completely covers the skirt (Figure 4.1). In many cases, the design extends over the bodice as well, although there can also be a separate bodice design similar to what is seen in the registers' variation. Floral elements comprise most of the designs, which can also include ribbon garlands, ropes, tassels, vases, and baskets, all framed by borders that define the hem and front opening of the dress. Embroidery on the sleeves may be limited to the edges or extend the entire length of the sleeve. Some examples also include appliqued fabric in a contrasting color, often used as the body of an embroidered basket. Detail is added through the use of sequins and small *tırtıl*.

Bindallı dresses generally were produced in workshops. Although the surviving examples present an extremely diverse range of motifs and design elements, it would not be surprising to find evidence of shared designs or the repetition of individual motifs from one dress to the next. The fact that designs existed on paper to be traced onto cardboard or transferred directly on the dress fabric suggests that workshops or individual embroiderers would have had libraries of *bindallı* patterns at their disposal in creating dress designs. Delibaş, for example, mentions that designs for dival work could be purchased from shops in the Kapalı Çarşı (Delibaş 1987: 54). The dresses illustrated in Figures 4.5 and 1.1 present just such evidence of shared design in the repetition of certain motifs. In both examples of the register type of pattern, the dresses have an elaborate motif decorating the sleeve at the ends, with smaller floral motifs scattered up the sleeves. These motifs share the same ogival framing elements and the same five-petaled flower supporting a five-branch leaf at the upper edge of the design. The flowers and subsidiary lines that fill the sleeve design on the two dresses are very close but not exactly the same, suggesting that larger patterns such as the ones on the sleeves of these two dresses were broken down into their individual elements in the process of designing the embroidery for an entire dress. The category of *bindallı* dresses, worn over many decades by Ottoman women, includes garments in a range of fabrics and tailoring modes, some clearly looking to European fashions, a trend that gained momentum with the adoption of the white wedding dress.

The White Wedding Dress

By the turn of the twentieth century wedding dresses for the elite women of Istanbul closely resembled those worn in the major cities of Europe or America. To understand how the *bindallı* dress of the mid-nineteenth century was so quickly transformed into something quite different, a brief look at wedding fashions elsewhere will be helpful, beginning with the dress worn by Queen Victoria at her wedding in 1840 (Figure 4.8). Married at age twenty, three years after she acceded to the British throne, the wedding of Queen Victoria and Prince Albert was a highly visible, carefully managed public relations event designed to enhance the reputation and

Figure 4.8 Queen Victoria's wedding dress, Mary Bettans, 1840. London, Royal Collection Enterprises Limited 2025/Royal Collection Trust. Photographer: Historic Royal Palaces, RCIN 71975.

popularity of the monarchy.[3] The queen was directly involved in planning many aspects of the ceremony, including her dress.

Queen Victoria's sartorial choices were deliberate and demonstrate that she understood very clearly the power of dress as a means of creating an impression and influencing the public. First, she declined to continue the royal tradition of wearing velvet and ermine state robes, perhaps wishing to signal that her primary identity on her wedding day was as a bride, not a monarch.[4] Second, the materials she selected for her dress, the silk satin woven at Spitalfields and the Honiton lace that decorated the dress in the shape of a deep bertha collar, frills at the sleeve, and a twenty-five-inch deep flounce on the skirt (not shown in Figure 4.8), were British made, both products of industries in decline as a result of industrialization and foreign competition. However, having made these decisions, the dress itself did not necessarily aim to set new fashion trends. "Her white satin and lace dress accords exactly with fashionable taste as exemplified in the fashion journals for 1839, following an already established fashion for simplicity and antique lace rather than setting it" (Staniland and Levey 1983: 6.)

The wedding received extensive coverage in the press. The *Times of London* sold thirty thousand copies of the February 11 edition covering the wedding, Madame Tussaud's Wax Museum displayed a wedding group for several months following the wedding, and illustrations of the wedding were widely available as prints. There were no photographs of the wedding, but Queen Victoria's dress was described in detail in the newspaper accounts of the wedding and could be seen in the prints and fashion plates that appeared shortly afterward.

Queen Victoria's wedding dress did not necessarily depart from the tastes of the day, but it nonetheless had an immediate and dramatic impact on wedding fashion. In popular thought, Queen Victoria is credited with the establishment of the white wedding dress as the fashion norm, but this is not strictly true.[5] Until the mid-nineteenth century, although brides could choose to wear white, they could just as commonly choose a dress in a different color that they could then wear on many other occasions after their wedding.

Within a few years of Queen Victoria's wedding, however, the influential American lady's magazine *Godey's Lady's Book* wrote, "Custom has decided, from the earliest ages, that white is the most fitting hue [for brides], whatever may be the material. It is an emblem of the purity and innocence of girlhood, and the unsullied heart she now yields to the chosen one" (Lee ibid.). In addition to affecting the growing popularity of the white gown as a bridal choice, the shape and specific details of Victoria's dress were also widely copied. To cite only one example of many, an 1859 wedding dress in the collection of the Costume Institute of the Metropolitan Museum of Art shows the same off-the-shoulder neckline, ornamented bertha, V-shaped bodice waistline, and full skirt with forward facing pleats, all executed in a white silk satin.[6]

The wedding fashions popular in turn-of-the-century Europe and America also made their way to Istanbul, as an elaborate bridal outfit from 1910 in the Sadberk Hanım Museum demonstrates (Figure 4.9). An elegant two-piece dress of cream-colored satin, the boned blouse has a high neck and full, elbow-length sleeves. The skirt is cut on the bias and has a train. The outfit, which was made in a fashion house for a woman named Rukiye Tahire Günsav, is elaborately trimmed with different kinds of lace, embroidery, and faggoting (Görünür 2010: 216). Rukiye's dress displays close similarities to a slightly earlier dress now in the collection of the Costume Institute. Dated 1902–1905, the New York dress is also a two-piece dress made of cream-colored silk. The similarities extend to the design of the blouse, with the high boned neck popular in these years; full, elbow-length sleeves; and the shape of the skirt. The New York dress is trimmed with extensive embroidery, beading, and lace, all in the same color palette as the dress fabric, much like the Sadberk Hanım dress. The overall impressions created by the two wedding outfits, separated by a few years in date and many thousands of miles, are extremely close, demonstrating a shared language for wedding fashion among elite women in major urban centers.

Ottoman Weddings: Who Wore What

The *bindallı* dress, particularly in shades of red, and the white European-style wedding dress worn by Istanbul women as well as urban women in other parts of the Ottoman Empire, were key components of wedding wardrobes over many decades. They remain so today, a phenomenon discussed in the book's afterword. However, they were not the only garments that made up bridal dress across the empire, as the lavishly illustrated 1986 work *Historical Costumes of Turkish Women* by Umay Günay amply demonstrates. The *bindallı* dress was worn in Anatolia, the Balkans, and Greater Syria, sometimes in combination with locally specific headdresses or other accessories. In other cases, bridal wear had regionally or ethnically specific traditions: for example, the heavily embroidered red *entari* that was particularly popular in the Kütahya and Eskişehir areas (Figure 4.10). Made of a red wool twill known as *tepebaşı* or *hüseyni*, embroidered with silk, metallic

Figure 4.9 Wedding dress, 1910. Büyükdere, Courtesy of the Vehbi Koç Foundation, Sadberk Hanım Museum, SHM 14072-k.786 a, b.

thread, and sequins in floral motifs, this example is an *üçetek entari* with a low neckline and long sleeves with elaborately decorated ends. Examples of garments made of *tepebaşı* survive from the eighteenth century as illustrated in Görünür (66–67), but the garment illustrated here can be dated to the last quarter of the nineteenth century, based on the presence of synthetic dyes in the silk embroidery.[7] Other outfits associated with weddings in the same region were *şalvar* and *cepken* of silk or velvet with specific patterns of embroidery, which gave the outfits their names, *çatkılı* (diagonal lines of floral motifs) and *eğrimli* (floral motifs in undulating lines) (ibid.: 112–17, 295).

In the tumultuous last decades of the Ottoman Empire, expectations and practices around weddings, and indeed marriage itself, were embroiled in the far-reaching political and social changes taking place, a full discussion of which is well beyond what I can consider here.[8] However, even considering the ways in which ideas about marriage and how it was formalized may been shifting, throughout this period women and men expected to marry, and in fact, the overwhelming percentage of the population did marry. According to Duben and Behar, only 2 percent of women did not marry before the end of their childbearing years, according to the surveys they consulted (1991: 103). The role of the bride and groom in choosing their partners began to alter, but marriage continued to be understood as an alliance between families, essential for raising children and continuing the family.

Figure 4.10 *Üçetek entari*, last quarter nineteenth century. New York, Metropolitan Museum of Art, Purchase, Irene Lewisohn Bequest, 1980.145.3.

In Muslim weddings, specific legal obligations on the part of the two families were spelled out in advance, and a series of public events marked the occasion (Hart 2009). The main steps of the marriage process began with the promise ceremony, which was an informal agreement between the two families that a marriage would take place. Engagement involved a contract describing some of the financial arrangements agreed upon by both families at this stage, which could include the amount of *mehr* or bridal gift to be paid to the bride by the groom, responsibility for the cost of the wedding festivities, and any property that might be transferred upon the marriage. Once the engagement had taken place, the marriage could follow. This was primarily a civil ceremony, although often formalized by a religious ceremony as well.

The celebrations of the wedding itself could go on for several days, involving separate events for the groom and the bride preparing both for their new roles, culminating on the day of the wedding in a public procession bringing the bride from her family's house to the home of the groom's family, where the ceremony would be performed. Both families might host wedding meals, and on the day following the ceremony, the bride would receive her friends and female relatives. If finances allowed, the bride would have separate outfits for each of the different ceremonies that were part of the wedding celebrations, which could then be worn afterward on special occasions. Apart from the legal formalities, the specific traditions for celebrating weddings, described here very generally, varied extensively from region to region with the Empire and according to the status of the families involved. The wedding practices of Armenian, Jewish, and Greek families, discussed below, shared certain characteristics with Muslim weddings, but in all cases, the wedding itself and the events that marked it served to demonstrate membership in a particular religious community, solidify communal ties, and signal the wealth and standing within the community of the families involved. Dress played a key part in these efforts.

The wedding dresses described earlier in this chapter were worn by Muslim women, but in some cases (Figure 4.5), also by women from other religious communities. Just as wedding celebrations across religious groups shared certain features, fashions in wedding costume crossed boundaries. Armenian, Jewish, and Greek brides often chose wedding dresses very similar to what Muslim brides were wearing. Their choices were affected by a range of factors, personal and communal, with clothing from disparate traditions being worn at the same moment by brides in different circumstances. Carolyn Paine, a British woman who spent a year, 1850–1851, in Istanbul, attended two weddings, one the son of the grand vizier and the second an Armenian ceremony. In the first case, a Muslim wedding at the most elite level, the bride wore a *bindallı* style outfit, lavishly embroidered with gold. In describing the dress of the Armenian bride, on the other hand, Paine writes, "Her dress, which was Parisian, with the exception of the bridal veil, was of white satin, with deep flounces of lace, a wreath of orange blossoms on the head, over which was thrown a white thread-lace veil that reached to her feet, falling over the back" (1859: 62, 82).

Armenian weddings, like those in other religious communities in Istanbul, involved a number of separate components, including events at the homes of the bride and groom's parents, and a wedding procession from the bride's house to the church and back to the house of the bride or groom's family for a feast.[9] The Armenian community embraced photography from its beginnings, and its archive of wedding photography is particularly rich, despite all the losses that resulted from the genocide. Wedding photographs were kept in family albums and saved as important reminders of lost family when people had to flee. Thus, they have have ended up in various archives, in Türkiye and in the Armenian, Greek, and Jewish diaspora. Many are no doubt still part of family collections, but they are also found in secondhand shops and flea markets, as the identities of those pictured become lost over time and the pictures are discarded.

Whatever their present context, wedding photographs are compelling documents of social history as well as fashion history. Ottoman weddings were recorded by photographers in large numbers, across different classes and ethnic groups, and in urban and provincial settings. The corpus of Ottoman wedding images demonstrates that as photography became more accessible in the last decades of the nineteenth century, the custom of marking a wedding with a photograph gained in popularity. In this context, wedding photographs generally take three forms: the bridal couple, typically in a photographer's studio setting, standing stiffly next to each other facing the camera; a studio portrait of the bride alone; or a group photo taken at or near the site of the wedding ceremony with the bride and groom surrounded by members of the local community. Each of these kinds of images served a different purpose, as the ensuing discussion demonstrates.

Once again, to understand Ottoman wedding photography, it is useful to look briefly at how this practice emerged in the history of photography more generally. In the Euro-American context, having portraits painted on the occasion of a wedding was an accepted custom for those who could afford it; and with the advent of photography, the practice of making wedding portraits become more widespread. Like wedding dresses, wedding photographs were more likely to be saved than quotidian images and thus may be found in large numbers in public and private collections, in photographic formats beginning with the daguerreotype. In Britain, wedding photography may be found among the work of well-known photographers such as Camille Silvy and Julia Margaret Cameron (Haworth-Booth 2010: 88–89) and was embraced by the royal family. The 1840 wedding of Queen Victoria was not recorded photographically, but subsequent royal weddings were well documented with photographs. For example, two of the wedding photographs of her daughter Princess Louise, who wed in 1871, were produced as cartes de visite and widely circulated (Perry 2012 and Plunkett 2003).

The royal enthusiasm for wedding photography and the circulation of those images encouraged the practice of wedding photographs; and as photography became more widely available, the custom of taking wedding portraits extended to couples across social classes in Britain and elsewhere. As photo technologies changed, wedding photography could take place at the ceremony itself, but in the early decades the bride and groom visited the photographer's studio, either on the day of the wedding, or soon afterward, to have the photograph made.

The captivating photograph of an Armenian Istanbul couple, dated circa 1898 and shown in Figure 4.11, documents the wedding of Dikranouhi Essefian Kalpakian and her new husband, Parsegh Kalpakian. The bride is dressed in the height of fashion. Her white dress has the exaggerated leg-of-mutton sleeves current in the 1890s, along with a tightly fitted bodice and a flat-fronted A-line skirt with a train in the back. The dress is decorated with ruffles, bows, and flowers, and she wears a long veil held in place by a floral crown. The couple is stiffly posed in the Beyazit studio of Nicolas Andriomenos, described as one of the city's most prestigious portrait photographers (Öztuncay 2003: 307). Although it is perhaps surprising that this couple did not choose an Armenian photographer to make their wedding portrait, the extreme fashionability of the bride suggests that they may have sought out an equally fashionable photographer for this occasion.

Photographs of the bride and groom (Figures 4.11 and 2.8), like the British examples discussed previously, were mostly taken in a photographer's studio, around the time of the wedding but not necessarily on the

Figure 4.11 Wedding portrait Dikranouhi Essefian Kalpakian and Parsegh Kalpakian, Nicolas Andriomenos, 1898. Watertown, MA, Project Save Photographic Archive, Courtesy of Nevarte Kalpakian Adrian, L1991.033.001.

exact day of the ceremony. It is tempting to read these images from a twenty-first-century perspective when wedding choices are often a matter negotiated between the wedding couple alone, and portraits of the newlyweds are ubiquitous. However, the image of the Kalpakians and similar photographs from this period were one of the very few aspects of the wedding where they were independent actors. Choice of partner, economic agreements, and all the different celebratory events associated with the wedding were family- and community-based. These portraits gave the wedding couple the chance to perform a different identity as an independent couple setting off on a new chapter of their lives, even though that new chapter would most likely begin with residing with the groom's family. For the time of the photograph and evidenced by the enduring materiality of that image, their independent conjugal identity was affirmed (Najmabadi 2021). It is possible that some portraits of Muslim couples depict a polygynous marriage (i.e., the bride is the second wife of the husband), although given the very low percentage of polygamy in the last decades of the nineteenth century (less than 3 percent, according to Behar 1991: 477), this seems unlikely.[10]

The dress in Figure 4.12, another example of Armenian wedding fashion, presents a very different appearance than that seen in the Kalpakian photograph. Given to the Metropolitan Museum of Art in 1991,

Figure 4.12 Wedding dress, 1881. New York, Metropolitan Museum of Art, Gift of Fimi M. Samour, 1991.55.

it was identified by the donor as her mother's 1881 wedding dress, worn in the region of Adana in southern Türkiye. The dress is made from a striking silk brocade with alternating violet and fuchsia stripes and extra weft gold floral motifs. Mostly machine sewn, the dress embodies a combination of traditional and European-style construction: the round neck and front opening are familiar components of *entaris* and *bindallı* dresses, as is the deep red cotton lining at the inside hem of the skirt. The set-in sleeves are borrowed from European tailoring, but the sleeves and bodice retain the loose fit of traditional garments, worn without corseting. The carefully pleated skirt, another feature of European dress construction, takes full advantage of the dramatic fabric, and when worn, the dress would have been very striking indeed.

Moving further east, the blue *bindallı* dress with matching *cepken* in Figure 4.13, dated circa 1860, belonged to a woman in the Armenian Jamgochian family, from the town of Agn, present day Kemaliye in the Erzincan province.[11] The short jacket and gathered skirt of this ensemble connect it firmly to traditional garment vocabularies, as does the gold *dival* embroidery that characterizes *bindallı* dresses. The blue silk is elegantly embroidered with gold designs in two registers across the gathered skirt, on either side of the front bodice opening of the jacket, around the shoulders and back of the jacket, and on the sleeves. The *dival* embroidery is perhaps less elaborate than some of the most expensive *bindallı* dresses worn in Istanbul, but it is a very fine

Figure 4.13 Two-piece *bindallı* outfit, 1860. Mission Hills, CA, Courtesy of Ararat-Eskijian Museum and Research Center.

interpretation of a *bindallı* outfit in an unusual blue color. Like the two previous examples of dresses worn by Armenian brides, this one demonstrates the diversity of bridal fashion in the Armenian communities in the last decades of the nineteenth century. Although the Istanbul bride fully embraced the latest European fashion in her dress, women who lived further from the sartorial centers created outfits that combined new ideas with traditional shapes and construction techniques, in the case of the Adana dress, or simpler versions of elaborate Istanbul fashion, in the case of the Jamgochian *bindallı* ensemble.

The *bindallı* dress was also popular among Ottoman Jewish women as historic photographs and museum collections demonstrate (Figures 4.5 and 4.14). Sephardi Jewish weddings in the Ottoman context involved a number of different elements, beginning with the betrothal agreement and ending with the week of seven blessings that followed the ceremony (Juhasz 1990:196–217). In the time that elapsed from the betrothal ceremony to the wedding itself, the making, and perhaps purchase of clothes for the bride was a major preoccupation of the bride's family, both for the wedding events and to prepare her for married life. The clothes worn for the wedding, whether a *bindallı* dress or a white wedding dress, would also be worn again for holidays and special events. *Bindallı* dresses in particular, once they were no longer being actively worn, were often donated to the synagogue, where they were remade into objects such as Torah Ark curtains, Torah mantles, or reader's desk covers (ibid.: 65–119; Maskareli 2022: 049).

Figure 4.14 [Bride wearing *bindallı* dress], photographer unknown, early twentieth century. Jerusalem, The Israel Museum, Photographic Archive of the Isidore and Anne Falk Information Center for Jewish Art and Life, courtesy of the Siman-Tov family, Israel Museum Photo Archive 5289.

Images of Jewish women wearing *bindallı* dresses dating from the late nineteenth century and into the 1920s survive in museum and archival collections from the Balkans.[12] A photograph in the Israel Museum provides an example of a bridal portrait that includes a *bindallı* dress (Figure 4.14). Taken in a photographer's studio the day after the wedding (Juhasz 2012: 312), the pensive bride leans against one arm of the small settee on which she is seated and looks away from the photographer out of the picture frame. She is holding a stem of white flowers in her right hand, and the details of the all-over embroidery of the dress and the white veil are very clear, although their visual impact is somewhat diminished by the competing patterns of the heavily ornamented settee and elaborately patterned wallpaper of the studio setting.

Bridal portraits play a very different role than the photographs of the bride and groom discussed above. Figure 4.15 is a portrait of Serpouhi Mendilian Encababian, taken on the occasion of her marriage to Karekin Encababian. It is one of five that document the wedding: four are photographs of the couple, and the fifth is the portrait of Serpouhi by herself illustrated here. That portrait, as well as the photograph of the bride wearing a *bindallı* dress discussed in the previous paragraph and other photographs taken of brides alone, are documents of major transitions in the lives of the women who are photographed. They record their appearance at an epitome of fashionability and beauty, before the changes their bodies will undergo as a result of childbearing and before their transition into their adult lives as wives and matriarchs. The women in the pictures are

Figure 4.15 *Serpouhi Mendilian Encababian*, Karek Encababian photographer, 1909. Watertown, MA, Project Save Photographic Archive, Courtesy of Kay Encababian Surabian.

enacting a fleeting moment (no longer the daughter in their birth household and not yet the newest member of their husband's family) that is intensely personal but also highly prescribed by communal norms.

A third photograph from around the same time, taken in Izmir in 1910, shows a very different way of documenting a wedding and demonstrates that wedding dress among Jewish brides varied widely depending on family circumstances, personal taste, location, and perhaps specific part of the wedding festivities. The Izmir bride in Figure 4.16 is at the center of a large party of extremely fashionably dressed people, carefully arranged to spill out of the entrance and down the stairs of a large residential building. The women in particular wear elegant dresses, with the narrow two-tiered skirts and elaborately constructed bodices of Euro-American fashion circa 1910. The bride, seen at left center, flanked by the groom, wears a white gown relatively closely fitted and beautifully draped. Given the number of discrete events associated with Jewish weddings, it is entirely possible that the trousseau of the bride pictured here, dressed in the height of European fashion, would also have included a *bindallı* dress to be worn at a separate event.

Until the advent of reliable indoor lighting for photography, it was difficult to take photographs of the actual wedding ceremony. However, the ceremony and the attendant participants could be documented in group portraits, often taken outside the wedding venue (Figures 4.16, 4.17, and 4.18). These images, where

Figure 4.16 [Wedding, Izmir], photographer unknown, 1910. Jerusalem, The Israel Museum, Photographic Archive of the Isidore and Anne Falk Information Center for Jewish Art and Life, courtesy of Dorette Gabay, Izmir, Israel Museum Photo Archive 5075.

Figure 4.17 [Cappadocian Greek wedding near Kayseri], photographer unknown, 1902. Private collection.

Figure 4.18 [Wedding ceremony at Malakopi (Cappadocia)], photographer unknown, *ca.* 1910. Athens, Courtesy of the Centre for Asia Minor Studies.

the bridal couple are surrounded and, in some cases, nearly obscured by the family and community members standing around them, emphasize the communal significance of weddings, as alliances are cemented or newly established, and the young couple claims a place in their community. They also serve to mark the continuation of particular religious and ethnic traditions in a multiethnic environment. At the time the photographs were made, the specific details of the group (who is standing closest to the couple, who is at the edge of the group, who was present, who was absent) would have been meaningful, but those meanings are generally lost over time. What remains important as these photographs move across space and time is the fact of the community and the performance of its religious events.

As was the case with bridal fashions in the Muslim, Armenian, and Jewish communities seen here, the wedding clothes worn by Greek brides differed markedly from region to region. In the fashion center of the empire, Istanbul, brides were wearing white European-style wedding dresses as early as the 1850s, as reported by Amelia Hornby, who attended a Greek wedding in 1856: "Here, on a divan, pale and thoughtful, sat a young lady in the simplest white dress, made after the English fashion, a light white veil falling from the Greek chaplet of flowers on her head, to the ground" (Hornby 1863: 422).

Further afield, wedding fashions in the Cappadocian region, with its sizable Greek population, were more diverse. A bridal costume in the collection of the Benaki Museum from Sille, near Konya, and dated generally to the nineteenth century, shows a lavish, multilayered ensemble of a silk brocade with a floral design, heavily embellished with gold. The outfit consists of full-length coat, worn open with long, full sleeves with wide bands of off-white fur trimming the sleeves and front opening. Beneath the coat, a floor-length dress of the same fabric has the very long sleeves falling open from the elbow and front opening typical of an *entari*, but it appears to be closed down the front, as a dress. An elaborate belt/sash holds the two layers closed at the waist. The beautiful brocade fabric and use of fur signal a wealthy bride, with costume elements drawn from multiple traditions.

The bride in Figure 4.17 has chosen a more modern wedding dress. The photograph is dated 1902, and the subjects are identified as Agioi Theodoros and Nikolaos Bostanzoglou.[13] Their wedding took place in Kermira, or present-day Germir, then a small town near Kayseri of Muslims, Greeks, and Armenians. The young couple stands in the midst of a large crowd, most likely after their marriage because they are wearing the floral crowns that were an important component of the Greek Orthodox wedding ceremony. At the very center of the photograph and looking directly at the camera, the bride wears a white veil and dress with a narrow waist (which would have required a corset), long, fitted sleeves, and softly gathered skirt. The dress is trimmed with ruffles and other decorative elements, difficult to see clearly in the image. Her jewelry includes, in addition to at least two more delicate necklaces, a long chain of gold coins reaching below her waist, thus incorporating a custom that crosses ethnic and religious lines in Anatolia, that of the bride wearing a significant portion of her wealth in coins at her marriage. Her necklace of coins appears to be the only concession to traditional attire in her otherwise surprisingly fashionable dress, especially considering her location in a small provincial town in central Anatolia, a reminder of the degree to which fashion knowledge traveled, along with people and goods, much more extensively than might otherwise be imagined.

A second wedding photograph from the Greek community in Cappadocia, this time from Malakopi, or Derinkuyu, and dated circa 1910, shows a very different sartorial choice on the part of the bride (Figure 4.18). She wears a dark-colored print dress, fitted but not highly tailored, trimmed with a lace flounce around the skirt and other bands of lace on the skirt, sleeves, and bodice. The bride and her groom both wear crowns, in the case of the bride, on top of a fabric headdress. The young girls visible in the image are all wearing dresses similar in style to the bride, suggesting that her dress was locally made. Perhaps family finances did not permit a trip to a nearby city to purchase a more fashionable dress, or she may have preferred a dress that could be worn on special occasions for years to come, as would be the case with the one she chose. Or the dress could even have been borrowed for the occasion.

The clothes worn by brides in the late Ottoman Empire are a kaleidoscope of design, fabric, trim, and color. They range from the highly fashionable and extremely expensive dresses of urban brides to the much more modest locally made outfits, in many cases incorporating elements from contemporary fashion and regional tradition to create wedding clothes that reflect the personal and social identity of the bride. A deeper investigation of these dress practices is well beyond what I can undertake here, but such a study would add immeasurably to the understanding of the relationships among different ethnic and religious groups, the way fashion trends traveled and were adapted to suit specific circumstances, and the factors influencing the fashion choices of Ottoman brides.

Wedding photographs of famous brides—European royalty, for example—were produced as cartes de visite or cabinet cards and circulated widely. From a dress history perspective, these were important as a means of disseminating information about the latest wedding fashions. In the Ottoman context, wedding photographs did not necessarily have the same public role, but they would have been shared in the form of cabinet cards, larger photographs mounted on cardboard, or postcards, with family and friends. Although the images served a number of purposes, detailed above, documenting details of the bride's apparel was a significant aspect of these photographs, for the bride, her friends, and family in the first instance, but now also for fashion history. Whether showcasing traditional bridal outfits or the latest European modes, the photographs tell the story of bridal dress as an index of the fashion choices that Ottoman women made.

In a 2015 article, in discussing pilgrimage photography, Lucie Ryzova describes pilgrimage as a liminal time, out of normative time that temporarily places the pilgrim in a different temporal and spatial regime. She goes on to say, "The ritualization of behavior in liminal time works as a kind of 'social stage' in which social identities are even more 'on display' than is the case in normative time" (2015: 165). Weddings are similarly liminal, time-limited, and drawing participants together to enact specific rituals and relationships. The wedding photographs considered here provide a material stage that allows the participants, whether the bridal couple, the bride alone, or the community to perform their ritualized roles. The photographs then become evidence of their successful performances after participants return to their normal lives, and over time, become iconic images in ways never anticipated at the moment they were made. The wedding photographs here all document moments in the lives of their subjects before the tumultuous events of the early twentieth century, when successive wars, genocide, and large-scale population exchanges changed the region in ways impossible to imagine when these weddings took place.

Conclusion

Wedding fashions, a small but very important subset of women's overall wardrobes, demonstrate the extent to which Ottoman women of all ethnicities turned to Euro-American modes in the last decades of the nineteenth century. Similarly, wedding photography reveals how photographs allowed women to display a high point in their fashionability, perform new identities, and signal communal membership. In the next chapter I consider how women learned about the new styles they chose for their clothing, how they acquired them, and the role that fashion media played in this process.

CHAPTER 5
THE FASHION ECONOMY IN ISTANBUL

Hanımefendi [Dear Madam]: The Ottoman Consumer

The transformation in the dress of the Ottoman women in Istanbul that can be traced over the course of the nineteenth century did not happen overnight. As I demonstrated in Chapters 3 and 4, it began with gradual changes in garment details and accessories, moving from there to more substantive alterations and the adoption of the dress. At some point in this fashion transformation, the changes became more dramatic, radically changing the appearance of many Istanbul women. In this chapter I examine the fashion economy, or the interrelated commercial, economic, social, and personal forces involved in producing and consuming clothes, considering the opportunities Ottoman women had to interact with European women, the new fashion media, and changes in how clothes were produced and marketed to Ottoman consumers. Without understanding their engagement with the fashion economy, it is impossible to understand how Istanbul women transformed their dress practices.

I begin with reviewing the ways in which the dresses and other garments worn by European and American women in this period were constructed. Dresses were complex structures, made up of many different shaped and sized pieces assembled into a garment that exactly fit the person for whom it was intended (Figure 5.1). Although nineteenth-century gowns were elaborate creations decorated with numerous ruffles, frills, flounces, and pleats, they depended for their ultimate effect on the way they fit the body of the wearer. Tailoring was a finely developed art that incorporated numerous tricks to achieve the desired effect for an individual consumer: the waistline of a dress could be lengthened to make a short women appear taller; shoulder seams moved inward to make a broad-shouldered woman appear less so; various parts of the garment padded to compensate for the deficiencies of the wearer, and so on. Many women were accomplished seamstresses who made their own clothing. But unlike their Ottoman counterparts who needed no equipment other than needle, thread, and straight edge, the European seamstress required extensive and detailed guides in the form of pattern books, paper patterns, instructions, and mannequins on which the clothes could be fit. Construction of a garment was a complicated business; Ottoman garments on the other hand were easily assembled, but the embroidery and trim required for their decoration were very time-consuming to execute.

The step from a stylish *entari* with cuffs (Figure 3.17) or a *bindallı* dress (Figure 4.6) to a fashionable wedding ensemble (Figure 4.12), for example, represents a major change in garment construction and sewing techniques. The complexity of tailored Euro-American dresses is well beyond what even an experienced tailor or seamstress could create without access to specific fashion information. Nor would the women who ordered these garments have been able to imagine them without being fully conversant with the current fashions of which these dresses are a part.

What had taken place in the fashion landscape of Istanbul to make such a change possible? For example, were new players involved in the fashion economy, as producers, merchants, or in other capacities? Did production methods change? Did new merchandising structures emerge during these decades? And how was fashion information communicated, both to Istanbul consumers and among the social groups wearing the new fashions? How did Istanbul women share or demonstrate their fashion savvy?

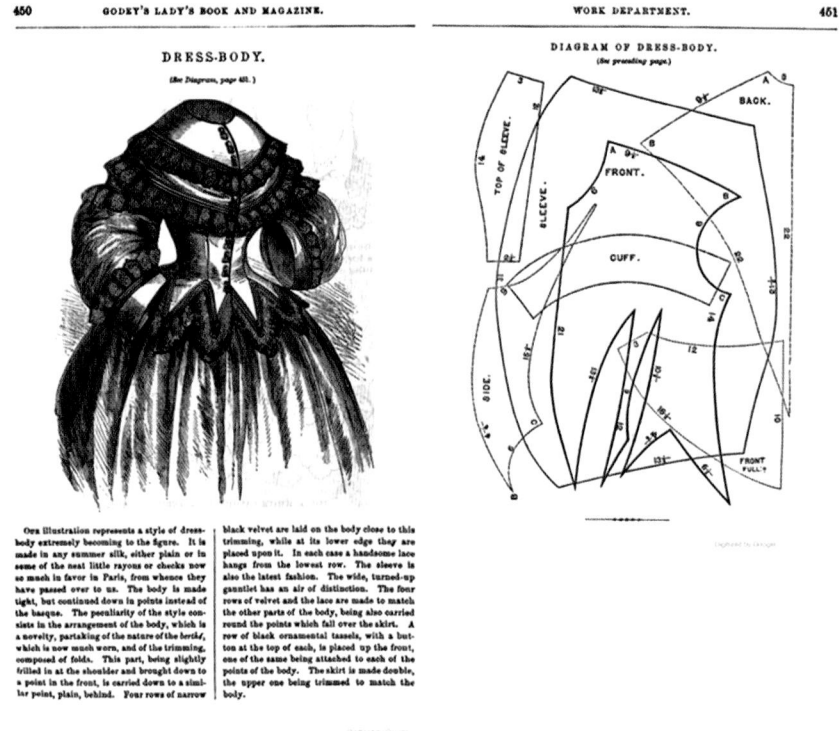

Figure 5.1 American dress bodice, *Godey's Lady's Book* 57, no. 5 (November 1858): 450, 451.

As these questions suggest, the adoption of European-style dresses by Ottoman women was only possible as a result of the emergence of a new, modern fashion economy in the city that placed Istanbul fashion consumers at the center of a network of information and access to goods. The clothing decisions these consumers made would have been informed by the fashion journals and local press that they read, the images of other women they saw, circulated by cartes de visite and other means, the clothes in the modern stores in Pera and Galata, advice from tailors and seamstresses, either local or foreign, who were well informed about the new fashions, and what their friends were wearing. Placing the consumer at the center of this network focuses attention on a range of disparate information, illuminating the complex process of fashion change. The four most significant circumstances the women of Istanbul encountered in terms of fashion were their expanded contact with other women, both foreign and local; the new availability of fashion media; changes in clothing production modes and shopping options; and an evolving consumer culture.

Interaction with European Women

Perhaps the single most important force in the spread of European fashion in Istanbul was the presence of European women in the city. Over the course of the nineteenth century, the numbers of European women visiting the city, either as short-term visitors or longer residents, grew substantially. Improvements in transportation were an important factor but not the only one. The increasingly complex economic and diplomatic entanglements between the Ottoman Empire and European powers brought more bankers, government officials, educators, businessmen, and others to Istanbul; in many cases they were accompanied by their wives, who set up housekeeping in the city. The Crimean War (1853–1856) brought English nurses to Istanbul, as well as nurses from other countries, with European nurses an ongoing presence into the early twentieth century, working alongside Ottoman women. Other professional women from Europe—writers, governesses and teachers, artists, seamstresses—also arrived in Istanbul in the second half of the nineteenth century, staying for weeks or even years.

Many of the foreign women, whether visitors or residents, wanted to satisfy their curiosity about Turkish women, who they could not easily meet publicly, so they visited as many Turkish homes as they could. Their Turkish hostesses received them hospitably, perhaps to satisfy their own curiosity about the Europeans (Figure 5.2). Nearly every woman author of the nineteenth century describes at least one visit to a harem; for the most part, the visits were slow-moving, awkward social occasions. In the first part of the century at least, the language barrier was formidable, although this became less of a difficulty when Turkish women began to learn French. (Very few European women attempted to learn Turkish.)

Reading multiple accounts of these visits, it is clear that there was a performative aspect to the events on the part of both the visitors and the hosts. Requests for visits were extended through intermediaries, and once a date was set, both parties knew what was expected of them. Visitors arrived at the agreed-upon time and were conducted to the harem, the women's quarters of the house, where they were greeted by the senior woman who was present. The European women often visited in small groups and were received by most of

Figure 5.2 Untitled, Mary Adelaide Walker, late 1850s, published in *Constantinople during the Crimean War* by Emelia B. M. Hornby, 1863, p. 352.

the women of the household. After removing their outer garments and shoes, the visitors were seated, and children were introduced and admired. Eating and smoking were standard activities, although few European women accepted the pipe when it was offered.

The 1891 book *Nisvan-ı İslam (Women of Islam)* by Fatma Aliye, the first women novelist in Turkish literature, presents a fascinating counterpoint to the standard European account of a harem visit, written from the point of view of the Ottoman women hosting the European visitors.[1] The book (a work of fiction) consists of three conversations among European and Ottoman women that had taken place in French, transcribed into Ottoman Turkish by a first-person narrator (the author), and taken from the harem visits of the European visitors to her home. Exchanges among Ottoman women are interspersed among the transcriptions from harem visits. Beyond the specifics of harem visits, the larger issues the author addressed have to do with the misunderstandings that European women have of Ottoman women, due at least in part to issues of translation, linguistic and cultural.

Fashion has a central place in the third conversation of *Nisvan-ı İslam*. The section begins with a discussion among three Ottoman friends of a dress issue that one of the three women has; in the course of the talk, the sartorial identities of each of three women are described. One is obsessively concerned with keeping up with the latest European styles, one dresses in traditional Turkish style, and the narrator wears both options as she chooses. These mirror the situation among elite Ottoman women more generally and allow a wide-ranging conversation about fashion economies and the larger moral issues involved in fashion choices. Later on, three French women arrive for a visit and are dismayed to find that their hosts are not wearing "traditional" Ottoman clothing as they had requested. Through conversation it emerges that the French women had expected their hosts to be wearing the dress of the harem women (paid models) pictured in the commercial photographs produced for the tourist market (such as Figure 2.7). This section of the book is a rich account of "cultural mistranslation" (Booth and Shissler: 343), told in the context of fashion and photography.

As the passage from Fatma Aliye's book and the accounts of European women (even taking into account the potentials for misunderstandings) demonstrate, clothing was very often both a central topic of conversation and one of the main activities in the cross-cultural encounters of these women. The clothes of the European visitors were touched to examine the fabric, skirts lifted to inspect stockings and petticoats, and hats and cloaks tried on. When the Turkish ladies were better acquainted with the European visitors or wished to impress them, they displayed their wardrobes to them, as happened to Emelia Hornby, the wife of a British official stationed in Istanbul during the Crimean War. Recounting an 1856 visit to a family in her neighborhood in one of her letters home, she wrote:

> Robe after robe, carefully pinned up in muslin, was produced, of every color and shade, for all the ladies ran
> to fetch their whole stock of finery. Dresses of light green edged with gold, and violet trimmed with silver,
> flowered dresses, embroidered dresses, shawls, scarfs and jackets were produced in endless array. (1863: 340)

In some cases, visits could be returned, as the same author reports: "They visit you and flatter you and beg the patterns of your gown and bonnet" (ibid.: 157).

Apart from reporting on harem life generally, some writers had a particularly keen eye for fashion. Julia Pardoe, visiting the city in 1836, was an invaluable observer as previously noted. Here is her description of the dress of a child in the harem of Esma Sultan, the older sister of Sultan Mahmud II:

> Her costume was an odd admixture of the European and Oriental. She wore trousers of pale blue
> cotton flowered with yellow; and an antery of light green striped with white and edged with a fringe
> of pink floss silk; while her jacket, which was the production of a Parisian dress maker, was of dove-

colored satin, thickly wadded, and furnished with a deep cape, and a pair of immense sleeves, fastened at the wrists with diamond studs.

(Pardoe 1837: 179)

Emelia Hornby was also an astute observer of dress. She has this to say about the dress of a pasha's twelve-year-old daughter in 1855:

The dress and trousers are of a thick kind of gauze, of a pale salmon color, and sprigged with silver. A green velvet cap, beautifully embroidered, covers her head, and her hair hangs down her back in numerous plaits … Her socks are of embroidered yellow leather, with peaks turning up in front, and she seems very proud of her gay-colored French parasol.

(1863: 73)

The foreign women who stayed longer in Istanbul had the opportunity to see Ottoman women in a range of settings. Those who set up housekeeping employed Greek and Armenian women in their houses and often lived among them in the villages along the Bosporus. The foreigners depended on their neighbors and domestic servants to understand local customs; the local women, in turn, could observe foreign women at close quarters, learning about their dress, their reading habits, and other aspects of their lives. The foreign women would also have socialized with the elite women in the minority communities at dinners, theater performances, and other cultural events, as well as the women's associations set up to provide relief to refugees, soldiers, and others. Wives of foreign diplomats and high-ranking government officials met, and in some cases became friendly with the wives of the Ottoman men with whom their husbands worked. For example, Lady Layard, wife of the archaeologist Sir Austen Henry Layard, British ambassador in Istanbul from 1877 to 1880, frequently mentions in her diary of both visiting and receiving visits from Ottoman princesses, the wife of Kamil Paşa, who was later Grand Vizier, and others.

Ottoman Women Among Themselves

Dress practices are at the same time private and public. Self-fashioning is an important part of expressing an identity, for oneself but also for a wider community. The interactions Istanbul women had with other women, local or foreign, were a crucial part of their fashion journey, when they could display their dress to each other and share information about the latest styles, best places to shop, favorite dressmakers, and so on. Istanbul women frequently visited each other in their homes (indeed, Fatma Aliye's authorial decision to structure *Nisvan-ı İslam*, discussed above, around such visits is indicative of their role in the social and intellectual life of women in this period).

For Muslim women, these were harem visits, but for members of other religious groups, family visits and social events that involved both men and women were part of their daily lives. Visits to the bath, shopping (discussed in more detail below), and visits to the Sweet Waters and other picnic spots were all occasions where women had the opportunity to meet with each other. Armenian and Greek women would have attended church, providing another regular social opportunity, while for Muslim and Jewish women, with the exception of specific holidays, religious observances mostly took place at home. In the last decades of the nineteenth century and into the early twentieth century, women's social lives became much more varied. The Western-style department stores in Pera, with their display windows, invited window shopping; pastry shops and restaurants catering to women only began to open; dressmakers opened shops; and cinemas and theaters presented afternoon performances for women.[2]

These new activities were directed at women of leisure, but in many cases, they were served by working women, whose lives had also changed dramatically. Istanbul women had always worked, but with some notable exceptions, most of that work took place within the home, as enslaved or free domestic servants, weavers, embroiderers or seamstresses doing piecework, midwives, and so on. Beginning in the second half of the nineteenth century, other kinds of employment possibilities emerged, in the new shops serving women, textile factories, hospital nursing, education, and elsewhere. (These new employment possibilities and their impact on the dress practices of working women are explored in Chapter 8.) At first these new positions were filled primarily by non-Muslim women, although Muslim women began working outside the home as social and economic circumstances changed in the early twentieth century. From a fashion perspective, the increased public presence of women and their expanded opportunities for interaction among larger social networks was a significant factor in the exchange of fashion knowledge.

Fashion and Media

The second half of the nineteenth century also saw the emergence of fashion images that circulated among Istanbul women, a major change in the image economy. The increasing availability of photography, the creation of fashion magazines, and the prevalence of newspaper advertising provided new ways of seeing dressed bodies. These representations were an important means of disseminating fashion information, and they gave women the opportunity to imagine (and in the case of photographic portraits, see) themselves in new, more modern ways—to try on new identities through images. From the 1860s onward, when photography began to be taught to the Ottoman military and photography equipment was both easier to use and more readily available, more informal, personal presentations of Ottoman women were created. These private, personal photographs are an important counterpoint to the fashion imagery of commercial print media.

Some of these photographs may have been taken by women photographers. Although not as numerous as studios owned by men, evidence indicates women-run studios in Istanbul from the 1840s onward (Berberoğlu 2023: 47). Many of the women photographers came from Europe, but Muslim Turkish women also operated studios. Of these Naciye Hanım (1881–1973) is the best known, opening her studio first in the Yildiz neighborhood of Istanbul in 1919, making portraits of Ottoman Muslim women and offering photography lessons (ibid.: 68). Operating in Istanbul before Naciye Hanım, Elisa Zonaro, the wife of the Italian painter Fausto Zonaro, had a photography studio from circa 1894 until she left Istanbul with her family in 1910. According to her advertisements, she specialized in taking photographs of women and children, and she was willing to visit her clients in their home to make the photographs (ibid.: 166).

In some cases, the name, or at least something about the women who appear in these photographs, is known. Even when that is not so, the images are still informative. For example, in the snapshot pictured in Figure 5.3, two women are seated outdoors eating grapes. They are sitting on bentwood chairs, with a third chair between them on which the platter of fruit is perched. The chairs, a recent design innovation from Vienna, were a frequent prop in Ottoman photographs, signaling modernity. The woman on the right is wearing a light-colored dress, belted at the waist, with a black lace collar. Her friend is dressed in a *ferace*, or outdoor coat, and has a scarf tied loosely around her head. The *ferace* is a fashionable one, with a wide collar trimmed with rows of darker braid, and the full sleeves that would have accommodated the leg-of-mutton sleeves popular on European dresses. Absorbed in their conversation and the grapes, they are not paying attention to the photographer, who was most likely a family member.[3]

Figure 5.3 Eating grapes outside, photographer unknown, *ca.* 1890–1905. Los Angeles, Pierre de Gigord collection of photographs of the Ottoman Empire and the Republic of Turkey. Getty Research Institute, 96.R.14 (CD7_001).

The photograph in Figure 5.4 is more formal in its presentation of the three young women who are pictured. Closely grouped in front of a backdrop evoking a palatial setting, two girls stand together behind a third seated figure; all look directly at the photographer. The photograph was taken by Ali Sami (1866–1936), a military photographer who taught photography and art at the military college and was appointed by the sultan to record various state events. Apart from his professional images, he took photographs of his family and friends, which provide an opportunity to see the dress of members of the Ottoman elite during his career. In this example, the seated figure is dressed in an elaborate gown of a silk brocade with tiered, flounced sleeves and an overskirt; she seems very pleased with her outfit. The two standing figures are wearing European-style clothes, too, but not nearly as elaborate as that of the central figure. The figure on the left, the youngest of the three, is dressed in a blouse of a print fabric and a dark skirt, both of which could have been made at home. The three are posed with their heads close together, indicating a close relationship among them. Without knowing the circumstances of the photograph, it would seem to mark an important occasion in the life of the seated figure, given her centrality in the composition as well as her clothing. The backdrop appears in other photographs taken by Ali Sami, one of which is dated 1906, a date in keeping with the style of the clothes. Ottoman women's access to photography and to their photographic images was a key component in their development of a new, modern sense of self and of their interaction with fashion, allowing them to see themselves and others in

Figure 5.4 Untitled, Ali Sami, *ca.* 1906. Los Angeles, Pierre de Gigord collection of photographs of the Ottoman Empire and the Republic of Turkey. Getty Research Institute, 96.R.14 (CD_002).

new, perhaps transitory or even experimental ways. In this case, the photograph documents a particularly fashionable moment in the life of the seated figure, when she was most likely wearing something very different than her everyday attire.

Unlike earlier images of Ottoman women in costume albums, travel books, and the like, in photographs such as these the photographer and the women pictured would have had some interaction. Women would have had a certain amount of agency in how they were represented, choosing their clothing, head covering, and to a lesser extent their pose and the studio setting with its props and backdrop. With the exception of women whose family members were photographers, for many having a photograph made would have been a relatively momentous event, most likely involving very specific choices in self-fashioning and presentation. The cartes de visite (Figure 5.5) and cabinet cards popular in Istanbul as elsewhere from the 1850s through the 1890s were designed to be shared widely. In the Ottoman context, the photographs that women had made of themselves would have most likely been shared among family members and close friends. Berberoğlu documents an example of a photograph taken in 1907 by Elisa Zonaro of a young Istanbul artist Müfide Kadri who has inscribed her photograph on the reverse to her friend, artist Vildan Gizer ("To my dear sister Ms. Vildan, a humble souvenir from me") (Berberoğlu 2024: 18). Exchanging photographs among women friends and family, while documenting a particular moment in their lives, was also a means of performing an identity not always publicly visible.

However, photography, although a critically important part of this story, is only one of the fashion media at play in nineteenth-century Istanbul. Fashion magazines from Europe, local newspapers, and toward the end

Figure 5.5 Portrait, carte de visite, Abdullah Frères, 1865–1870. Istanbul, Ömer Koç collection.

of the century, the newly introduced women's press in Istanbul, all worked together to create a vibrant fashion conversation for interested consumers. Fashion magazines had their start in Europe in the late seventeenth century in the form of fashion plates circulated to generate interest in new designs. By the mid-nineteenth century, they were a big business: by one count ninety-four fashion magazines and trade journals were published in Paris in the years 1850–1870 (Koning and Verhaak 2015: 140). They had varying success; some disappeared after only a few issues, but others reached as many as fifty-two thousand readers in one year (ibid.). Fashion magazines directed at female consumers at varying economic levels were also produced in Britain and the United States, all influenced by competing publications from other fashion centers. In many cases sold by subscription, these would have also reached Istanbul, where they would have been read and shared among local and foreign fashion consumers (Figure 5.6).

Magazines directed at women focused on fashion, but they also included recipes, household hints, serialized stories, and more. The fashion information they provided was both aspirational and practical. On the one hand, they presented the latest fashions from Paris and London, often in color, but they also published patterns for embroidery, knitting, and crochet. Some periodicals also included patterns for garments illustrated in the issue so that the clothes could be made at home (Figure 5.7). These patterns, compressed into a single sheet,

Figure 5.6 A Woman at a Brion Sewing Machine, *Le Miroir Parisien, Journal des Dames et Demoiselles*, July 1870. Amsterdam, Rijksmuseum, M. A. Ghering-van-Irlent Collection Inv. no. RP-P-2009-3554.

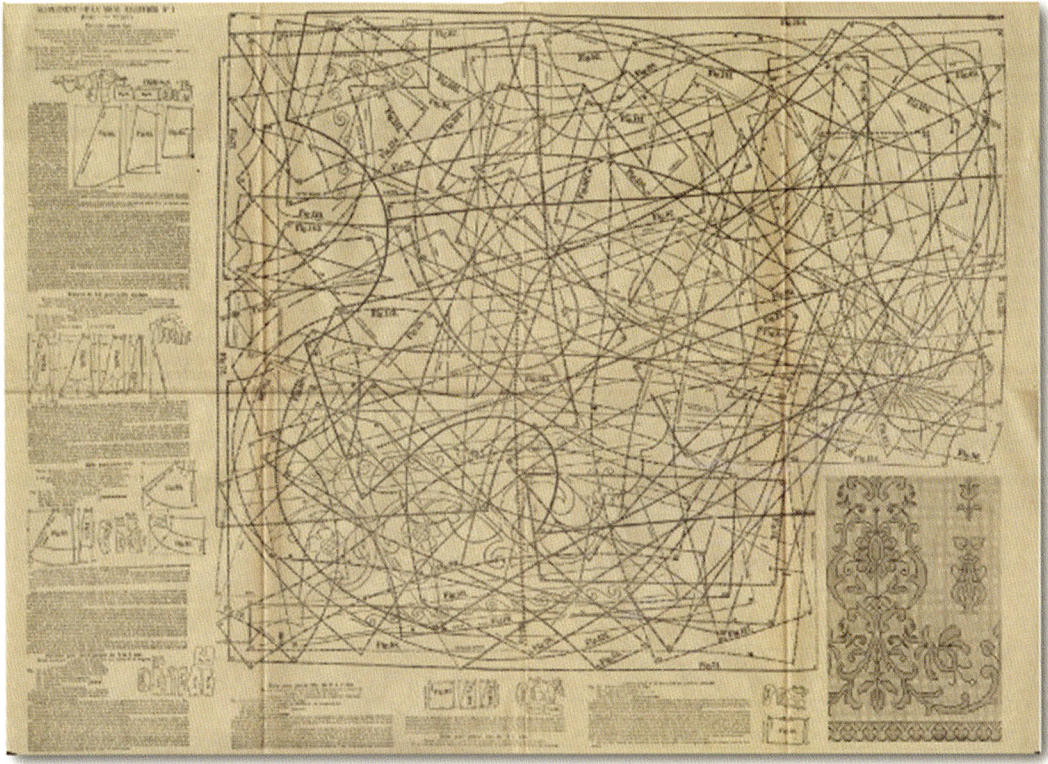

Figure 5.7 Pattern Sheet, *La mode illustrée*, 1870, no. 36. Collection of the author.

were not for the faint of heart. The double-sided pattern page illustrated here, from an 1870 number of *La mode illustrée* includes pattern pieces for fifteen different projects: corsets, jackets, collars, blouses, girls' dresses, and more. Deciphering the pattern pieces that corresponded to a specific garment and copying them onto tissue paper would have been a time-consuming task, and the sewing instructions provided were minimal at best.

A group of seven fashion plates in the Topkapı Saray archives provides important insights into how these fashion illustrations circulated and how Ottoman women used them to shape their dress practices (Figure 5.8).[4] The seven pages in the Topkapı were compiled from three different fashion magazines printed in Paris and dating from 1873 and 1874 (*L'elegance Parisienne*, *La Saison*, and *Penelope*, in Greek). One of the sheets is stamped with an address: 32 Passage Hazzapulo, Pera. The compilation of sheets from different journals as well as the fact that they seem to have been delivered to a shop in the Hazzapulo Passage, in the modern shopping district of Pera, signals that they were part of the stock-in-trade of seamstresses catering to elite women seeking to wear the latest fashions from Paris. Although some women were able to order their dresses direct from Paris, for many others, copies made locally based on the latest fashion illustrations were a reasonable alternative.[5]

The pages are annotated with notes: in some cases, written directly on the page; in other cases, pinned to the sheet, with specific directions about what the woman ordering the dress wanted. Most of the pages also have fabric scraps pinned to the sheets. For example, the example illustrated here from the journal *Penelope* has two notes in the margins of the page as well as two fabric samples pinned to the page. The notes read: "Navy blue velvet looks the same as this picture. Back skirt five *arşın*, [an old Turkish measure of length,

Figure 5.8 *Penelope*, Paris, fashion illustration with fabric samples attached, April 1874. The Directorate of National Palaces Topkapı Palace Archives Collection Inv. No. TSMA. D.10739/4.

equal to about 27 inches] front skirt four *arşın*. Light cloth(?) will be cut and sewn as in this picture. The back skirt is five *arşın*. The front skirt is four *arşın*."[6] The notes on the other pages are similar, specifying fabric type, length, and other details for the dresses. In the case of the imperial palace, harem servants, most likely enslaved women, acted as fashion intermediaries between the palace harem and the dressmaker's shop, but in other cases, women may have visited the shops themselves. When the clothes were ready to be fitted, the dressmakers would visit the harem with their work.

Beginning around the middle of the nineteenth century, a very active and rich newspaper culture developed in Istanbul. The newspapers serving the diverse population of the city also provided fashion information, as well as revealing the goods and services available to local consumers. The newspapers published in English and French, because of the dominance of London and Paris as fashion centers, were important fashion influences for Ottoman women, although these were not the only newspapers produced in the city by any means. Ahmet Emin Yalman's 1914 Columbia University PhD dissertation, *The Development of Modern Turkey as Measured by Its Press*, documents forty-seven newspapers in the city in 1876, of which thirteen were in Ottoman Turkish (Yanatma 2015: 30). The remaining thirty-four included newspapers in Arabic, Armenian, Bulgarian, English, French, German, Greek, and Ladino, with the Greek, Armenian, and French being the most numerous. The population of Istanbul was a polyglot one, so although the newspapers each included content of interest to their specific readership, the newspapers, particularly the Ottoman, French, and Armenian would have been read across the city. In addition to local newspapers, foreign newspapers were also received by the European community. *Le Temps*, published in Paris, was sent to Istanbul, and the London newspapers reached the city as well.

The Istanbul newspapers of this period are filled with lively firsthand descriptions of local politics, social events among the foreign community, activities of the court, visits of foreign dignitaries, and much more. In addition to the local news, the papers all carried international news, with extensive commentary and miscellaneous news items of interest from the outside world. This material reached Istanbul via telegraph, established there in the 1850s, and through the international news agencies, primarily Agence Havas and Reuters. Shipping and commercial news with published shipping schedules and local commodities trading, as well as other financial news, was also included. Serialized novels or other literature were an important feature of most newspapers.

Accounts of social events, theater performances, the arrival and departure of members of the diplomatic community, and the activities of the court were recorded meticulously. This description of an evening entertainment from 1884 is typical of such offerings:

> A most delightful soiree was given on Thursday evening by Mme D. Pandjiri which was attended by a large portion of the elite of Pera society. Among the guests present were Nusret Pasha, aide-de-camp general to the Sultan, Ahmed Djelaleddin Bey, Chief of the Political Cabinet of His Majesty … etc. Before dancing began Mme. d'Edelberg, the well known prima donna, sang two operatic pieces which were much applauded. At 2 a.m. a most sumptuous supper of 150 covers was served, after which dancing was resumed with a brilliant cotillon lasting until nearly 7 in the morning.
>
> *(The Oriental Advertiser/La Moniteur Oriental, March 1, 1884)*

In April 1884, the Austrian crown prince and his wife made a five-day visit to Istanbul. Details of the planning for this visit, both on the part of the court and the local Austrian community, appeared in the paper every day for at least a month in advance of the visit, which was the practice for most visits by state officials. The brief references to Archduchess Stephanie's visits to the royal harem are particularly interesting. On April 12 the paper reports:

> We have learned that by order of His Majesty the Sultan, Mlle. E. Dadian, daughter of His Excellency Artin Effendi Dadian, under-secretary of State for Foreign Affairs, will attend in the Imperial Harem, on the occasions when the Royal ladies will be visited by the Archduchess Stephanie, to act as interpreter.

A week later, the paper notes that Mlle. Dadian had received "the second class of the order of the Chefkat [*Şefkat Nişanı* or the Order of Compassion created by Abdulhamid II in 1878] set in brilliants" from the sultan, and on April 25 reports:

> His Majesty the Sultan has been pleased to appoint Mlle Dadian, daughter of His Excellency the under-Secretary of State for Foreign Affairs, permanent interpreter to the Imperial Harem, in token of His satisfaction of the able manner in which Mlle Dadian performed those duties on the occasions when the Royal ladies were visited by the Archduchess Stephanie.

The fact that in 1884 the imperial harem required a permanent interpreter indicates that the women of the court had increased opportunities to meet with foreign women and perhaps also wished to know more about their visitors than language limitations on the part of harem residents and their visitors had previously allowed.

Newspapers of the day were modest in comparison to the full-color, lavishly illustrated versions produced in the twentieth century. Most of the Istanbul newspapers were four pages, with official announcements, nonpolitical news (inventions, construction of bridges and railroads) and local news on the first two pages. Financial information and business news was provided on the third page. Serialized novels were often presented at the bottom of one or more pages, and advertisements ran on the third and fourth pages. Their images (in ads or shipping notices) were limited to line drawings, so could not compete with beautifully illustrated fashion magazines. Nonetheless, the newspapers, especially the advertisements, were important sources of fashion information.

In the absence of pictures, the ads presented copiously worded descriptions of the goods their customers would find when they visited their stores (Figure 5.9). In the January 16, 1848, edition of the *Journal de Constantinople*, the Bon Ton department store ran this ad: CONFECTION DE CORSETS A LA DERNIERE MODE DE PARIS [Corsets made in the latest style from Paris]. In much smaller print, the next lines read

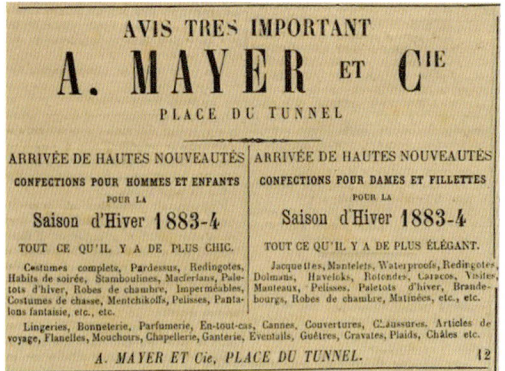
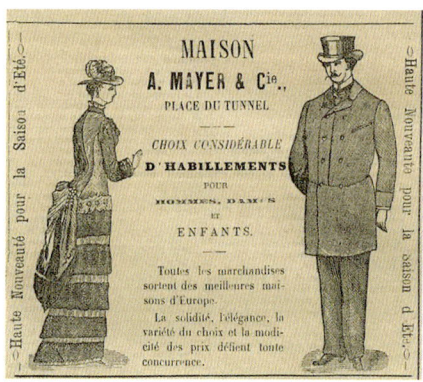

Figure 5.9 Ads from Istanbul newspapers: *Oriental Advertiser*, April 16 and 18, 1884.

Independamment de la vente des Etoffes de Soie, et de tous les Articles de Nouveautes necessaires a la Toilette des Dames, tels que Chapeaux, Manteaux, Mantelets,… QUI SORTENT DES MEILLEURES MAISONS DE PARIS. [Independently selling silk fabric, and all the new goods necessary for ladies dressing, such as hats, coats, cloaks, … coming from the best houses of Paris.]

The ad also informs readers that their corsets were "a un prix modere" [of a moderate price], and in the latest style are easy to wear. The ad provides the store's address on the Grande Rue de Pera and reiterates that its goods come from the makers in Paris. A similarly loquacious ad was placed in the January–mid-April 1884 numbers of the *Oriental Advertiser* by Maison A. Meyer & Cie, listing in painstaking detail the "Haute Nouveautes" [best goods] for the winter season for men, women, children and young girls (Figure 5.9). However, just two days after its wordy winter season ad appeared in the paper, the ad of April 18 describing summer goods displayed a modern new design. The sharply reduced amount of text was flanked on either side by the fashionably dressed figures of a man and a woman. The woman, shown in profile, wears an outfit very much à la mode, with a long, slim bodice, close-fitting sleeves, a modest bustle, and tiered skirt. An 1897 ad from a different Istanbul department store, Carlman and Blumberg, which includes the figures of two women sporting highly fashionable jackets with nipped-in waists and leg-of-mutton sleeves, indicates the continuation of this new trend in advertising design.

In addition to fashion-related advertisements, the newspapers ran short pieces about fashion, in some cases extracts from French or British papers. *The Oriental Advertiser* also had an occasional column, "Courrier parisien de la mode." The piece that ran on March 13, 1884, was devoted primarily to the subject of winter coats and jackets. After first advising the reader that it was more important to adjust one's fashion choices to the actual temperature rather than the name of the season, the column then describes outerwear recently seen in Paris:

> *J'ai vu quelques pardesus de demi-saison qui m'ont semble jolis; entr'autres; une pelisse charmante en pacha gris acier, c'est a dire en alpaga a gros grain.* [I saw a few mid-season overcoats that seemed pretty to me; among others; a charming pelisse in steel grey pashmina; that is to say a grosgrain or ribbed alpaca.]

The writer goes on to deplore fashions that are unhealthy for the body (skirts too tight for walking, heels too high) and endorses healthier trends. The next article, on March 20, is concerned with defining the morning gown (*la matinée*) and detailing a few examples. The column also includes news about spring fashions and closes with disparaging words about current trends in hats, which the author finds lacking in taste. The column ends by advising: "*Dans la rue, à pied, un chapeau de couleur sombre et sombrement garni est toujours de meilleur ton.*" [In the street, walking, a hat in a dark color and trim is always in the best taste.] The columns are at the same time extremely detailed in their descriptions of specific garments and quite authoritative in advising readers on their fashion choices.

The French language papers were of particular importance for fashion and would have had broad readership because French was the common language for many sectors of the Istanbul population. However, the newspapers published for the Armenian, Greek, and Jewish communities of Istanbul are worth looking at briefly to get a sense of the attention paid to matters of fashion and other consumer goods. The two main Ladino newspapers serving the Jewish community were *El Tiempo* (1872–1930) and *El Telegrafo* (1872–1931), which had a combined print run of about fourteen hundred, reaching perhaps eight to ten times as many readers, because the papers would have been shared in cafés and libraries (Cohen 2012: 251). The content of the papers was similar to the English and French newspapers but with a focus on political and economic news relating to Ottoman Jews and Jewish communities internationally, as well as Istanbul news and events,

Figure 5.10   Above: Singer advertisement, *El Telegrafo*, 1896. Courtesy of William Gross; Below: Printemps advertisement, *El Tiempo*, 1905. National Library of Israel.

literature, shipping news, and so on. Both newspapers carried ads for a range of goods and services, illustrated in some cases. These include fashion-related items—for example, a 1905 ad in *El Tiempo* in French from the Paris department store Printemps advertising its mail order-catalogs and postal arrangements,[7] and an ad for Singer sewing machines, with two cherubs operating the machine, in *El Telegrafo* in 1896 (Figure 5.10).

The Armenian press in Istanbul was extremely active, with eleven newspapers in the city by 1872. That number varied over the years, but the Armenian press was consistent in its presence in the print culture of Istanbul, with the exception of 1894–1897, the time of the Hamidian massacres of Armenians in Anatolia. The Armenian newspapers, all suspended by the government in that period, were allowed to resume publication within a few years. The papers resembled other newspapers of the day in their format with advertisements on the third and fourth pages. The ads in the Armenian papers, as well as those in the other newspapers examined here, provide a very useful picture of the goods and services the readers for each paper needed, or perhaps more accurately wanted, for their homes and themselves. In the case of the Armenian papers, ads for physicians and various remedies were the most numerous. Sewing and washing machines also appeared regularly in the papers' ads. The ads for clothing, shoes, perfumes, and hair dyes that appeared in the Armenian papers resembled those seen in other papers, often from the same merchants. The advertisements were for specific goods and services, but they were selling their readers modernity and sophisticated consumption.

The Greek community in Istanbul was served by numerous newspapers over the course of the nineteenth century, beginning in 1835 with *Othomanikos Minytor.* Published in Greek and Ottoman Turkish, it remained in production until 1841 and was followed by a succession of papers of longer or shorter duration. One of the longest running of the Istanbul papers was *Konstantinoupolis*, published by Dimitris Nikolaidis from 1867 until he passed it along to his son in 1909 (Balta and Kavak 2017). The format of the paper was very similar to the French, English, Ladino, and Armenian newspapers already mentioned. Among the ads in an 1893 copy of *Konstantinoupolis* preserved in a Greek archive is one for a sewing machine, an indication of the broad reach of the marketing for the new invention.[8]

Beginning in about 1869, dozens of periodicals targeted at Ottoman women began to appear, nearly all published in Istanbul (Figure 5.11).[9] These were inexpensive serial publications, some lasting for only an issue or two, others for longer. Their names were clearly designed to attract women readers: *Aile* (*Family*, 1880), *Şükufezar* (*Blooming Garden*, 1886), *Parça Bohçası* (*Ragbag*, 1889), *Demet* (*Bouquet*, 1908), and *Mahasin* (*Beauties*, 1908), among many others. The content of the magazines was far-reaching, touching on matters of education for women, household management, raising children, becoming modern, beauty and health, fashion, politics and literature, among many other topics. Some content was reproduced from European sources, but a great deal was the work of local authors, both men and women. Although many of the contributors were well-known journalists or literary figures, subscribers also wrote in with questions or comments on earlier issues, creating an ongoing conversation among readers. Circulation numbers for the periodicals are difficult to find, but the subscription information for one example, *Hanımlara Mahsus Gazete*, or *The Ladies Own Gazette,* which offered different prices for readers purchasing their copies in Istanbul or receiving them in other parts of the empire or abroad (Enis 2013: 142–47), seems to indicate a fairly wide readership. Literacy rates for women were still relatively low, but literate women could have discussed what they read with their nonliterate friends or household members, and copies certainly would have been passed around, expanding the readership of the periodicals.

Most, but not all the nearly forty women's periodicals that appeared beginning in 1869 included some fashion-related content, the exceptions being journals that focused specifically on social or political issues. In some cases, fashion was an explicit part of a journal's mission: for example, the journal *Mahasin* (*Beauties*), which brought out twelve issues beginning in 1908, defined one of its aims as "being a perfect fashion and fine arts magazine, and… that women would not need European fashion magazines anymore" (Karaman 2016: 118).

Figure 5.11 *Hanımlara Mahsus Gazete (The Ladies Own Gazette),* August 31, 1895. Collection of the author.

Fashion-related content in the women's magazines had a number of sometimes contradictory goals. Readers should be careful consumers, spending within their means and making sensible choices. It was important to be aware of new fashion trends (and patronize the magazine's advertisers) but not follow them slavishly. Specific clothing items, particularly the corset, generated numerous articles, warning about the health dangers they presented as well as considering which shapes were best suited to specific dress styles or body types. Many articles presented practical sewing how-to instructions and patterns. At the same time, more philosophical pieces appeared: for example, an essay titled "*Moda Nereden Çıkıyor*?" [Where Does Fashion Come From?], written by Gülistan İsmet in a December 1900 issue of *Hanımlara Mahsus Gazete* (ibid.: 283), in which the author ruminated on the enigma of fashion as a concept.

Hanımlara Mahsus Gazete (HMG), in print from 1895 through 1908, was the longest-lived of the early women's periodicals. Initially, it was published twice a week, but within its first year, it became weekly; generally, it consisted of 8–10 pages, although that could vary (Enis: 148). The publisher was İbnülhakkı Mehmet Tahir, a journalist who also wrote for the newspaper *Tarik*. Tahir's wife, author Fatma Şadiye, was deeply involved in the local fashion economy, running her own studio producing fashionable clothes and employing women dressmakers and designers. Magazine subscribers were offered discounts on goods and tailoring services, and the journal set up its own mail-order business through which subscribers could order goods and patterns from Istanbul (Frierson 1995: 23).

The place of fashion in the journal's pages was complex, as was the magazine's editorial position. The magazine presented fashion through a number of different avenues within its pages: the ads it carried for local stores, seamstresses, and tailors meant that readers needed to be encouraged to patronize those businesses, as well as the related enterprises of the magazine itself. Many readers wanted the latest, most detailed information on the newest styles from foreign fashion magazines as well as patterns and instruction for knitting, lacemaking, and sewing for clothes and household goods. Readers and authors carried on active and sometimes heated conversations, in many cases concerned about guiding readers to make healthy, moral, and financially responsible decisions about their dress practices. The panoply of often contradictory fashion discourse within the pages of *HMG* must have been confusing, even daunting, for some of the journal's readers.

The corset, a highly structured undergarment considered to be necessary for wearing close-fitting European dresses, became the entry point for wide-ranging discussions about modernity for Ottoman women, health, and the definition of beauty, as well as more mundane concerns about specific corset styles and construction techniques. The conversations are important because they reveal the tensions underlying seemingly personal, even inconsequential fashion decisions that Istanbul women were making. Why did it matter if Ottoman women began to wear the corset instead of the much less-structured undergarments that had accompanied their traditional apparel?

As a piece of intimate attire, the corset signaled a completely different regime of body management for Ottoman women, one that was much more revealing than previously. In addition, health concerns about the use of the corset raised in the Euro-American press made their way into the Ottoman journals. Embracing the corset could be taken as a sign of the wholesale adoption of European fashion by some Ottoman women, which raised both economic and moral concerns.

The range of voices participating in the corset conversations, both in *HMG* and elsewhere, are diverse, confirming the role of the corset as a "sociocultural benchmark," to borrow Burçak's term (2023: 3). The women who wrote for the journal included well-known figures such as the author Fatma Aliye and her sister Emine Semiye (a regular contributor to the journal and board member, respectively) along with women teachers, other professional women, and subscribers to the journal.[10] Men included physicians, as well as members of the Ottoman political and intellectual elite. The prolific journalist Ahmed Midhat Efendi wrote about women's fashion and related health concerns in his 1886/1887 book *Kadınlarda Hıfz-ı Cemal*

[*Preserving Female Beauty*]. Fatma Aliye addressed fashion in her book *Nisvan-ı İslam*, discussed above; and her sister Emine Semiye wrote an article, "Fashion and the Corset" in *HMG*, to name only a few. These public conversations indicate changing conventions in Ottoman society—previously, women's outdoor dress had been regulated by court sumptuary laws, but the discussions shaping those laws would not have included women; at the same time, decisions concerning women's indoor dress then remained within the purview of the individual and her family.

The health risks thought to be associated with the corset opened the way for a public conversation about women's intimate dress practices, or as Burçak writes, "a scienticized public debate which represented moral virtue and patriotic duty towards the larger goal of communal and imperial wellbeing" (ibid.: 1). Women's fashion choices, including the adoption of the corset, became tied up with health, patriotism, and Muslim identity, in addition to the more usual concerns about family budget, personal style, and so on.

Fashion choices may sometimes just be about choosing a flattering style, a favorite color, finding an unexpected bargain, but the decisions that Ottoman women in Istanbul were making about their wardrobes carried weightier messages. This 1904 passage from *Hanımlara Mahsus Gazete*, published in response to a reader's article, is worth quoting at length because it gives a good sense of some of the larger concerns behind the seemingly simple choice of dress.

> Even though we temporarily stopped publishing fashion photos for a couple of months, we did not intend to put women off fashion … Our intention is merely to protect women from the harms of fashion. We approve of fashion for the ladies who abide by the rules of courtesy and elegance. However, why would what we call 'fashion', cost one year's maintenance of a family? Why would a lady spend everything she has (on fashion)? Why would a woman, whose husband is not well off, bother with having new dresses made or follow changing fashions? Now, to the matter of publishing pictures in our newspaper: it is our mission. Our aim is also to serve women who have their dresses made once or twice in a year and to encourage them to make a selection from our newspaper or sew the dress themselves, and not have to pay a dress maker. We know that modest women are not harmed from following fashion … Is it not doubtless that the pictures we issue serve the interests of these ladies?

(ibid.: 295)

The diverse media that have been highlighted here, foreign fashion magazines, Istanbul newspapers, and women's periodicals, all provided the women of Istanbul with information about dress. Depending on what they were reading, they learned about the latest fashions in the European fashion cities, the Istanbul shops where they could buy ready-made clothing or accessories, which seamstresses or tailors they might patronize, and how women in their city were thinking about their dress choices.

In particular, the women's magazines provided a locally based, culturally specific conversation about dress. Although they reported on the latest fashion trends and published pattern details and other instruction, the active and sometime heated discussion on the ethics or morality of fashion choices, the dangers of extravagance, and other pressing fashion-related issues also reflected the anxiety on both individual and societal levels associated with the new fashions. Extravagance in dress practices and changes in style had always provoked commentary in Istanbul, but in earlier times the responses had been confined primarily to matters of women's street dress and would have been written by men. The new women's periodicals published articles written by men and women on the subjects such as extravagance that had always generated comment, but now they extended into more intimate personal matters, particularly the wearing of the corset and what constituted appropriate indoor dress for Ottoman women. Personal fashion choices, previously a matter of concern within a relatively narrow family or social circle, had become a topic of discussion in a much more public context. The women's press provided a new, robust venue for Istanbul women to engage with fashion and challenged them to find their way among conflicting viewpoints as they developed their own sartorial identities.

New Clothes and Shopping

Traditionally, Istanbul women acquired their clothing in several different ways, making choices based on their economic resources and socially accepted practices. The three most common ways of adding to their wardrobes were through the goods sold by door-to-door merchants (Figure 5.12), buying ready-made clothing in the Grand Bazaar or smaller neighborhood markets for more modest consumers, or making new clothes to order, either by professional seamstresses or at home.

The *bohçacı*, or woman who peddled a variety of goods directly to women at home, was a familiar figure in most Istanbul neighborhoods, selling jewelry, trinkets, fabric, ready-made clothing, cosmetics, and perfumes, among other things. Swoboda's painting shows a visit of one such woman to a wealthy household. Three women are seated on divans, each holding a piece of jewelry from what the *bohçacı* is selling. It is impossible to know the status of the three harem inhabitants—they could be enslaved or free, depending on the family circumstances. In contrast to their more colorful outfits, the older woman in a dark coat and white headscarf

Figure 5.12 *Shopping in the Harem*, Sandor Alexander Swoboda, mid-nineteenth century. Istanbul, The Directorate of National Palaces, Painting Museum, Istanbul, Türkiye, Inv. No. 13/9.

has her box of wares open on the floor in front of her. She is looking at the woman in a red *entari*, who, based on both her expansive pose and bright garment, is likely the person who might make a purchase. Such merchants had a reputation for gossip; because they went from house to house, they were often an important means of circulating information on a variety of topics, including fashion.

Istanbul women could also venture outside to make purchases. Charles White, writing in the 1840s, and Leyla Saz, recounting shopping habits at mid-century, both describe the goods sold in the Kapalı Çarşı and smaller bazaars and markets: textiles of all kinds, both locally made and imported, ready-made clothes, embroidered goods, lace, furs (Figure 5.13). The shops in the Kapalı Çarşı sold higher-quality goods for a wealthier clientele, while women of more modest means patronized the smaller weekly markets that took place around the city. Saz writes,

Figure 5.13 *Silk Bazaar*, Amadeo Preziosi, 1858, *Stamboul. Recollections of Eastern Life*. Philadelphia, Kislak Center for Special Collections, Rare Books and Manuscripts, University of Pennsylvania.

The ladies of the small bourgeoisie would generally do their shopping at the weekly markets of their own quarter where they could buy all the things they needed—from linens, printed cottons to food. The great ladies never went to these markets; when they did go, either by whim or out of curiosity, they would preserve the strictest incognito in their dress and would cover their face with their thickest veils in order not to be recognized.

(Saz 1994: 117)

The "great ladies," as Saz calls them, did their shopping in the Kapalı Çarşı, although they would not actually enter the bazaar. Typically, the ladies of the Imperial Harem would stop in the *hünkâr kasrı*, a private space reserved for the use of the imperial family, of the nearby Nurosmaniye Mosque so that the merchants could bring their wares for the eunuchs [castrated male servants who guarded harem women] to show to the women. In other cases, elite women would send their servants to the bazaar to make purchases (ibid.: 115).

Once cloth had been purchased, it would be taken or sent home, where it would be sewn. This might be done by the women of the household, mistresses or servants, or by professional seamstresses. Contemporary accounts are full of references to sewing at home. Mary Adelaide Walker, the British artist discussed in Chapter 2, has this to say about one household she visited:

Arriving at the house on an "old General" to paint a portrait of his wife, I found the household in a state of great excitement. The hanum [General's wife] had been up half the night manufacturing a "Frank" dress for the occasion. It was copied from a stray number of the "*Modes Illustrées*." The lady had cut out and fitted it herself, and her women were hard at work stitching the parts together. It is a handsome crimson velvet bodice trimmed with white lace, shapely and stiff with whalebone.

(1886: 120)

Elsewhere Walker mentions the dress worn by another of her clients, Fatma Sultan, whose portrait was discussed in Chapter 2. Wishing to appear fashionable, Fatma Sultan chose to wear a specially made garment of white French silk with a European-style bodice and a traditional *entari* skirt, with *şalvar*. Such hybrid outfits, combining elements of European and Ottoman fashion as a way of embracing the new fashions, were worn in the last decades of the nineteenth century (Metinsoy 2023: 52), although they do not survive in museum collections.

Expert seamstresses, professionals who made their living with their needles, made clothes for Ottoman women. In some cases, wealthy households employed live-in seamstresses, but more often women would be summoned when needed. They would either stay in the house for days or weeks while they were making clothes for the household (this would often take place at the change of seasons when new clothes were needed, or for *bayrams*) or they would visit the household to receive their instructions and return as needed for fittings.

Beginning in the mid-nineteenth century, the place of seamstresses in the fashion economy began to expand. The itinerant, independent seamstress who traveled, sometimes staying in the homes of her clients, continued to be one model, but others began to open ateliers where their clients could visit them to see the latest fashion magazines, choose fabric and patterns, and have fittings. As the businesses expanded, these ateliers employed other women and established reputations among the well-to-do fashion consumers in the city. The names of many of these dressmakers or their shops have come down to us via contemporary fashion media, commercial directories, and other sources. One particularly informative document is an order book in the Topkapı Palace archives recording orders placed with a seamstress called Mademoiselle Kokina, discussed in Chapter 6. Some ateliers and dress shops produced their own labels, to be sewn into their dresses.

Dresses in the collection of the Sadberk Hanım Museum, for example, include a wedding dress with a label in Turkish and French that reads "Hüsn-I İntihab Mağazası—Kani İpekçi, Au bon gout Kiani İpekdji," and another dress with a label from "Mme N. Galatis Robes et Confections Pera Constantinople."

Known as *modistras*, from the French *modiste* (Eryavuz 2023: 170), many but not all these accomplished professionals were Greek women. Others, mentioned by Fanny Davis, were the Jewish Fegara and the Shaki sisters, and the French de Milleville sisters (1986: 191). Muslim women, too, were sometimes engaged in the clothing trade: for example, a bridal shop run by Raşide Hanım in Beyazit was praised in a 1900 issue of *Hanımlara Mahsus Gazete* for its reasonable prices for ready-made clothing and bridal gowns (Frierson 1995: 27–28). In an effort to keep up to date with the latest designs, ambitious dressmakers traveled to Paris and London to see new styles and bring back the newest fabrics and accessories. They also subscribed to European fashion magazines that they could share with their clients.

The nineteenth century brought other changes in shopping opportunities to Istanbul. By the 1840s, shops carrying European goods had begun to open in Pera and Galata. Charles White mentions ladies buying "silk or cotton web gloves [themselves a fashion innovation] from the Frank traders of Pera" in 1844 (1845: 81). Throughout 1848, for example, the *Journal de Constantinople* ran ads for Le magasin le Bon Ton, detailing the varied and highly fashionable fabrics, "tous les Articles des Nouveautés nécessaires à la toilette des Dames" [all the new merchandise needed for the dressing of ladies], articles of clothing, perfumes, corsets, all "adoptés par les dames de la haute société de Paris" [adopted by the high society ladies of Paris]. The ads describe the location of the store on the Grande Rue de Pera, in the second story of the Bazar Parisien, which had formerly been the Gracie store.[11] The new stores in the early years of commercial development of the shopping district along the Grande Rue de Pera were modest enterprises, hence the location of the Bon Ton on the second story of a building that also housed other retail establishments. It was not long, however, before large department stores on the model of those opening in London, Paris, and New York made their appearance in Pera.

Among those most-often mentioned in contemporary sources are the Bon Marché, so well-known that its name entered Turkish as the word (*bonmarşe*) to describe any department store; Orsodi-Back; Carlmann and Blumberg; and Baker's (or Maison Baker), most of which were established in the 1850s. Each of these has its own long business history, a particular combination of partners that shifted over the years, and a place in the commercial history of Istanbul. They also have important commonalities: most were set up for both retail and wholesale trade, and they were part of large international networks of trade in both raw materials and finished goods. Unlike the Kapalı Çarşı, which also sold a staggering variety of goods under one very large roof but in individually owned shops, the department stores were a single business, each owned by one person or one partnership, and the staff was all employed by that owner. Many department stores maintained multiple locations in the city, including Eminönü/Sirkeci and the neighborhood of the Kapalı Çarşı. Pera was certainly the heart of the modern shopping district of Istanbul, but the department store owners realized that if they wanted to attract a diverse clientele, their shops would have to be accessible to consumers living across the city.

With their display windows and carefully arranged merchandise, the stores aimed to create a new shopping experience for their customers, where aesthetic appeal was almost as important as utility and price. With so much of the stock arranged for viewing, browsing became a new kind of public activity—a very different experience from shopping in the bazaar where the merchant controlled access to the wares and displayed specific goods to the shopper. The stores vied with one another to bring new goods to their Istanbul customers. Orsodi-Back, for example, is credited with introducing *bonneterie* (machine-made hosiery), a category of goods that included "socks, stockings, but also vests, waistcoats, cardigans, shawls, baby clothes and underwear" (Kupferschmidt 2007: 38), an innovation that was soon picked up by its competitors. The department stores sold both ready-to-wear and made-to-order clothing, employing their own seamstresses and tailors for their customers.

As the century progressed, more and more shops opened in Pera and other neighborhoods. The big department stores offered all kinds of goods, but smaller shops could specialize. Thus Madame Vapillon's shop was stocked with Parisian accessories, Madame Trophe's was a millinery shop (Çelik 1986: 134), and there were numerous corsetieres where women could be fitted for corsets, described by one author as the ultimate sign of status and the new lifestyle for women who wished to be fashionable (Başcı 2005: 73). As the conversations in *Hanımlara Mahsus Gazete* and elsewhere demonstrated, the corset was a controversial garment, but it was an indispensable part of European-style dressing and thus an undergarment that would have been in high demand.

Another important shopping innovation appearing in Istanbul in these years was the *pasaj*, or shopping arcade. Some of these—for example, the *Avrupa* (European) *Pasajı* of 1874—were modeled on similar structures in Europe such as London's Burlington Arcade, with glass ceilings and small shops lining a central corridor open at both ends. The 1908 *Suriye*, or Syrian, *Pasajı* and the *Fransiz Geçidi*, built in 1860 in Karaköy near the port, have similar plans. The *Pasaj Hazzapoulu*, mentioned above as the site of a dressmaker's studio, opened in 1871 by a Greek family, takes a different form, with a central courtyard ringed with shops on two stories, accessible at each end from two roughly parallel Pera streets. Apart from whatever businesses these arcades may have offered, they would have been attractive shopping destinations for Ottoman women who were not necessarily completely comfortable being seen on busy commercial streets.

The modern department stores and shops in Pera, Galata, and other Istanbul neighborhoods were not the only new purchasing venues available for fashion-minded women in the city. According to Carolyn Paine, writing in 1850–1851,

> Parisian etiquette, manners and customs, prevail in all the circles of society that have felt the influence of Franks. Nowhere are the laws of fashion *à la mode de Paris* so rigorously observed. There are numerous boutiques furnished with elegant and fanciful decorations in French millinery, and the richest of silks, velvets and laces; yet many ladies are in the habit of importing their wardrobes directly from the city of modistes.
>
> (Paine 1859: 28)

"Importing their wardrobes directly from the city of modistes" could be accomplished by various means. The most direct way was to travel to Paris or London and purchase garments on the spot, on option available to wealthy women who had the opportunity to travel. In some cases, Istanbul seamstresses could order garments for their clients to be shipped directly to them. Women who were able to purchase couture garments from Europe on a regular basis could order directly from the fashion house, which would have had their measurements on file.[12] Lady Layard makes a brief mention in her diary from June 1878 about the fact that her two gowns from Paris had just arrived via ship and were delivered to her by messenger.[13] Men who traveled outside the Empire, whether on government business or for their own commercial interests, brought fashion news home with them, and in some cases, fabric, novel trimmings, and even ready-made garments.

The mail-order business, what has evolved in our time into online shopping, began in the mid-nineteenth century. The owner of the Bon Marché department store in Paris, Aristide Boucicaut, published the store's first mail-order catalog in 1855 (Tortora 2010: 165). As noted above, a second Paris department store, Printemps, began mail-order sales in 1868 and ran advertisements in Istanbul newspapers. Locally, the *Hanımlara Mahsus*

Gazete ran its own mail-order service for subscribers (see above). *Bindallı* dresses, the subject of the previous chapter, were sometimes called *kutu içi entari* or *kutu entarisi* (box dress) because they could be purchased or shipped ready-made in boxes (Görünür 2010: 51).

Conclusion

The women and men of Istanbul, and indeed of the Ottoman Empire more generally, had always been engaged in the manufacturing and trade that was a hallmark of the Empire. Foreign goods had long had a place in the Ottoman economy, but beginning in the seventeenth and eighteenth centuries, with the increased consumption of coffee and tobacco and an increase in the import of Indian textiles, imported goods played a larger role in the economy (Quataert 2000a:10). The nineteenth century saw an even more dramatic expansion of Ottoman consumption of foreign goods, and women's fashion had a major part in that trend. Increased exposure to European women and expanded opportunities for socializing outside the home, fashion media, and new ways of shopping all contributed to a shift in how fashion information and fashion goods were consumed by the women of Ottoman Istanbul, who by the second half of the nineteenth century had a new visibility and greater influence in shaping markets (Başcı 2004: 61; Fleet 2016: 119).

The changes that took place in the fashion economy of Istanbul in the second half of the nineteenth century, as well as changes in expectations regarding women's presence in public places and increasing educational and employment opportunities, affected all the women of the city, at least to some degree. The next chapters explore the ways in which various populations of Ottoman women embraced the new fashions, beginning with the elite women of court circles, the fashion tastemakers.

CHAPTER 6
THE TASTEMAKERS: ROYAL AND ELITE WOMEN

There have always been women (and men) whose dress and fashion sense were emulated by their contemporaries, or who set fashion trends from their positions as dressmakers or designers with powerful clients. Today tastemakers or fashion influencers (apart from designers) might be actors, artists, politicians, or social media pundits, but in the nineteenth century they were generally women of wealth and social position. Empress Eugénie of France, Princess Alexandra of England, and other royal women were renowned for their beauty and fashion sense. In the United States, fashion royalty was more likely to come from the ranks of elite society or to be found among the wives of important men of politics or industry.

The assumption that fashion influence is a trickle-down process, with trends moving from the wealthy elite down the social and economic scale, is a long-standing convention of fashion history, today complicated by a more nuanced and inclusive view of how influence works, an issue which will be taken up in the following chapters. The most powerful fashion tastemakers in Ottoman Istanbul would have been women of wealth and social position, across ethnicities and religions. Style influence among Ottoman women was disseminated through personal contact and social interaction, as well as by the published images of European-style leaders and the fashion media discussed in the previous chapter.

Wealthy and stylish women in the Greek, Armenian, and Jewish communities would certainly have been regarded as fashion leaders within their own circles. Their close associations with members of the foreign communities in Istanbul, with whom they would have interacted socially, gave them access to fashion information not so readily available to Muslim women. The lives of even the most important women in the minority communities of the city are poorly documented for the most part, and their clothing does not survive in any great numbers. Thus, without losing sight of the role of fashion influencers outside palace circles, my focus here is on royal and elite Muslim women, an unwieldy and potentially confusing cast of characters.

Royal Muslim women generally were a large, influential segment of the Ottoman elite, connected by family and marriage across Ottoman society. Their names—and in some cases, their biographies—have come down to us, examples of their clothing survive in museum collections, and many of them were also enthusiastic consumers of photographic portraiture, so more documentation concerning their fashion choices exists than for many other Ottoman women. In this chapter, I look at that evidence to understand the social circumstances in which they operated and how they engaged with other elite and foreign women to stay abreast of current fashions.

Who's Who: Understanding the Cast of Characters

From the mid-nineteenth century through the end of the Ottoman sultanate in 1922, there were six sultans, all of whom had multiple sexual partners, and who sired forty-four daughters, twenty-five of whom lived to the age of marriage (Uluçay 1980:139–87). The imperial harem was a structured, hierarchical organization, and depending on circumstances (sultan's preferences and birth of children, among others) the sexual partners of the sultan had different titles (*kadın*, *ikbal*, or *gözde*), in decreasing levels of status and ordered by seniority within those ranks. In the Ottoman system, only direct descendants of a sultan or a prince were considered to be members of the imperial family. Thus, female children of *kadıns*, *ikbals*, or *gözdes* were royal princesses, but their mothers were not, and the children of princesses were not royal. However, all these women, royal or not, had close associations with the imperial palace, or in the case of the married princesses, their own palaces, had servants both enslaved and free, and had access to substantial wealth.

The circles of elite Muslim women in Istanbul widened beyond palace circles to include *askeri* women (wives and daughters of high-ranking palace officials and military officers, as well as the wives and daughters of important members of the *ulema*, or Muslim religious hierarchy). These people all would have been members of the *askeri* class, but not all *askeri* would have been part of these elite circles: wealth, family, and political importance were important factors in determining social status.

Royal women lived in palaces: either the imperial palace, if they were the consorts of the sultan or his unmarried daughters; or in the case of married princesses, in their own palaces. During the second half of the nineteenth century and through the end of World War I, the Ottoman sultans lived primarily in three palaces, Dolmabahçe, Çırağan, and Yildiz. Other imperial palaces—for example, Beylerbeyi Palace—were built as more temporary residences, although following his dethronement Abdülhamid lived there from 1912 until his death in 1918.

Upon their marriage, royal princesses moved to their own palaces, in some cases built for them by the sultan. If the palaces were not ready, temporary residences would be rented for them. Often located along the Bosporus, the princess's palaces had extensive harems, replicating the structure of the imperial harem on a smaller scale. Many of the princesses had active social lives, receiving other women, both Ottoman and foreign, engaging in charitable activities, and playing important roles in the social landscape of elite Ottoman women.

Fehime Sultan

Among royal women, some lived more in the public eye than others and are thus better known. One of these is Murad V's daughter, Fehime Sultan, a relatively rare figure in Ottoman costume history because garments associated with her as well as photographs have survived, along with mentions in contemporary sources, thus allowing a certain picture of her engagement with both fashion and photography to emerge. Specific to her in some ways, in others her story sheds light on the self-fashioning of royal women more generally.

The photograph of Fehime Sultan illustrated here (Figure 6.1) has fascinated me since it was first published (Renda 1993: 249). In the photograph she faces the camera directly and signals clearly that music is extremely important to her by placing her hand on the music displayed on the piano. The setting is modern, even luxurious with the piano, other furniture, and the large palm in the background. Her dress is very much of the moment, elegant and in keeping with current fashion, with no visible connection to the traditional dress that a woman of her position would have worn fifty years previously. In a second photograph from this same occasion, presumably taken by the same photographer, Fehime is seated at the piano, as if playing, although it is clear from the way her skirt is arranged and her pose that the image was carefully composed.

By the time these two photographs were taken, circa 1912, royal women had been sitting for photographs for several decades. Until the first years of the twentieth century, photographers' access to the imperial family was strictly controlled, with the designation "court photographer by appointment to the sultan" being highly sought after by Istanbul photographers. The Abdullah Frères were the first to receive this title, from Abdülaziz in 1865, and they retained it until 1876 (Öztuncay 2010: 38). As photographers by appointment to the court, they were

Figure 6.1 [*Fehime Sultan*], photographer unknown. 1912, Istanbul, The Directorate of National Palaces, Painting Museum, 17/435.

entitled to use the sultan's official monogram, or *tuğra*, on their work, which set them apart from other local photographers and increased their commercial success. Over the next decades, the title of court photographer moved among different photographers, but by 1894 it was no longer an exclusive award. Even before that, access to the palace was given to photographers besides the official court photographer (Öztuncay 2010: 48).

Yildiz Palace, the residence of Abdülhamid beginning in 1877, had a photographic studio, but royal clients also visited the Pera studio of Vasilaki Kargopulo, court photographer from 1878 until his death in 1886. Some of the royal princesses were enthusiastic consumers of photography, having their own portraits made and buying other photographs that were compiled into albums or displayed in their homes. Abdülmecid and Abdülhamid were both engaged with photography so it is not surprising that their children would also have been enthusiasts. Two of Abdülmecid's daughters, Fatma Sultan and Refia Sultan, sat for portraits by the Abdullah Frères in about 1865 wearing European dress and with their hair uncovered, a striking display of modernity for that time.

Refia Sultan, shown in Figure 6.2, was a particularly avid patron, paying Abdullah Frères substantial amounts for photographs in the 1870s (Öztuncay: 43–48). Photography was an engaging way for court women, and indeed Ottoman women more generally to the extent that their finances allowed, to document two key aspects of their lives: their families, especially their children, and their clothing. The photographs

Figure 6.2 *Refia Sultan*, Abdullah Frères, *ca.* 1865. Istanbul, Ömer Koç Collection.

memorialized children, many of whom did not survive into adulthood, and captured the women as their best selves, exquisitely dressed and bejeweled.

Just as the women discussed in Chapter 4 wished to mark their weddings with photography, so did royal brides, who also commissioned wedding portraits, in some cases together with their bridal party. In these cases, circumstances dictated that the photographer visit the bride, as opposed to the bridal couple traveling to the photographer's studio. The photographers chosen for such assignments were generally the professional photographers already associated with the palace, whose work was of a very high quality, and who were accustomed to working with palace clients. Their subjects would have been equally familiar with the process of being photographed, unlike some of the brides whose photographs were illustrated in Chapter 4. The portrait illustrated here of Sabiha Sultan (Figure 6.3), daughter of Sultan Vahideddin, was taken by the firm of Sébah and Joaillier, one of a few images from her 1920 wedding. Sabiha Sultan is positioned in the center of the image, framed by drapery above her and decorative elements to either side. Her white dress with its long train, white veil, headdress feather, and her light-colored skin all stand out against the dark background, drawing the viewer's eye to her. She sits with her legs crossed at the ankles, at a slight angle to the camera, and looks directly at the viewer, apparently quite relaxed in front of the camera.

Sabiha's portrait, like the image of Fehime Sultan illustrated above, is a highly accomplished work by a professional photographer. By the first decades of the twentieth century, photography had become a familiar form of marking important events and performing a modern identity, especially among Istanbul's elite, who could well have afforded the cost of a visit to the photographer's studio or perhaps even have owned their own cameras. The formal portraits of earlier times were supplemented by more informal or personal images. In the

Figure 6.3 [*Sabiha Sultan*], Sébah & Joaillier, June 29, 1920. Istanbul, Dolmabahçe Palace Inv. No. 100/4859.

case of Fehime Sultan, for example, in addition to the two formal portraits already mentioned, at least eight other photographs document different moments in her tumultuous life in the last decades of the Ottoman Empire and during her exile in Nice.

Fehıme Sultan was born in 1875, the only child of Murad V's fourth wife, and one of his seven children. Her father, Murad V, was put on the throne in 1876 following the deposition of his uncle Abdülaziz and reigned only ninety-three days. Following his deposition, Murad, who died in 1904, and his family lived in various palaces, carefully watched over. Fehime Sultan was married twice, first in a marriage arranged for her by her uncle when she was twenty-six, and then following a divorce, to a military officer in 1910. In 1924 when the Ottoman royal family was exiled, she went to Nice and died there of tuberculosis in 1929 at the age of fifty-four, penniless (Uluçay 1980: 242–43).

Like most members of the Ottoman royal family, Fehime was educated in the palace. In her case, she developed a strong interest in music, no doubt influenced by her father, who apparently was a prolific and at least somewhat talented composer. She was also, according to one source, a very strong supporter of the Nationalist Movement (Committee of Union and Progress), which forced Sultan Abdülhamid to establish a constitutional government in 1908 and had effective control over the government, beginning in about 1913 (Zürcher 2010). In support of the movement, Fehime Sultan composed a piano sonata, *Pour la Constitution*, in 1911, and it is almost certainly that work commemorated in the two photographs discussed above. (Criss 1999: 120).

Fehime Sultan had a reputation for enjoying expensive fashion, and certainly the dress she is wearing in the two photographs with the piano support that reputation. Two garments in the Topkapı Sarayı collection are connected with her, (Scarce 1987: 84–86). One of those resembles the one that Fehime Sultan is wearing in the photograph, but it is not the same one. Each is designed to create the impression of a multipiece outfit, but the Topkapı Sarayı dress at least is a one-piece garment that relies on the complex construction and the use of multiple fabrics to give the impression of a robe overlaying a blouse and skirt. White polished cotton, pink silk taffeta, lace, and pink velvet as well as ruffles, sashes, and a large bow all are used to create an elaborate confection that must have been the height of fashion when it was made. Indeed, a review of surviving examples of French fashion in the period preceding the outbreak of World War I reveals gowns with comparable profiles and equally elaborate combinations of luxurious fabrics and trimming. One such example in the collection of the Metropolitan Museum of Art from the Parisian House of Worth (1982.304) shows close similarities to Fehime's dress. We know that some wealthy Ottoman women traveled to Paris to buy clothes and fashion accessories, but given Fehime Sultan's restricted movements for much of her life, it is more likely that her dress either was ordered from Paris or made for her by a dressmaker well acquainted with the latest modes.

Fehime Sultan's photographs with the piano are so obviously composed images, it is difficult to imagine that they were taken at a public or quasi-public event such as a concert or recital. And in fact, most photographs of royal girls and women are similar in their careful composition, taken by professional photographers either in the palace or the photographer's studio. The photographic technology of the time did not allow candid photos of events, and thus the many occasions in which palace women and other elite women met do not have visual records; fortunately, written descriptions survive of some of these events.

The Occasions

In our media-saturated time, it is difficult to imagine how fashion influencers would have functioned without constantly circulated images of themselves and their looks. Given the absence of today's social media, the palace events that brought royal and elite women together in real life were crucial opportunities to display the latest fashions and most elaborate jewels. These occasions, mostly weddings and palace receptions, were formal events that unfolded in prescribed ways, as were the visits made to the imperial harem by visiting royalty from Europe. Social calls among royal and elite women were also an important part of late Ottoman social life; some European women also participated in these events.

The weddings of royal princesses in the last decades of the Ottoman Empire were elaborate affairs, taking place over a number of days. Until their marriage, the princesses lived in the imperial palace, moving with their husband and entourage to their own residence at the time of the wedding. A few days before the actual wedding, the trousseau of the bride was displayed in the palace, after which it was taken from the imperial palace to the bride's new residence. On the day of the wedding, the bride was enthroned in her new home, receiving female guests and displaying her magnificent gown and jewels. At some point a meal was served, with guests seated according to rank, followed by music and dancing. A second day of celebrations took place along similar lines. Leyla Saz writes about the impact of these events on the guests for the 1857 wedding of Refia Sultan:

> most of the ladies who were invited, I would say almost all of them, were seeing a festival of this importance for the first time. They were quite thunderstruck and for good reason: it is impossible to imagine the elegance, the luxury of such an event if one has not seen with one's own eyes this spectacle straight from a fairy tale.

> *(Saz 1994: 176)*

Leyla Saz was writing several decades after the weddings she described, talking about a period she said was the happiest time in her life, so her descriptions of these events may exaggerate their opulence and are no doubt sentimentalized. Even making allowances for hyperbole, the royal weddings would have been perhaps the most important occasions for displaying fashion among the royal and elite Muslim women of Istanbul.

Carolyn Paine, visiting Istanbul in 1850–1851, attended the wedding of the son of the grand vizier, reporting on the dress of both the bride and some of the guests as well as other aspects of the event. She estimated that about two thousand women attended the wedding, providing plenty of opportunities to see and be seen in the latest, most elaborate styles. The bride's dress "was of scarlet cashmere, heavily and tastefully wrought with gold, the antari and trousers being of the same material," while one of the Sultan's consorts was "sumptuously attired in a dress of rose-colored cashmere, with gold and silver embroidery" (Paine 1859: 63–65). Leyla Saz, writing of three royal weddings at about the same time, describes magnificent silk gowns in blue, a deep red, and garnet, embroidered in gold and decorated with pearls and diamonds, some so heavily embroidered that attendants needed to walk behind the bride to carry the long train of the *entari* (Saz ibid.: 177–92).

Greek and Armenian women had begun to wear white European-style wedding dresses in the 1850s, as Carolyn Paine noted in her description of an Armenian bride, quoted in Chapter 4. However, not until several decades later did Muslim brides begin to wear white wedding dresses. Princess Naime, a daughter of Abdülhamid II, was married in 1898 in a white gown described by her sister Ayşe Osmanoğlu as being in "the old style" (Brookes 2008: 160); reportedly, she was the first Ottoman princess to be married in white. Other elite Muslim brides were more fashion forward in the 1890s, choosing to wear highly fashionable, European-style wedding dresses in shades of white.

When Şehsuvar Hanım married Caliph Abdülmecid Efendi in 1896, she wore an elaborate gown of gold and off-white satin, with a fitted bodice and full-length skirt with a long train (Figure 6.4). The bodice has a lace yoke edged with a deep lace flounce, stand up collar, and long, tiered sleeves trimmed with lace and sequins (Eryavuz 2023: 114). The dress is au courant in a number of ways: the use of different fabrics in a range of related tonalities, the extravagant lace embellishments made possible by the availability of machine-made lace, and the high, modest neck all link this wedding dress to fashion trends seen in European gowns of the same period.[1]

Invitations to the palace for weddings or other events were an opportunity to wear the most fashionable, most elegant outfit in a women's wardrobe. Leyla Saz in particular has many references to what she and the women and girls around her wore to royal weddings, including the story of her mother and another guest at the wedding of Münire Sultan in 1857 turning up in exactly the same costume, the fabric and trimmings having been sold to them by a merchant who affirmed to each that no one else would have that fabric (Saz 1994: 202). A few pages later Leyla Saz has more to say about the dress of wedding guests:

> Here is a rapid glimpse of the costumes worn on the second day of the wedding ceremonies. The Kadın, the mother of the Sultane wore, like the evening before, a very simple white dress. Adile Sultane also wore a white dress with three trains [*üç etek entari*] covered with very light embroideries; she also wore a basque bodice according to the style of the day with a diadem and a brooch. Fatma Sultane had a costume consisting of a double skirt in white satin embroidered with flowers whose stems were in gold, the leaves in pink silk and the petals in velvet silk. Her bodice was cut quite low in front and the double sleeves came just to her elbows … The ladies of the city wore dresses of all different colors in voile, a sheer fabric much used in those days, and naturally all the dresses had three trains and were worn over baggy pants [*şalvar*].
>
> (205)

Figure 6.4 Wedding dress, 1896. Büyükdere, Courtesy of the Vehbi Koç Foundation, Sadberk Hanım Museum, 18028-K.1231.

Fifty years later, invitations to royal weddings or palace receptions still demanded the most elegant outfits, but styles had changed substantially. Court appearances required that dresses have a train, but otherwise there were no specific constraints. The two dresses of about the same date illustrated here most likely would have been worn at palace events. The gray silk taffeta dress in Figure 6.5 belonged to Leyla Saz, when she would have been in her fifties or perhaps older. It is plain and rather conservative in style, with a V-neck, long set-in sleeves, and extra fullness for the skirt added by gores at the side, a design feature that would have been familiar to her from the *entaris* of her youth. The dress is trimmed with tulle at the neck and sleeve ends, and it has the long train suitable for court functions. The sophisticated dress illustrated in Figure 6.6 also has a long train, but apart from that the two dresses are very different. A two-piece outfit that originally had long sleeves, the blouse and skirt are made of a light-colored silk fabric with a woven pattern of flowers; a pleated insert of a light green satin is in the front of the skirt. The bodice, which buttons up the back, is highly structured and would have been fitted on the wearer. The dress is trimmed with silver braid, pearls, beads, and butterflies constructed of silver wire. It was made for Zeynep Hanım, the wife of one of the palace physicians in the time of Abdülhamid II, by a Greek dressmaker, Mme N. Galatis, who had a shop in Pera (her label is sewn into the waist tape of the dress). This dress would have been suitable for the palace events to which Zeynep Hanım,

Figure 6.5 Dress belongıng to Leyla Saz, early twentieth century. Büyükdere, Courtesy of the Vehbi Koç Foundation, Sadberk Hanım Museum, 19885-K.1737.

as the wife of a palace official, would have been invited (Görünür 2010: 240). The dresses belonging to Leyla Saz and Zeynep Hanım demonstrate the range of choices that elite Istanbul women made at a period when fashions were changing rapidly. Older women often preferred the styles that evoked the traditional garments with which they had grown up, whereas younger women were more fashion forward, looking to European fashion capitals for the latest styles.

The major religious holidays in the Muslim calendar, *Eid al-Fitr* and *Eid al-Adha*,[2] were celebrated by the imperial palace with great pomp and splendor, bringing together royal women, married princesses, and the wives of high government officials. Another religious event, the Friday *selamlık*, when the sultan traveled publicly to the noon prayer at a nearby mosque, provided a more frequent opportunity for palace women to visit with women from outside. The *selamlık* ceremony, an aspect of Ottoman political life from the fifteenth century through the abolition of the caliphate in 1924, allowed the sultan to be seen, to receive petitions from his subjects, to review troops, and to demonstrate his piety. Abdülhamid II (r. 1876–1909), famously averse to public appearances, was said never to have missed the *selamlık* over all the years of his reign.

During Abdülhamid's time, the public aspects of the ceremony, which was attended by thousands of troops, members of the harem, government officials, invited visitors, and any members of the public who wished to

Figure 6.6 Two-piece dress, early twentieth century. Büyükdere, Courtesy of the Vehbi Koç Foundation, Sadberk Hanım Museum, 12414-K.586 a, b.

Figure 6.7 *Salut de Constantinople. Revue militaire. Le Selamlik*, photographer unknown, *ca.* 1900–1907. Nicholas Catsimpoolas Collection, Boston Public Library.

watch, consisted of a long procession of carriages and troops accompanied by music from military bands, all converging on the mosque (from 1886 on, this would have been the Hamidiye Mosque) (Figure 6.7). When the sultan arrived in front of the mosque, he was joined by his government ministers and entered the mosque for prayers. Members of the diplomatic community who had been invited to watch did so from the nearby ambassador's kiosk (Müller 1897: 45). Following the prayer service, the sultan returned to the palace, along with any guests who might have been invited.

In her memoire, Ayşe Osmanoğlu, a daughter of Abdülhamid, writes that the Princess Mother, who stood in the role of the sultan's mother, and the High *Hazinedar* or *Hazinedar Usta*, the highest-ranking administrator of the harem, were required to attend the *selamlık* each week; imperial princesses and the sultan's consorts could attend if they wished. Mrs. Max Müller, a British visitor in the late 1890s, described the arrival of the harem women like this:

> We had hardly taken our places [in the ambassador's kiosk] when someone said: 'Here come the ladies of the harem' and a procession of about six closed carriages, splendidly appointed, descended from Yildiz, and, passing in front of our windows, turned in at the iron gates of the court of the Mosque. Here they are drawn up one behind the other, the horses are taken out, and the ladies see what they

can from under the half-drawn blinds … As the carriages passed us, we could only catch a glimpse of the brilliant pink and blue and yellow brocades worn by the ladies.

(Müller ibid.)

After returning to the palace, the younger princesses were free to spend the rest of the day in the parks of Yildiz Palace with their mothers, servants, and other young royal visitors. Older women also visited with each other, as recounted by Ayşe Osmanoğlu:

After the Mosque Processions the Pasha Mother (the mother of the Khedive [Egyptian ruler]) would proceed to the Chalet Villa [*Şale Köşkü* or Pavilion, part of Yildiz Palace], where the *kalfas* [attendants] of the High Hazinedar waited upon her respectfully, and where she passed the time in the company of one of the Princesses. If any wives of ministers of state had attended the ceremony, they too were received with all due honors in the harem, and they took the evening meal in the palace. At 8.30 they made their way to the theatre. Together with the princesses who had come from outside the palace, they were received by the Sultan in the Small Salon, entering their boxes when the performance was to begin.

(Brookes 2008: 178)

Unlike the more formal events marking major religious holidays, the Friday *selamlık* gave women in the imperial harem, married princesses living outside, and other elite women the opportunity to interact in more relaxed and intimate settings. Although still governed by social custom and protocol, these visits would have been opportunities for the exchange of news on an array of topics, including dress, and a time to show off their latest fashions.

When members of European royal families visited Istanbul, the women of the parties would pay formal calls on the Ottoman imperial harem, as was the case when the Austrian Crown Prince and Archduchess Stephanie visited in 1884, mentioned in the previous chapter. These visits were no doubt stiff and possibly awkward events, with conversation hampered by the need for translation, but from a fashion point of view they were significant. Of the many such visits that took place in the last decades of the nineteenth century, two in particular stand out: the visits of Princess Alexandra of England and the French Empress Eugénie, both in 1869. Both women were fashion icons in their own circles, and their impact on the dress practices of the women with whom they came in contact in Istanbul would have been substantial.

Prince Edward and Princess Alexandra (1844–1925), the Prince and Princess of Wales, visited Istanbul for ten days in April 1869 as part of a longer tour of Egypt, Crimea, and Greece. They traveled on a luxurious royal yacht, the *Ariadne*, and while they were in Istanbul, stayed in one of the royal palaces as guests of Sultan Abdülaziz. The royal couple were young and popular; Alexandra was regarded as "one of the most stylish women in Britain" (Strasdin 2017: 1), and this was their first extended international trip. Abdülaziz had visited England as part of a European tour in 1867 and wanting to repay the welcome he had enjoyed there, he filled their time in Istanbul with receptions, state dinners, official luncheons, as well as theater visits, incognito trips to the Covered Bazaar, and innumerable other activities.

The local newspaper accounts of their visit were alert to the fact that the state dinner that the sultan hosted at the Dolmabahçe Palace, which included foreign women, represented a sharp break in social custom. From the *Levant Herald* of April 3, 1869:

For the first time in the history of the country, foreign ladies will sit down at the same table as the Padishah. In addition to the Princess of Wales—who will not, as was first expected, be entertained by the ladies of the harem, but will be present at the imperial table, the Hon. Mrs. Elliot [wife of the British Ambassador] and Madame Ignatieff [wife of the Russian Ambassador] have received invitations.

Mrs. Grey, the princess's companion, also attended the dinner. Members of the imperial harem could not appear at the state events that the sultan hosted, but after the dinner Princess Alexandra and, Mrs. Grey, together with the wives of the British and Russian ambassadors, were escorted by the sultan to the imperial harem where they were received by the Sultan Valide (sultan's mother) and the most senior of the royal consorts, who according to Mrs. Grey "was dressed quite in the European style: a low evening-dress, covered with lace, and a long train, the Turkish star and ribbon over her shoulder, and, in short, dressed like any European princess" (Grey 1869: 160). For their part, according to the report in the *Levent Herald*, the visiting ladies were *décoletées* (meaning their dresses had low-cut necklines) and wore gowns of blue silk, light gray trimmed with black lace, maroon moire, and white watered silk, respectively (*Levant Herald*, April 5, 1869).

Princess Alexandra visited with Ottoman women once or twice more, and also with members of the foreign diplomatic community. She would have been observed by the elite women of the minority communities of the city at the theater and opera performances they attended. The journalist William Russell, who accompanied them on the trip, described one such event at the Naum Theatre:

> The Princess was beautifully dressed; the Prince and suite were in full uniform. On their entering the state box, in the centre of the tier, all the audience rose, and it needed an effort to believe we were in Constantinople, so brilliant and Europeanized was the spectacle. There were no Moslem women, but Syrians, and Levantines, and Perotes, Greeks, and, above all, Armenian ladies shone in jewels and costly dresses.
>
> *(506)*

They also attended a Sunday church service at the British Embassy chapel, which was, according to the slightly tongue-in-cheek report in the paper, "filled with such a congregation as only royalty can draw" (*Levant Herald*, April 5, 1969).

Their trip was documented by the drawings of the artist who traveled with them, as well as by photographs. Traveling as they were in the heyday of cartes de visite and cabinet cards, it is not surprising to read in Mrs. Grey's account of the voyage that women in the harem of the Egyptian viceroy's mother gave them photographs and "were charmed with some which the Princess gave them of herself" (Grey 1869: 134). In Istanbul, Prince Edward visited the Abdullah Frères studio and had some photographs made, then engaged the photographer to visit their yacht on their last day to photograph their party, including Princess Alexandra (Figure 6.8). Russell writes: "Abdullah attended early, photographed the Royal party, and took some cabinet photographs of the Princess, which were very good" (Russell 1869: 512).

The year 1869 was an important one for royal visitors to Istanbul. The opening of the Suez Canal in November, marked with five days of festivities, drew distinguished guests from all of Europe, due in part to Khedive Ismail's personal invitations, presented during his European tour in the summer of 1869. Although Egypt under khedival rule enjoyed a certain amount of independence, it was still a part of the Ottoman Empire, and protocol required that guests pay their respects to the Ottoman sultan in Istanbul before journeying to Egypt (Roxburgh 2022: 236). Thus, the French empress Eugénie; Franz Joseph, emperor of Austria; the crown prince of Prussia; and Prince Henry and Princess Amelia of the Netherlands, as well as other dignitaries, visited Istanbul in the weeks leading up to November 16.

Cabinet Portrait
ABDULLAH FRÈRES
PERA DE CONSTANTINOPLE.
PHOTLE IMPLE

Figure 6.8 Princess Alexandra, Abdullah Frères, 1869. Royal Collection Enterprises Limited 2025/Royal Collection Trust.

All these visits were occasions of great ceremony, but not all royal guests generated the same degree of attention. The visit of the prince and princess of the Netherlands lasted only two days and received two short notices in the *Levant Herald*, although a state dinner was given in their honor, and the princess visited the Valide Sultan. Empress Eugénie of France, on the other hand, remained in the city for six days, extending her visit twice beyond what had been planned originally. Her visit was covered extensively in the local press, providing an extremely detailed account of her reception among both the Ottoman elite and people on the street. French newspapers also covered her visit, publishing views of trip highlights (Figure 6.9).

The newspaper accounts of her visit published in the *Levant Herald* describe what must have been a blur of social events, giving her the opportunity to see and be seen by women and men from different parts of Istanbul society. Her travels around the city were hardly inconspicuous, as this account of her visit to the Sultan Ahmet neighborhood reveals:

Figure 6.9 The empress receives the diplomatic corps in Constantinople, Turkey, during her Mediterranean voyage to Egypt for the opening of the Suez Canal in 1869. 1869, *L'Illustration, Journal Universel*, v. 54, p. 309.

She occupied an open four-horse chariot, and was accompanied by her nieces, the Mlles. D'Albes, and a lady of honour. M. Bouree, Djemil Pasha, Raouf Pasha, and a numerous suite followed in other court carriages, the whole being escorted by a half squadron of mounted gendarmerie. The chief points along the route taken were thronged by crowds of eager Stamboulees—nearly half of them Turkish women—whose frequent cheers were very graciously acknowledged by the illustrious *mussafir* [guest].

(Levant Herald, October 15, 1869)

The newspaper reports similar enthusiastic receptions by Turkish women on other of Eugenie's excursions. In addition to the gathering she held for members of the foreign diplomatic community and her visit with the French colony and Roman Catholic clergy and convent heads, she held a reception for the Turkish wives and daughters of high-ranking Turkish officials.

As a visiting head of state, standing in for Napoleon III, ruler of France, Eugenie was received with all the protocol that her rank merited. When her ship arrived at Beylerbeyi Palace, Sultan Abdülaziz boarded and conducted her personally to the palace; and after her reception by state ministers, staff, bodyguards and others, he took Eugenie to her apartments. She was accompanied by the sultan to numerous events, dined with him several times, and was the guest of honor at a formal state dinner that also included all the foreign diplomats and their wives. Unlike the state dinner given for the Prince and Princess of Wales a mere six months previously, the presence of foreign women at the sultan's table did not merit special notice in the press.

Eugenie did not neglect the women of the imperial harem. She called on the Valide Sultan on the day of her arrival, a visit that occasioned this note in the *Levant Herald*:

And lastly, we are assured by an eye-witness that when her Majesty's caique [barge] touched Dolma-bahtche stairs, the harem windows were thrown up, and a crowd of houris[3] thronged every opening to gaze-*sans* yashmak and brilliant in velvet and jewels—on the beautiful *Fransa Imperatrizassy* as she landed from the barge.

(October 15, 1869)

According to the published schedule of her visit, the Valide Sultan would have returned the empress's visit the next day at Beylerbeyi Palace.

The opportunity to see and be seen by visiting royalty would have impelled Ottoman women to wear their most elegant and fashionable clothing and likely to acquire new outfits for these very special occasions. The fact that the senior consort of Abdülaziz received Princess Alexandra and the other guests in a low-cut evening dress ornamented with a sash and jeweled Turkish order is notable: that is not the outfit she would have been wearing on an ordinary evening. Based on contemporary accounts, Eugenie's visit generated even more attention than had that of the Princess of Wales, and she would have been seen, even from a distance, by many more women. She was renowned for her fashionability—she is said to have commissioned 250 dresses from the elite fashion designer Charles Frederick Worth for her appearances at the Suez Canal (and presumably her visit to Istanbul).[4] Although some reports of Eugenie's impact on Ottoman women's fashion may be apocryphal, there is no doubt that her dress was carefully studied by the women she encountered in Istanbul. According to Zeyneb Hanoum (an Ottoman Muslim woman writing from Paris in 1907), Eugenie's hair styling was copied, her high-heeled shoes were adopted, and there was a "craze for everything French" (Zeyneb Hanoum 1913: 98). Zeyneb Hanoum describes clearly the "trickle-down" mechanism by which Eugenie's fashionability spread among Istanbul women, first among the women of the court and then more broadly:

> the women of the palace and the wives of the high functionaries copied as nearly as they could
> the appearance of the beautiful Empress … As might be supposed, the middle class soon followed
> the example of the palace ladies and adopted Western costume.

(Zeyneb Hanoum, 96–98)

Apart from the formal visits of European royalty, Ottoman royal women also had social contacts with some of the European women who visited Istanbul or were resident there while their husband held diplomatic posts or other assignments. In some cases, these visits took place outside the palaces, as when Annie Lady Brassey hosted Ottoman friends on her yacht, the *Sunbeam*, in 1874. Visiting Istanbul for about a month as part of a longer Mediterranean voyage, Lady Brassey and her husband, Thomas Brassey (later Earl Brassey), having spent a great deal of time in Egypt, were acquainted with members of the Khedival family. Lady Brassey called on Princess Aziza and Princess Nazli, nieces of Khedive Ismail Paşa, several times during her time in Istanbul and visited other Ottoman women at home. They spoke French or English, discussed contemporary politics, women's situations in England and Istanbul, and admired each other's dress and jewels. Upon leaving Istanbul, her Ottoman friends gave Lady Brassey "a feridjee and yashmak, all arranged ready for me to put on, and the most lovely embroidered dress as a present" (Brassey 1880: 112).

A few years later, Lady Enid Layard, the wife of the archaeologist Austen Henry Layard, who served as British ambassador to the Ottoman Empire from 1877 to 1880, wrote about her experiences with Ottoman women. Layard kept a copious journal for fifty-one years, running to some eight thousand pages; while she was in Istanbul, she was kept busy with diplomatic affairs (she assisted her husband with correspondence), relief work, managing a large household and an extensive social life among the diplomatic community and the Ottoman elite. Lady Layard called on the wives of Ottoman officials with whom her husband worked, and they in return visited her, usually accompanied by a companion or servants, as she describes a visit from Princess Nazli in 1877: "Princess Nazli Khanum came to pay me a visit & stayed from 3 till 5. She asked to see Henry & saw him unveiled. She brought a companion Miss Meyrick with her. Gave her coffee & cigarettes & tea." Some of her entries mention dress as in this one, again from 1877: "She was beautifully dressed in a damask greyish blue dress embroidered with birds nests & lady birds." But generally, Lady Layard's diary entries are quite short. Her description of a visit to the imperial harem in 1877 is more detailed:

After a time H.M. asked me to accompany him to the Harem to pay a visit to his Sultana apologising for leaving Henry alone. We set out on foot I, the Sultan, Said & Kiamil Pashas, to walk across the garden to the Harem a few steps off. At the gate of it Said & Kiamil stopped & we were met by 2 men one of whom was Black. We went thro' a long kind of hall till we came at the end of it to a staircase where stood a young slave girl & the Sultan said in French "La dame d'honneur." She made bows & led us up & half way up stood a little fair woman dressed in pink damask & a purple velvet jacket & the Sultan said "ma mere"—at the top stood the Sultana & H.M. said "Madame la Principe." She shook hands & then the Sultan & I walked into a large kind of hall like the one below—there were chairs & divans all round & the Sultan placed me on a divan & took a chair next me & the mother sat opposite & the Sultana after much pressing sat next the Sultan, the slave standing opposite me.[5]

Her description continues, although in this case conversation was hampered by the translation efforts of the enslaved woman tasked with communication as well as the presence of the sultan for much of the time, which created a high degree of formality for the visit.

The general impression of the lives of the women of the imperial harem, particularly in Orientalist imagery and writing, is one of constraint and isolation. Yet as is abundantly clear from memoirs written by Ottoman women, European women's accounts of their engagement with harem women, newspaper reports and more, that was not the case. Palace women and royal princesses socialized with the wives and daughters of court officials and ministers on numerous occasions, and they received visits from visiting royalty and members of the European diplomatic community in Istanbul, even returning those visits on occasion. At home they had governesses, tutors, music and language teachers, and other women, both Ottoman and foreign, who stayed with them for weeks or months. Their ability to move about freely in public settings was certainly circumscribed, but they interacted frequently with women of different ethnicities and nationalities in a variety of different contexts.

In other words, women in the imperial harems had ample opportunities to be seen by other Ottoman women and to observe what a wide range of women, Ottoman and foreign, were wearing. These occasions, when they were visible to so many, facilitated their places as tastemakers in the city and the spread of their fashion sensibilities among women of different social and ethnic groups.

Palace Wardrobes

Palace women could select expensive fabrics and elaborate trims and have their clothes made by the most accomplished dressmakers (Figure 6.10). By the early twentieth century, when the dress illustrated in fig. 6.10 was made, such fashion-forward, elegant ensembles would have been commonplace for elite women in palace circles. The two-piece dress is made of pink silk with small flowers worked in gold. The bodice would have been fitted for the wearer and has a high neck and set-in sleeves. The back of the bodice was designed to be close-fitting, but the front is pleated and would have been slightly blousy. The pleated bodice, high neck, and ruffled sleeve treatment ending in lace all link this outfit to current styles popular elsewhere. (See Edwards 2017: 123 for a useful comparison.) The long skirt is flat across the front, with pleats at the center back and a train, which would have made it suitable for palace functions.

However, not everyone chose to dress in the latest European fashions. Women of the palace and the married princesses embraced a range of dress styles, depending on their age and personal taste, among other variables. In some cases, older women preferred the traditional garments, as reported by Leyla Saz and Ayşe Osmanoğlu. Describing the celebrations attending Abdulaziz's return from Europe in 1867, Saz writes,

Figure 6.10 Two-piece dress, early twentieth century. Büyükdere, Courtesy of the Vehbi Koç Foundation, Sadberk Hanım Museum, 18031-K.1233 a-b.

At this period, the young ladies and girls had completely abandoned the old dresses with three tails or trains and the baggy pants underneath; fashion now demanded skirts with a single train which was caught up and attached to the belt—there were now petticoats instead of *şalvars* or the baggy pants previously worn.

(162)

Apart from noting that nearly everyone was wearing green, "the colour of satisfied hopes and wishes as well as joy," Saz describes the garments worn by the older women merely as dresses, but the implication that they were the "old dresses" is clear. Describing the outfits worn by two of her aunts, Ayşe Osmanoğlu writes that one always dressed in brown, in the Turkish style, while another wore gowns in the European fashion (Brookes 2008: 142). Whatever their specific tastes, the clothing budgets for the sultan's consorts and royal princesses were lavish. Some women, Fehime Sultan for one, were reputed to be particularly interested in fashion, and in some cases, excessively extravagant. Emine Nazikeda Kadınefendi, the wife of Sultan Vahideddin (r. 1918–1922), ordered an "expensive and superbly designed outfit" at least every two weeks, according to her lady-in-waiting (Eryavuz 2023: 174).

Simple clothes, such as underwear and wrappers, continued to be made by harem seamstresses, but as the annotated fashion plates discussed in the previous chapter indicate, palace women engaged outside dressmakers for their more complex garments. An order book from a Greek seamstress, Mademoiselle Kokona, or Maryioga Mavrudi, in use from 1871 through 1875, in the Topkapı Palace Archives (TPM D.4962), describes the clothes that the harem ordered, as well as the details of payment and delivery (Ipek 2012). Particularly intriguing are the orders placed by the princess, most likely Refia Sultan, according to Ipek (2012: 59) for members of her household. Married in 1857, Refia Sultan lived in Defterdarburnu palace with her husband and servants, enslaved and free. Included in the order book are *entaris* and other garments for high-ranking women in the harem (*hazinedar usta* [head harem administrator], *kahveci usta* [head of the coffee service], *kalfas*, or senior servants, and others), as well as other named women (ibid.). The orders confirm that religious holidays were occasions for new clothes, as were royal weddings and other court events. Royal women could order clothes when they pleased, but other harem inhabitants received clothes at holidays and the change of seasons. In her memoirs, Leyla Saz includes frequent mentions of receiving gifts of clothing or fabric from "her" princess, a practice that was widespread in the imperial harem. Such gifts were prized because of their fashionability as well as their royal association.

The work of the harem was divided by task, each organized under the supervision of an *usta* or head, the *çameşuy usta*, in the case of the laundry. The women responsible for the palace laundry may have attended to details of clothing acquisition, but they were also responsible for the care and storage of the expensive and often fragile clothes of the royal princesses and sultan's consorts as well as the sultan. As fashions changed for Ottoman women, so did aspects of taking care of their clothing. The traditional garments, *gömlek*, *şalvar*, *entari*, *cepken*, and others, were constructed in such a way that they could be easily folded and stored flat. Leyla Saz has provided a very useful description of how clothes were stored:

> The dresses were arranged on the shelves of armoires, wrapped up in a double envelope of silk and covered by a piece of calico. The *feraces*, the *yaşmaks* and the handkerchiefs were all carefully folded and wrapped up. In those days fashion demanded that creases should be very evident; therefore, large tiles of marble were placed on the folded clothes so that they could be carefully pressed while on the shelf.
>
> *(Saz 116)*

European-style clothes, with their very full, gathered skirts and complex bodice structures provided different storage challenges. They were also stored flat (clothes hangers, or "shoulders" as they were originally called, did not come into common use in England until the early twentieth century) (Walkley and Foster 1978: 169), but they did not benefit from being compressed by the weight of other garments. Creases and wrinkles from being stored were not fashionable, so the dresses would have had to be aired or carefully pressed before being worn.

The laundresses responsible for palace wardrobes would have been familiar with taking care of delicate cottons and gauzes, silks, woolens, and the elaborate trims that decorated traditional garments. The rigorous washing methods used for cotton and linens were not necessarily the best way to care for lavishly decorated silk *entaris* and *şalvar*. They could be taken apart for cleaning and then resewn; the cotton linings were replaced when they became soiled (Baker et al. 1996: 48). The structure of the European-style clothing would have been different, but in many ways the care that the dresses, corsets, and petticoats required would have been much the same as the traditional garments. For any new laundering or care challenges the European fashions presented, the seamstresses and tailors who supplied the new garments would likely have been able to provide some guidance.

Conclusion

The focus here has been on the fashion influence of royal and elite women in palace circles and the various ways in which their dress practices were shared and observed by other women in the city. The servants who lived in the imperial harem and princesses' palaces, enslaved and free, would also have been completely aware of the fashions that their mistresses adopted, but so far little attention has been paid to their wardrobes or their own sartorial engagement. The fashion stories of domestic servants, enslaved or free, which have so far been omitted from Ottoman fashion history, are the subject of the next chapter.

CHAPTER 7
THE ELUSIVE FASHION STORIES OF ENSLAVED WOMEN AND DOMESTIC SERVANTS

Living in the same households as the elite fashion influencers examined in the previous chapter, enslaved women and domestic servants are generally left out of Ottoman fashion history. With this chapter, I turn my attention to these women, seeking to uncover the hidden stories of their clothing and their dress practices. In considering how best to proceed with very limited evidence at hand for the specific garments of enslaved women in Ottoman Istanbul, I looked to the work that has been done on the fashion history of enslaved African American women in the United States in the same period, approximately 1850–1920. Although the circumstances of these two groups of enslaved women bear significant differences, they also share striking similarities, particularly in terms of the material that survives to tell their fashion stories. Perhaps most importantly, the scholarship of the past two decades on the dress of enslaved and newly freed Black women in the United States provides a roadmap for undertaking similar work in the Ottoman context.[1]

My foray into the dress history of enslaved Black women in the United States has given me three insights about investigating the elusive dress practices of enslaved Ottoman women. First, although virtually no garments can be securely identified with an enslaved person, this may change as more family heirlooms come into public view. Second, when evaluating research subjects who have so far fallen outside mainstream narratives, it is essential to rethink the standard criteria of assessment applied to the research materials and even the subjects themselves.[2] Given the temporary nature of enslavement in the Ottoman context, the variety of positions occupied by enslaved women, and the different relationships that often existed between mistress and dependent, the status of figures pictured in a harem scene cannot be reliably identified. Likewise, often it is not known for sure who might have owned a specific garment. The certainty regarding provenance, date, or other facts that scholars like to claim for their research subjects may not be possible for much of what could be associated with enslaved women. Third, paraphrasing from Tiya Miles's brilliant 2022 book, *All That She Carried: The Journey of Ashley's Sack, a Black Family Keepsake*, the conclusions that might be reached about the dress of enslaved Ottoman women must be "grounded interpretations based on evidence, comparison and context, … [but also] supposition and imagination," particularly in the face of archival deficit (Miles 2022: 17).

Enslaved Women and Their Clothing

Slavery was a central element of the American economic system from the earliest years of the colonial period, with enslaved Africans arriving in Virginia as early as 1619.[3] By the time the U.S. slave trade was officially abolished in 1808, the enslaved population stood at about four million. In the areas of the country where slavery was most prevalent (the southeastern quadrant of the United States), on average, the enslaved constituted just over 30 percent of the population for much of the nineteenth century,[4] a much higher percentage than in Ottoman Istanbul. The two systems have other important differences.

For one, the treatment of the enslaved in the United States was intentionally brutal and degrading, with virtually no legal protections for them until the end of the Civil War in 1865. Although the enslaved were able, with the permission of their owners, to buy their freedom and that of their families in some cases, they did not necessarily maintain an ongoing relationship with their former owners or receive financial support from them. In the decades following the Civil War in 1865, the modest gains made by the Black population in terms of personal freedom and economic security were accomplished despite the dominant culture, not with their support. Legal protections were passed slowly and often ignored.

As was outlined in the introduction, the experiences of enslaved women in the Ottoman context varied widely depending on their circumstances, with the most important distinction being between those working in urban households, including the palaces, and those (mostly men) working in agriculture and industry. My focus here is on women working in Istanbul households as servants, not the elite women who may have been enslaved as children or young women before making a successful marriage. Unlike women trapped in Atlantic slavery, domestic enslavement in the Ottoman context was generally temporary. Domestic slaves expected to be freed after a certain period, typically about seven years, at which time they often received financial support from their former mistresses and remained in contact with them.

Most of the clothing that belonged to the millions of enslaved people in the nineteenth-century United States has long since disappeared. This is due in large part to the inferior fabric with which the enslaved were provided to make their clothes, as well as their limited wardrobes and the hard wear to which their clothes were subjected. Even given these circumstances, a handful of garments have been identified as having belonged to enslaved women. Following the Civil War, with increased mobility and prosperity, at least for some, Black women had greater resources for self-fashioning, and more garments from these later decades survive in public collections.

Similarly, it is difficult to identify any specific garments with enslaved Ottoman women. However, estate records and other archival sources do provide insight into the possessions of some enslaved women, including their wardrobes. Argit's 2020 book *Life after the Harem: Female Palace Slaves, Patronage and the Imperial Ottoman Court*, based on her examination of two sets of court records from 1714–1732 and 1773–1775, is a rich source of information about the clothing this group owned in the eighteenth century.

During their time in the palace, enslaved women received salaries and clothing. They may also have been given gifts, depending on the generosity of their mistresses and specific circumstances.[5] Argit cites an example of an enslaved child who received trousseau items from her mistress that included "three furs of different qualities, fifteen caftans, twenty dresses, and other clothing items" (Argit: 72–73). Although there would have been a great range in the wealth of palace slaves after they left the imperial harem, or of manumitted women more generally, in some cases they accumulated significant assets, including textiles and clothing. Here is one of Argit's several examples:

> Sarayî Ülfet's caftans and dresses were surprising: she possessed several caftans made of various fabrics and in a variety of colors … Her thirty-seven dresses were made of a variety of colored and embroidered fabrics, such as *sevayi* (silk mixture) *germsud* (silk), *şeritli* (striped) *germsud*, *telkâri* (woven with gold or silver thread), *şali* (cashmere).
>
> *(ibid.: 190)*

According to her research, the inventories of clothing owned by palace women (formerly enslaved women) and other women shared many similar items, with economic status apparently more of a determinant of similarity than formerly enslaved or free (ibid.).

Argit's work is an invaluable contribution to understanding the material culture of one segment of enslaved women. Hopefully, similar work will be undertaken for the nineteenth century, and for a more diverse group of enslaved women, to the extent that they appear in the archival records. Perhaps such work will lead, in turn, to a greater focus on the actual objects, including clothing, by which enslaved women fashioned their lives.

The Visual Evidence

In the absence of extensive collections of actual dress, visual representations of enslaved women in both the African American and Ottoman contexts are crucial sources of information regarding their dress practices. Depictions of the harem and of harem women are ubiquitous in the visual record of the Ottoman Empire. Travelers, photographers, Orientalist painters, Ottoman painters working for the court and privately, among others, all produced images of the harem, and of Ottoman women more generally. These range from the completely fictional to reasonably accurate depictions of Ottoman home life, and from the frankly erotic to gently romanticized views of Ottoman women. The harem women who appear in these paintings and photographs occupy a range of different positions, both enslaved and free, within the complex structure of the harem. The evidence that this body of work presents for the dress practices of harem women over an extended period is incomplete and often contradicts information gleaned from other sources, but it is nonetheless valuable for understanding the dress history of women who are otherwise elusive in the fashion record in this period.

For African Americans in nineteenth-century America, photography was an important means of claiming their own identity, showing themselves as they wished to be seen. It was also a business that required few resources, leading to the establishment of Black owned studios in many cities, thus putting the control of their images in the hands of their own communities. The wealth of photographic imagery of Black Americans is a key resource for reconstructing the dress practices of enslaved women, although using these photographs often presents significant challenges. As is the case with Ottoman photo history, many photographs have survived with very little information about the sitter, the photographer, or the context of the image. The circumstances surrounding the making of the photographs could include portraits made at the request of the sitter as well as at the request of an enslaver. Black Americans of all economic classes appear in front of the camera, which may or may not have been wielded by Black photographers.

Comparing photographs of enslaved women from the American and Ottoman contexts is enlightening. The disparities and similarities of their situations are thrown into high relief, as the two pairs of images here will demonstrate. The first pair shows enslaved women, or perhaps domestic servants in the Ottoman case, in very different outdoor settings, each reflecting the circumstances enslaved women confronted at various moments. The carte de visite in Figure 7.1[6] provides a rare view of a contraband camp, a Civil War experience for hundreds of thousands of enslaved people.[7] Dated circa 1863, the photograph shows a large group of people, mostly women and children with a scattering of men, standing and sitting on the grounds of two or three wooden frame buildings in Baton Rouge, Louisiana. At the time that this photograph was taken, the population of the camp was more than a thousand.[8]

The people in the image are certainly aware of the photographer—many of them are looking straight at him. But it is also clear that the photographer did not have full control of the group; some of the children in the front have moved during the exposure time of the image and are very blurry. A group of women sit in a circle in the center of the photograph, others are nearby, and a larger crowd stands at the back. About sixteen women can be picked out individually from the crowd, and their clothes show the range of dress that could have been found among a group of enslaved women from plantations or houses of varying sizes who had been doing different kinds of work. Everyone wears a head covering of some kind but that, too, shows a degree of variety. The woman standing alone in the center right of the image wears a dress and apron of plain fabric, very

Figure 7.1 *Refugee Camp, Bullard Plantation,* William D. McPherson and J. Oliver, 1864. National Gallery of Art, Washington, DC.

worn, with no visible corseting or petticoats, and a loosely draped head wrap. Several of the seated women wear plaid or striped dresses and more tightly wrapped head cloths of printed fabric; others wear lighter colored, perhaps plain, dresses and head wraps. One woman standing at the left edge of the group wears a more elaborate dress of a printed fabric with a white collar or neck scarf and a short apron. Her skirt is full enough that it could be supported by crinoline or hoops. Another figure at the other edge of the crowd is also garbed in a more structured dress with a longer apron. Most likely the plain-colored dresses are made of Negro cloth, the coarse fabric specifically manufactured for clothing the enslaved, particularly those working in the fields and at other rough jobs. Women working in the house who might have been seen by the enslavers and their guests would have had somewhat more presentable clothing, and many enslaved women owned a fashionable dress that they made for themselves for special occasions and church, perhaps what the woman standing at the far left is wearing.

The Ottoman example, a snapshot that dates to several decades later (the 1890s), was taken in very different circumstances, showing a family group enjoying a tea party outdoors (Figure 7.2). One of a group of fifty-nine now in the collection of the Getty Research Institute, the dating is based on the dress of the women, and they were all taken within a few years of each other (Micklewright 2010: 249–56). From information gleaned from the snapshots as a group, this is a Muslim family whose military standing places them in the *askeri* sector of Istanbul society. This snapshot illustrates the dress of children, servants, adult female family members and friends, a relatively rare and valuable piece of fashion history.

Taking part in a garden party, women and girls are seated or standing at two tables in a forest setting drinking tea together. The boys and men who are also part of this family grouping were not seated with the women but could well have been nearby, because it is likely that the photograph was taken by the male member of the family who I have surmised elsewhere was an enthusiastic amateur photographer. Four adult

Figure 7.2 Untitled snapshot (Outdoor tea party), photographer unknown, *ca.* 1890. Los Angeles, Pierre de Gigord collection of photographs of the Ottoman Empire and the Republic of Turkey. Getty Research Institute, 96.R.14 (CD7).

women, one of whom has been caught in the act of filling a teapot from the samovar, are participants in the tea party; two servants stand behind them. Of the five figures seated at the table, two wear hats, two wear *yaşmaks* (the sheer white scarves worn by Ottoman Muslim women in public), and one, a younger girl, is bareheaded. Because they are dressed for public view, I surmise that the two women wearing *yaşmaks* are not family members, perhaps neighbors or close friends. The two women wearing hats are part of the family—one of them is acting as hostess by attending to the tea.

Looking again at the two women standing behind the table, given the date of this image, it is perhaps more likely that these two women are servants, not enslaved women, but it is impossible to know for sure. With the exception of the Black woman standing at the back right, everyone else has appeared in other snapshots in this set. She faces the camera directly and looks slightly bemused, perhaps the consequence of being part of a household with an amateur photographer who enjoys directing his camera at household members. She wears a long-sleeved, high-necked dress, or perhaps a skirt and blouse, of light-colored fabric; her head and shoulders are covered by a thin white scarf, suggesting that she is Muslim. The woman standing next to her is also wearing a light-colored, high-necked garment with long sleeves. She appears in a few other snapshots, often with the young children of the family, so most likely she is the nanny. In those other views, she wears long-sleeved, full-skirted dresses of printed or striped fabric, often with an apron.

The contraband camp image shows an enslaved population at a time of extreme dislocation, when they would have fled from their enslavers toward the Union army in hopes of freedom. The clothing of the various women reveals the range of dress available to enslaved women, depending on their status as house or field hands, their age, and perceived value. With one or two exceptions, the clothing is worn and ragged. The Ottoman photograph, on the other hand, shows a very different moment in the lives of the two servants, when they appear to be comfortably embedded in their household group, well-dressed and at ease.

In the second half of the nineteenth century when photography became more readily available and the nanny or baby nurse was an important figure in a family context, photographs of nurse and baby are common. In very many cases, the nurse is not identified by name, which is the case in the next two photographs I consider.

The first of these, dated 1871 on the glass plate negative, shows an unnamed Black nurse holding a White baby, who is identified as Huestis Cook (Figure 7.3). The fact that the photograph was taken by the baby's father, George Cook (1819–1902), a professional photographer in Richmond (Chaffin 2011), may explain the relaxed pose of both sitters and the unusually direct gaze of the baby out of the photograph to the photographer, his father. As an employee in the family of a photographer, the nurse would have been accustomed to the practice of photography and perhaps more comfortable in the studio than others may have been. Both subjects of the image are carefully outfitted, the baby in a very long dress with petticoats and the nurse in an immaculate, fashionable morning dress and white apron. The clothing in which the nurse and baby are dressed suggests a special occasion: the nurse's gown is more fashionable than her everyday garment would likely have been, and the baby's dress would have completely prevented him from moving about freely once the photograph had been taken and he was set down.

The name of the nurse in the photograph has not yet been found, and it is possible that her name was never recorded. The photograph has been published at least twice: in a 1954 celebratory volume of the photography of George and Huestis Cook, *Shadows in Silver*; and in Joan L. Severa's monumental 1995 work, *Dressed for*

Figure 7.3 *Baby Cook*, Cook Studio, 1871. The Valentine, Richmond, Virginia, Cook Photograph Collection. 1563/PHC0047.

the Photographer, Ordinary Americans and Fashion, 1840–1900. In *Shadows in Silver* the authors note that the nurse was "but a brief remove from slavery" (211), although it is possible, of course, that she had been a free woman prior to the end of the Civil War. Although they make no mention of her dress, elsewhere they write, "Since most Negro women were unskilled in sewing, except of the plainest and coarsest types, they paid good prices to have their best frocks fashioned by White dressmakers" (229), a statement very much at odds with other sources or surviving garments. Severa, on the other hand, provides a detailed description of the nurse's dress, saying that it is "of a most current fashion for morning dress" (Severa 1995: 281). She also says that as a house servant, the nurse would have been seen as an "extension of the family's means and taste."[9] Although this was generally true, framing the nurse's appearance only in that way removes her own agency in her self-fashioning. Wearing a fashionable dress with correct corseting, a cameo brooch, neatly coiffed hair, and the whitest collar and apron, the woman presents herself to the photographer as a self-possessed, calm, and gracious figure. She does not appear to be anxious in front of the camera, but neither is she obsequious, smiling, or otherwise acknowledging it.

Enslaved African women in Ottoman households are generally assumed to have been relegated to demanding jobs in the kitchen or laundry, but the cabinet card seen here (Figure 7.4) depicts a royal nanny with her infant charge, taken about 1885 by the photographer Pascal Sébah (Öztuncay 2010: 104). The royal baby is the focus of the image, the whiteness of its skin and elaborate ruffled pillow standing in sharp contrast to the dark background, skin, and clothing of the nanny. She looks down, her face in shadow, perhaps at the direction of the photographer or perhaps to avoid undue attention. The nanny is wearing an elaborately trimmed velvet *cepken* over a light-colored *entari*, the long sleeves of which extend from the shorter sleeves of the *cepken*. Her

Figure 7.4 *Royal Nanny*, Pascal Sébah, *ca.* 1885. Istanbul, Ömer Koç Collection.

hair is partially covered by an embroidered velvet cap with a long tassel. It seems likely that she is wearing these clothes for the occasion of the photograph, because they already were old-fashioned by the time that this photograph was made; more important, they were completely unsuitable for taking care of a small infant.

The Black nanny from the 1871 Virginia image faced the camera with a certain degree of confidence and is clearly wearing her own clothes, whereas the royal nanny in the Ottoman photograph is not at ease. She would not have known the photographer as the Virginia nanny did, and she could well have been unfamiliar with photography as a practice. It is also possible, given her young age, that she was a relative newcomer to the palace and still ill at ease in her new surroundings given what would have been a traumatic and dangerous journey from her home.[10] And the circumstances of this photograph are unclear—for whom was it taken? The nanny seems an unwilling subject, and the baby has no agency, so perhaps it was taken at the behest of the infant's mother, who may have enjoyed dressing up both baby and nanny for the picture. Most likely the exact context for this image or even the name of the nanny will never be known, but as a rare photograph of a working member of the royal harem, it remains an important document.

These two photographs are striking in the degree to which the women in each claim their subjectivity. The Richmond image shows a woman facing the camera with confidence, wearing her own stylish clothing. But despite her calm manner, she does not look directly at the viewer, conforming to contemporary expectations of the demeanor, posture, and direction of the gaze of enslaved and free Blacks in the company of Whites (White and White 1998: 63–85). The Ottoman nanny, on the other hand, is dressed in a costume and avoids the viewer's gaze, almost completely repudiating any claim to her subjectivity in the image.

The photograph of two women in Istanbul (Figure 7.5) was first published in 1915 in *An English Woman in a Turkish Harem* by the English writer and feminist Grace Ellison, and together with the book's text, provides

MISS "CHOCOLATE"

Figure 7.5 Miss "Chocolate," unknown photographer, 1913, published in Grace Ellison, *An English Woman in a Turkish Harem*, 1915.

another look into the lives of enslaved women.[11] On her third visit to Türkiye in 1913, Ellison spent several months in the home of a well-off female Ottoman friend. Ellison is pictured here, together with the enslaved woman, initially identified as "Cadhem Hair Calfat," who she renamed "Miss Chocolate," assigned to take care of Ellison during her visit. The picture is informal, with the two women seated next to each other on a bench in front of a mashrabiyya screen, most likely in the home in which they lived. Both dressed in similar street clothes (although Ellison carries a large fur muff), Ellison is looking at her companion, who in turn gazes out of the picture frame. Both subjects seem relaxed, although Ellison is clearly more at ease in front of the camera than is her servant. Ellison traveled with a camera, taking her own images, and purchased photographs, using both in her books. Although she may have wanted this image as a souvenir of her visit, it is also likely that she intended to use it in her book as it would have related directly to her subject.

In her book, Ellison relates what she knows of her servant's history and long service to the family. According to Ellison, because all the enslaved members of her friend's household had repeatedly been offered their freedom and declined, "Slavery, then, can be considered as no longer existing." (Ellison 1915: 26). It was a subject that she apparently discussed at length with her host. Based on her observations as well as what her host told her, she reported that enslaved women were treated kindly and were "perfectly happy." At the same time, she deplored their limited horizons and boring day-to-day routines. Like other women writing about Ottoman domestic life in this period, Ellison wanted to present what she encountered in a positive light to dispel some of the worst of the public misconceptions about the Orientalist harem. This also involved making a clear distinction between the circumstances of enslaved women in elite Ottoman homes and the more widely known horrors of Atlantic slavery, perhaps even putting aside some of her discomfort with Ottoman practices of slavery.

Next, I examine four paintings produced by foreign and Ottoman artists from the eighteenth century through the late nineteenth, showing women in a range of settings. Although a great many more artists could have been included here, these four paintings represent the kind of images that can be deployed in reconstructing the dress history of harem women. Taken as a group, the four reveal details of household relationships, the work that domestic servants carried out, and especially the dress of domestic servants, enslaved or free.

The first of the works is *Women Drinking Coffee* by the Flemish artist Jean-Baptiste Vanmour, introduced in Chapter 2. Vanmour lived in Istanbul for nearly forty years until his death in 1737, the date by which this painting must have been completed (Figure 7.6). One of a series of paintings the artist painted of specific moments in women's lives, the work shows six women and a child in a large room, enjoying coffee together. The artist has paid particular attention to dress in the painting, and his representations of the seven figures present some surprises. Two women, one standing and one seated, are the most elaborately dressed. They both wear *entaris*, with embroidered or woven decoration, buttoned down the front and closed by belts, over *şalvar* and *gömlek*. Fur-lined coats or *hırka*, lined with ermine in one case, are worn over their elegant *entaris*; elaborate turbans decorated with ropes of pearls complete their outfits. The other two ladies and the young girl wear outfits comprised of the same elements, but depicted in less detail, with fewer jewels and plainer fabric making up their garments.

Of the two attendants in the group, one wears a plain *entari* with tucked-up skirts over *şalvar* and *gömlek* and a less elaborate version of the headdress worn by all the women in the painting, the clothing expected of a servant. The second attendant, stepping away and carrying a tray, in contrast wears a richly colored *entari* over her *şalvar* and *gömlek* and a fur-trimmed *hırka*. Her clothing and her activities contradict each other: dressed as the other higher-ranking women in the scene, she is acting as a servant.

Figure 7.6 *Women Drinking Coffee*, Jean-Baptiste Vanmour, before 1737. Istanbul, Suna and İnan Kıraç Foundation Orientalist Painting Collection, Image copyright holder Suna and İnan Kıraç Foundation, @Uğur Ataç.

A late-eighteenth-century image from the *Zenanname* or *Book of Women* illustrates different costume, the *ferace* [long coat] and *yaşmak* [head covering] that Ottoman women wore when outside. Written by the Ottoman poet Fazıl Enderunlu or Fazıl Bey, the long poem is illustrated by paintings showing the dress of women from around the world, as known by the Ottomans (Figure 7.7).[12] The costumes of the *Zenanname* figures generally are described as deriving from the popular genre of costume albums.[13]

The page illustrated here from the Istanbul University Library manuscript shows two women walking outdoors, a servant following her mistress. They are most likely going to or from the bath. The Black woman on the left, an enslaved or free servant, carries a bundle, or *bohça*, of red and gold brocade, containing the bath supplies. Accompanying their mistress on outdoor excursions was an important part of the duties of domestic servants, serving to communicate the status and respectability of their employer or owner.

Dressed for the outdoors, few details of their indoor dress are visible, although what can be seen indicates much plainer dress for the servant. The *ferace* worn by the servant and that of the other woman do not look significantly different, although the *yaşmak* of the woman on the right (the mistress) is draped more elaborately than that of the servant and allows a bit more of her face to be seen. Her servant, walking behind her, has her eyes on her mistress. The two women are wearing similar cream-colored socks or stockings and slippers.

Dress and a description of harem activities are at the center of the highly decorative harem scene that Amadeo Preziosi painted about fifty years later (Figure 7.8).[14] Originally a watercolor, reproduced for sale as a lithograph, *La tasse de café*, circa 1858, shows three women in an interior space, signified as a harem by the furnishings. It is entirely possible that all three women are enslaved, but their differing status within

Figure 7.7 *Women going to the bath, Zenanname,* late eighteenth century. Istanbul, İstanbul Üniversitesi Nadir Eserler Kütüphanesi, T5502, p. 225.

the harem is indicated by their clothing. The woman most accessible to our gaze is reclining on a low couch, leaning against a pillow. She holds the mouthpiece to a water pipe in one hand and a set of beads in the other, indicating that she is at leisure. Dressed in *şalvar, cepken,* and *gömlek,* the colors and textures of her garments are carefully depicted: her *şalvar* are silky, the blue velvet of her *cepken* is smooth and lustrous, and her *gömlek* is fine and transparent. She is attended by two other figures, a musician and a Black woman offering her a cup of coffee. The musician, also seated on the couch, wears a figured garment with sleeves gathered at the wrists; her clothes are less carefully depicted and almost blend into the wall behind her.

The third figure in the scene is a Black woman standing in front of the couch. Nominally the subject of the painting, according to the title, the viewer must look carefully to find the cup of coffee. The eye is much more taken up with the riot of colors and textures that make up the outfit of the Black servant. She wears plain-colored *şalvar* that fall down over her feet, a striped *entari* with lace trim and a contrasting lining on the overly long sleeves, a *gömlek* under the *entari,* and a short, red *cepken* with gold trim on top. The long skirts of her *entari* would drag on the floor, but they are tucked up into a belt or sash that is not visible for ease of movement. Her hair is completely covered by a brightly colored scarf knotted around her head, and she wears large hoop earrings. The layers of fabric and decoration, although colorful, are painted with dark

Figure 7.8 *La tasse de café*, Amadeo Preziosi, *ca.* 1858. Kislak Center for Special Collections, Rare Books and Manuscripts, University of Pennsylvania.

undertones, echoing the woman's skin tones and creating a sharp contrast to the more brightly colored, fair-skinned women on the couch.

Preziosi used dress in a much more explicit way than the two artists considered above to direct our gaze to the figures he believed to be of the most interest to his audience. The reclining figure, dressed in the most sensual and carefully depicted clothing, should be understood as the "favorite," the woman who engages the sexual attention of the harem's owner. The musician, a person of lower status within the harem hierarchy, is positioned behind the favorite with clothing that literally blends into the background. The Black servant offering coffee is lowest in status but is exotic to the European eye because of her skin color and thus painted in such a way to attract the viewer's attention. Despite the sensuality and activity implied in the scene: music, smoking the water pipe, the clicking of the beads, the smell of the coffee, the image is curiously blank. The figures do not engage with each other, and each seems frozen in place.

The 1891 painting *Yaşlı Halayık* [Old Slave Woman] by the Ottoman artist Halil Paşa (1852–1939), an active figure in the Istanbul art world, and today regarded as one of the most important painters of the late Ottoman and early Republican periods, stands apart from the three other paintings considered thus far

Figure 7.9 *Yaşlı Halayık* [Old Slave Woman], Halil Paşa, 1891/Private Collection.

(Figure 7.9). Painted in oil on canvas, it commands attention by its size (140 cm. x 106 cm.). It is a portrait of a specific person, not a generic type, although the subject is not identified by name. Lost in thought, the woman is seated on a backless stool in the center of the painting, looking out of the picture frame but not making eye contact with the viewer. She wears a worn, red quilted *hırka* over a faded blue skirt. Her hair is partly covered by an old pink scarf folded up at the sides of her head, and on her feet are scuffed red slippers. She wears no jewelry and holds out her hands, heavily veined and care worn, for the warmth of the small brazier (*mangal*) in front of her. The space in which she sits is virtually bare except for the *mangal* and coffee implements on the floor in front of her, and the surrounding walls of the room in which she sits are murky, creating the sense that darkness and poverty weigh heavily on her. In sharp contrast to the elaborately costumed, exoticized representations of harem women in the works by Vanmour and Preziosi, and indeed by most artists, European or Ottoman, the *yaşlı halayık* in Halil Paşa's painting is an old woman, alone and visibly poor. Her depiction is a stark reminder of the poverty that was often the fate of enslaved women who had spent their lives in the service of others.

This sample of representations of Ottoman harem women and domestic servants, enslaved or free, small though it is, provides a set of images across a range of dates, in different media, by European and Ottoman artists for very different audiences. With the possible exception of the garden tea party snapshot, each image is created to make a specific point or to cater to a particular audience. Despite these circumstances, though, the images provide certain impressions of how Black women were positioned, how enslaved women or domestic servants dressed, and the clothes they wore. In contrast to what is routinely recounted by historians, Black enslaved women were not all confined to the kitchen or the laundry, at least according to the images examined here. Servants, whether enslaved or free, seem to have worn elaborate, colorful outfits, despite reports that they were meant to dress plainly. In these examples it is sometimes difficult to distinguish between the clothing of servant and mistress, although this could be due to artistic license.

The Texts

A second key body of information here is the written records that provide information not available via visual representations. Fashion historians working on the dress history of African American enslaved women have augmented the scanty costume evidence with a deep mining of contemporary written material, particularly newspaper ads and plantation records, as well as diaries, commercial archives, and correspondence. A key source are the advertisements that enslavers placed in local newspapers seeking information about runaway slaves because they often included a description of the clothes they were wearing. For example, "A woman named Milla ran away in 1772 wearing 'short striped Virginia cloth gown and petticoat, *oznabrig* [the coarse linen or hemp fabric used for making clothes for the enslaved] shift and bonnet'" (Baumgarten 1988: 57). Taken as a whole, these thousands of runaway ads provide the clothing vocabulary in use at the time, shorthand descriptions of the garments themselves and insight into how people in desperate circumstances used clothing as a way of assuming new identities. Plantation records detail the fabric allotments for the enslaved as well as the sources and costs of the fabric; they also provide instructions for the distribution of clothing among the plantation's enslaved. Historians have access to the voices of the enslaved themselves, through a compelling corpus of diaries and memoirs written by formerly enslaved people, and the *Born in Slavery: Slave Narratives from the Federal Writers' Project, 1936 to 1938* project, housed at the Library of Congress in Washington, D.C., which contains more than twenty-three hundred first-person accounts of slavery, collected by mostly White out-of-work writers as part of the Depression-era Works Project Administration.

Similarly, for the dress practices of enslaved women and domestic servants in the Ottoman context, a rich and extensive written record exists, although it is not without its challenges of interpretation, as detailed in Chapter 2. Sources include the writing of foreign visitors who described the Ottoman institutions of enslavement and the harem, as well as memoirs and other writings by Ottoman women who participated in those institutions. Taken together, these provide a sense of how enslaved women in elite households were dressed and how clothing was acquired by women working as domestic servants, whether free or enslaved. The sources are less helpful for details of specific garments, perhaps not surprising considering the limited opportunities that foreign visitors had to examine actual garments and the fact that the Ottoman women were often writing about events that had taken place decades earlier.

Among foreign women who visited Ottoman harems, beginning with Lady Mary Wortley Montagu in the early eighteenth century, through the nineteenth century, nearly everyone is struck by the number of enslaved women in the households they visit, the magnificence of their clothing, and the elegance of the high-ranking enslaved or formerly enslaved women they encounter. Julia Pardoe, staying in the city in 1835, has this to say about a young girl she saw on a visit:

My attention being attracted to the rosy, happy-looking little slave-girl who stood near me, with her chubby arms crossed before her, her large pink trowsers completely concealing her naked feet, and her long blue antery richly trimmed with yellow floss-silk fringe, lying upon the carpet.

(114)

E. B. M. Hornby, who lived in Istanbul in the 1850s, described her visit to the household of a "Pasha" in great detail, including the dress of the enslaved Circassian woman who she said had been presented to the pasha as a gift from the sultan:

I must now tell you her dress. Her trousers, and the robe which twists round the feet, and trails behind, were of the most brilliant blue, edged with a little embroidery of white. Her cashmere jacket was of pale lilac (like the double primroses), lined with a gold-colored fur. A delicate lilac gauze handkerchief was twined round her head; among the fringe of which, diamond heartseases, of the natural size, glittered on golden stalks which trembled at the slightest movement. Lilac slippers, embroidered with seed-pearls, completed her toilet.

(241)

Her account of this visit is particularly useful because she also had occasion to see the two nurses who brought in a baby to be displayed to the visitors and provided a description of their clothing as well, thus giving her readers a tantalizing glimpse of the hierarchies of dress among the servants of a large household. She writes:

The nurse who carried him was a lovely young woman: she was dressed in trousers and jacket of a bright green, and wore on her head a pale-yellow handkerchief, fastened with a large diamond. The other was an immense black woman, dressed entirely in scarlet silk, with a little edging of white, and a snow-white handkerchief bound round her woolly head.

(250)

Some of the Ottoman women writing provide key information about how domestic servants, free or enslaved, were supplied with clothing. Many palace women were also accomplished seamstresses. Filitzen, a high-ranking member of the household of Murad V beginning about 1876 through his death in 1904, wrote about the sewing practices in Çırağan Palace during these years:

> But if there was one thing nearly all of us knew, it was how to cut and sew cloth. Bolts of fabric would arrive from outside the palace whenever we requested them. Every kalfa [harem attendant] made her own clothes, with the Senior Consort in particular so skilled that she could have been considered an expert seamstress. Several times she even made clothes for our master.
>
> *(Brookes 2008: 113)*

Describing her home, an elite Ottoman household with close ties to the Egyptian royal family at the turn of the century, Emine Fuat Tugay offers a detailed account of the means by which servants in a large household were clothed, worth quoting in full:

> In spring and autumn bales of printed cotton or of flannelette would arrive at our house to be made up into dresses for the maids and kalfas. The former were dressed alike, but the kalfas and bacis [household servants] were allowed to choose their own materials and style. A Greek seamstress who lived in the neighbourhood took possession of the sewing-room and, assisted by maids who were clever with their needles, undertook the task of clothing the female staff. Each maid received four cotton dresses for the summer, two for work and two for the afternoons, and four made of flowered flannelette, as well as a woollen dress for the winter. The gowns which they wore at Bayram and on special occasions were of satin or brocade, and cut in the current fashion with long skirts ending in a train. Besides these items, slippers, shoes, handkerchiefs, and every article of underwear were also provided. One of the kalfas cut out white calico foundation garments which the maids sewed together themselves. They were also taught to darn, to knit, and to do fine embroidery. Each maid received jewels appropriate to her position and her term of service. Beginning with a plain gold brooch, she possessed by the time she was ready to marry an enviable assortment of diamond jewels.
>
> *(Tugay 1963: 217–18)*

So far, I haven't found any of the cotton flannelette maid's dresses that Tugay describes, but even a written description provides insight into the clothing hierarchies among domestic servants and the process by which they were outfitted. Taken as a whole, the written accounts, especially those from the 1850s onward, reveal a world in which dress was a preoccupation among Ottoman women across economic and ethnic lines. Whether free or enslaved, domestic servants were involved in making and caring for their own and their mistresses clothing, and depending on their seniority, accumulated their own wardrobes of dresses and jewels over time. Leyla Saz Hanımefendi, whose memoirs describe palace life in the 1850s–1870s gives a clear picture of the centrality of dress within a royal harem, particularly the women's involvement in determining their own wardrobes, even sewing their own dresses in some cases, as well as the manner in which gifts of clothing from royal women to servants and others were regarded as marks of great favor and highly treasured.

The Garments

Significant challenges are involved in finding garments that might have been worn by enslaved women or domestic servants, from either the American or Ottoman contexts. In the case of African American women, a small number of surviving dresses are thought to have belonged to enslaved women; in the Ottoman context, I have so far not identified anything that can be securely attached to a specific or even an unnamed woman.

With its concerted effort to build a collection, detailed in Chapter 2, the National Museum of African American History and Culture (NMAAHC) has a small number of pieces that form one of the largest groups of slave-era clothing in one museum. In addition to the two or three nineteenth-century dresses associated with enslaved women, the museum also has a number of pieces belonging to Harriet Tubman (the Black American abolitionist) including the silk lace and linen shawl sent to her by Queen Victoria. Other garments, shoes, pockets, petticoats, and personal objects that may have belonged to enslaved women can be found scattered in other museum collections and historic sites, difficult to find without extensive searching online and in person. As is also the case for Ottoman examples, it seems likely that some pieces are still in private hands, treasured objects that have been passed down through the generations.

The two dresses associated with enslaved women from the NMAAHC collection (Figure 7.10) that I was able to examine present the challenges involved in reconstructing this dress history and are thus instructive for my Ottoman project.[15] The first of these, on the right, is a brown and cream-colored striped dress, dated by the museum circa 1865–1875 and collected by Lois Alexander Lane for the Black Fashion Museum,

Figure 7.10 Left: Day dress, 1845–1865. Collection of the Smithsonian National Museum of African American History and Culture, Washington, DC, Gift of the Black Fashion Museum founded by Lois K. Alexander-Lane, 2007.3.4. Right: Day dress, 1865–1875. Collection of the Smithsonian National Museum of African American History and Culture, Washington, DC, Gift of the Black Fashion Museum founded by Lois K. Alexander-Lane, 2007.3.34.

mentioned in Chapter 2. The dress fabric is a printed cotton plain weave, with the stripes used thoughtfully by the seamstress to create interest and emphasize the dress's structure. The bodice construction, treatment of the skirt hem, joining of the skirt and bodice, and the use of self-piping at the waist are all consistent with dressmaking techniques of this time and show considerable skill on the part of the maker. The dress is in good condition but shows sign of wear with worn fabric at the cuffs and one elbow, staining in places, and fading.

The second dress was also collected for the Black Fashion Museum and was described by Ms. Alexander-Lane as a "slave dress," but it is not clear why she thought so. Like the dress discussed previously, it is made of a printed cotton plain weave, but this fabric is much more colorful and complex in its design, with a striped pattern in five colors of alternating bands of floral and geometric motifs. The dress is dated circa 1845–1865, based on an assessment of the dress style and the fabric plus X-ray analysis of the dyes and materials, which yielded a pre–Civil War date. The size of the dress suggests that the wearer was several inches shorter than five feet. Although the dress was clearly worn, it has been extremely well-preserved; the dress fabric still has a sheen and given the condition of the fabric, does not seem to have been laundered very frequently.

These two dresses were made meticulously and skillfully, with design and construction details that indicate an awareness of current sewing practices and fashion elements. Their fabric and relatively simple, unornamented structure identify them as belonging to women of modest means. They could have been made by or for enslaved women, or they could have belonged to free Black or White working-class women. If they belonged to enslaved women, it seems likely that the brown striped dress was a garment worn for everyday work by a woman working in the owner's home. The more colorful dress, on the other hand, fits the description of the dresses that enslaved women owned as their "good" dress, one that would be worn to church and for special occasions.[16]

If there are details of the past history of these garments that I cannot know, the dresses do reveal a great deal. In each case, they were made by someone who took care in the design and construction of the garment. Nothing about these pieces is sloppy or unfinished. The sewing is exact, the stitches are almost invisible, and the fabric is used carefully. Each demonstrates a desire on the part of the maker or wearer to maximize the fashionability of a relatively modest garment. If the brown striped dress was indeed a work uniform, it was a well cut, neatly assembled dress that could have been worn with a certain amount of pride whatever the status of the wearer.

The story of the second dress is less clear. It does not seem to have been worn very much, and it has been carefully preserved. If its original owner outgrew it, why wasn't it passed down and worn by others? For women of limited means, setting aside a well-made, barely worn garment would have been a choice made for very specific reasons. Perhaps the story of the dress involves a loss, possibly the death of the person for whom it was made, or her abrupt departure, and the dress was carefully saved as a memory of that person. It is impossible to know for sure, but we do know that among the enslaved, families were broken up, medical care was very poor, and the sudden loss of a woman young enough to wear this dress would not have been an uncommon occurrence.[17] Whatever the circumstances, this modest dress was carefully treasured for a century before being donated to the Black Fashion Museum.

These two dresses are separated by culture and geography from the clothing worn by enslaved women in Ottoman Istanbul, but their examination is nonetheless enlightening for my project. Their presence in a national museum collection is a reminder that the clothing and other personal possessions belonging to people of very modest means do indeed survive and can be tracked down and preserved. The dresses themselves show clear connections to current fashion trends and construction methods, a connection that becomes even stronger when they are compared to the dress of working women from Britain and Istanbul in the next chapter.

Apart from the similarities in dress style and construction demonstrated by these two dresses and examples considered in the next chapter, other aspects of the dress practices of enslaved women and domestic servants in the Ottoman and American contexts were radically different. Enslaved African Americans were provided with scanty wardrobes made of uncomfortable, coarse cloth. Anything more fashionable was made on their own time and using their own resources, and their appearance was rigorously policed to ensure that suitable distinctions were observed between the dress of enslaved Black women and free White women.

In the Ottoman context, as both the visual and written sources have made clear, the distinction between the clothing worn by harem mistresses and servants was murky; clothing often was given from mistress to servant, and high-ranking servants sometimes possessed elaborate dresses for special occasions. When enslaved women and girls were dressed lavishly for display to harem visitors, they "performed a mannequin function for palace audiences" (Lewis 2021: 84); at the same time, they were taking on the status conveyed by the outfits, even if only temporarily. They were also learning the body management required for elaborate dress and had the opportunity to develop their own fashion identity. When palace women were manumitted and married, they took the garments they had made or been given while enslaved with them to their new lives. With the fashion sensibilities that had been shaped by their palace experiences, they served as tastemakers in neighborhoods of diverse economic and social population, an important reminder that fashion influence is not just a top-down phenomenon. This stands in sharp contrast to the situation that newly freed African American enslaved women faced: their clothing was a visible—and no doubt despised—mark of their enslaved status, to be discarded as soon as circumstances allowed.

The relatively temporary time frame of Ottoman enslavement also makes it difficult to attach clothing to any specific legal status on the part of the owner. A further complication is the undocumented history of many surviving garments from this period, perhaps passed down within a family, given away, or sold when circumstances dictated. And it is always possible that an extended search in museum collections will reveal a garment or two that entered the collection with information about a specific family member whose past had included a period of enslavement, or that such pieces are still being preserved in family collections.

Reconstructing the fashion history of a specific group of people is a chancy exercise at the best of times, even more so for nonelite women whose individual stories and possessions have not survived. In the case of domestic servants of Ottoman Istanbul, enslaved and free, I have uncovered a certain amount, and there is a great deal I will most likely never know. The primary sources examined here (texts, images, and costume) reveal that depending on their circumstances, some of these women owned expensive clothing and jewelry in addition to their everyday clothing, and that in many cases, they could make their clothes for themselves. They were often paid in clothing, and fine garments circulated as signs of patronage and affection among women of differing social status.[18]

Evidence of the impact of individual circumstances on fashion is clear—enslavement and domestic servitude were not monolithic categories of experience but were shaped by the economic standing of specific households, the work assigned, an individual's ethnicity or religion, and historic accident, among others. These same variables were in play for the dress practices of the women of Ottoman Istanbul who, beginning in the last decades of the nineteenth century, began working in greater numbers outside the home, the subject of the next chapter.

CHAPTER 8
DRESSING FOR WORK

Ottoman women began to enter the public work force in Istanbul in the last decades of the nineteenth century and in much greater numbers in the turbulent first decades of the twentieth. Long *entaris* with their full sleeves and baggy *şalvar* would have been unsuitable for much of the work that women carried out in these more public settings, so the new working women would have needed to adopt different dress practices. They might have looked to European working women in Istanbul, and to the European fashions they saw in shops, which they would have made or had made in more affordable versions to suit their budgets.

Given museum collecting practices and the ravages of time, it is challenging to find clothing that would have belonged to the women who worked in factories, banks, shops, and classrooms in late-nineteenth and early-twentieth-century Istanbul, so casting a wide net for images and relevant examples is essential. In the period leading up to World War I, women working outside the home were still a relatively small subset of the population, but over the course of the twentieth century, their numbers grew substantially. In this chapter I want to understand how these first working women engaged with dress. Tracing their fashion engagement in this early period lays the groundwork for studying what is still an overlooked area of fashion history in twentieth-century Türkiye.

Education and Work for Women in Late Ottoman Istanbul

Educational reform was a key element of the Tanzimat Period, a time of reform and modernization beginning in 1839, but those reforms did not immediately extend to education for girls. The first *rüşdiyye* (middle or secondary school) for girls only opened in 1859, and by 1874–1875 there were only 361 girls enrolled in eleven schools (Aydinlik and Kenan 2021: 401, 403).[1] However, in these years girls in Istanbul had educational alternatives. Elite families preferred to educate their girls at home and employed foreign governesses for this purpose, which also served to provide access to European modes of dress, literature, and other aspects of domestic life for all the women of the household. Jewish, Armenian, Greek, and other Christian communities established their own schools for girls with women teachers. In the case of the Jewish community, for instance, in some cases, individual women offered classes in their home for small groups of girls, but these were considered illegal and were often closed by the government. Licensed schools were operated with the involvement of the Alliance Israélite Society, a French organization working internationally to advance education among Jewish communities in the Middle East. Many of the teachers at the Istanbul schools were local women who graduated from those same schools, in some cases also having attended the Alliance's teacher training school in Paris (Gün 2024: 173–93). The curriculum of the Jewish schools for girls, as well as the girls' *rüşdiyyes* and other girls' schools, always included sewing, tailoring, and/or embroidery, among other subjects.

More specialized institutions provided training directed at future employment for their students. The first vocational schools for girls opened in Istanbul in 1869, the first teacher training colleges in 1870 (Metinsoy 2023: 50). The American College for Girls, founded in 1873 as the Constantinople Home, became accredited to award BA and BS degrees in 1890 (Goffman 2015). Midwifery training programs had existed since the mid-century; and in the early years of the twentieth century, the need for nurses led to the development of specialized training programs (Segev 2024: 358–59).

Historically, many women in Ottoman Istanbul had worked to generate income, both from their own homes and in other locations, and their employment opportunities expanded in the late Ottoman period. Women and girls had worked as domestic servants, laundresses, bath attendants, peddlers, and in a variety of jobs in the textile industries, both from home and in workshops (Zarinebaf-Shahr 2001: 143), as well as midwives, slave traders, and legal representatives for women in court (Fleet 2016: 122–23). In the last decades of the nineteenth century, women began opening dressmaking studios; working in the new European-style department stores; working as teachers, hairdressers, and in textile and tobacco factories, discussed below. By 1913, Turkish women were employed by the Istanbul Telephone Department as operators and inspectors; and as cashiers, ticket collectors on the ferries, secretaries, and as clerks in the Post and Telegraph Offices (Metinsoy 2023: 59–60). Women's employment became even more diversified during World War I as they were pressed into service to replace men called to the front. Women continued to work in textile factories, now supplying the war effort, but also moved into white-collar jobs (Os 2018).

In the context of this project, the sewing machine, available in Istanbul beginning in 1886 (Metinsoy: 52), is of particular significance in terms of women's employment. In his "Social History of the Sewing Machine," Kupferschmidt quotes French journalist Paul Fesch,[2] who estimated that in 1907 there were ten thousand sewing machines owned in Istanbul (Kupferschmidt 2004: 201). Sewing machines became a part of dowries, allowing women to make clothes for their families, as well as to design and sew their own clothes (ibid.: 207; Metinsoy ibid.), thus allowing them to control their own self-fashioning. Possession of a sewing machine also provided women with a measure of financial independence because they could then make clothes for individual clients and even open dressmaking studios. In addition, women (and men) could work from home or in small workshops, producing clothing, umbrellas, and shoes to be sold to local department stores (Quataert 1992: 22–25).

Looking for the Dress of Ottoman Women at Work

Visual sources and a few written descriptions help illuminate the fashion history of Ottoman working women, but for the garments the women may have worn I needed to search elsewhere to understand how they may have fashioned themselves in these new contexts. Muslim women seeking fashion information would have looked to the working women in the Armenian and Greek communities in Istanbul who followed European fashions, but unfortunately the clothes that those women wore have also largely disappeared.

Another important source is the dress of the foreign working women who were in Istanbul as governesses, nurses, teachers, companions, and secretaries. These women, who were present in some number, would have been visible in public places. English nurses came to Istanbul with the Crimean War, along with nurses from other European countries, the beginning of a continuing presence of foreign nurses in the city. In the second half of the century, foreign governesses (British, French, and German) became a mainstay of the education of girls in elite families. Newspaper and periodical ads indicate an ongoing need for tutors, piano teachers, and art teachers. As more schools for girls were opened in the same period, foreign women came to serve as teachers in those schools, with the younger teachers in particular serving as fashion models for their students as well as for the Ottoman teachers (Figure 8.1).

With the increasing interest in European fashion among Ottoman women, foreign seamstresses were also drawn to the city, as noted in Chapter 5. With the exception of the foreign seamstresses who made it their business to be completely au courant with current fashions, the other working women to whom working Ottoman women may looked to for fashion guidance would not have been seen as fashion leaders at home.

Figure 8.1 Teachers at the American College for Girls, from left to right, Clara Hamlin, Mary Mills Patrick, Mary Hamlin and Mrs. Williams, *ca.* 1890s. Robert College Archives.

They may well have been interested in fashion, but their resources and employment circumstances would not have allowed them to wear the highly fashionable clothes of elite women. Their potential as tastemakers for a certain segment of Ottoman women is an instance of the lateral transmission of fashion knowledge, as opposed to the top-down model discussed in Chapter 6.

An important subset of the foreign women who were present in Istanbul, British women were also entering the public workplace in the last decades of the nineteenth century and faced some of the same challenges in dressing for these new roles as did Ottoman women. Looking at the clothes that British working women wore helps to explicate the dress practices of Ottoman women at around the same time. But even in Britain, with its rich and deep collections in public museums of women's dress, it is not always easy to find examples of the clothing that might have been worn by middle-class women and those earning their living in the jobs that had begun opening up to women in the later part of the nineteenth century.[3]

Ottoman examples are even more elusive. Even if these garments, most likely European in style, had survived, they would not necessarily have been passed down as family treasures in the same way as late Ottoman garments were. Nor have they been of particular interest to collectors or museum curators in Türkiye because they were not of the best quality fabric or construction. Nonetheless, by looking further afield in terms of both time and geography, it has been possible to identify several pieces most likely worn by nonelite Ottoman women in the late nineteenth and early twentieth century. Fabric type, garment style, and tailoring; quality of workmanship; provenance information; and collection context are all criteria that help to identify the possible history of a dress.

In the Victorian period in Britain, working women, particularly governesses, but also seamstresses, teachers, and to a lesser extent factory workers, were popular subjects for painters and photographers. Although the messages of these images are often concerned with social or economic issues related to the changing roles of women in this period, they are also useful to understand the dress practices of working women. For example, *The Seamstress* (Charles Baugniet, 1858) depicts a young woman working on a white silk dress, perhaps a wedding dress or a ball gown.[4] She is seated in a domestic interior, likely the home of her client because a dressmaker's shop would not have been furnished so elegantly. Although some dressmakers maintained their own shops, others were itinerant, working in the homes of their clients, a practice that was common in the Euro-American context in the nineteenth century and in Istanbul well into the twentieth century.

The seamstress wears a plain, neat brown dress with white collar and undersleeves, which could have been removed for laundering. The bodice is tied at the neck with a small black ribbon, and a pair of sewing shears are suspended from a black ribbon at her waist. Black earrings are her only jewelry. But despite its plain fabric, the dress is fashionable (as one might expect of a seamstress) with its dropped shoulders and full sleeves, a reminder that fashion engaged the attention of women across the economic spectrum, as their circumstances allowed.

Governesses also would have been expected to dress modestly; and given their extremely low wages, they would have had to be very frugal in their clothing expenditures. The central figure in British artist Edmund Leighton's 1894 painting *The New Governess* (Figure 8.2) presents a somewhat romanticized version of what a governess might have worn as she arrived at a new post. Standing at the front door, perhaps having just paid

Figure 8.2 *The New Governess*, Edmund Leighton, 1894. Private collection.

off a cab, she is looking at the small reticule (or purse) in her hand, with an umbrella and satchel at her feet. She wears a light-colored dress with a small print, likely a floral motif. Displaying none of the fashionable excesses of clothing of the period, her dress has a high neck; long, narrow sleeves; and a gathered skirt edged with a fabric ruffle. She wears a white fichu, a black lace shawl, and a black hat. It is a respectable, modest but not fashionable garment; eschewing the latest trends in trim or cut, it could have been worn over a long period of time.

A dress in the collection of Killerton House, an eighteenth-century estate near Exeter (Figure 8.3), shares certain features with the governess's garment in Leighton's painting. Dated circa 1860, the dress is made of a lightweight self-striped wool muslin (mousseline de laine) with a printed design of scattered floral sprigs, resembling the fabric in the dress in the painting. It is mostly machine sewn with finishing and alterations done by hand. The dress opens down the front, with a front closing for the full, gathered skirt. Ruched trimming made of the dress fabric is used at the yoke, extending over the shoulders, and at the sleeve ends. There are two horizontal tucks around the lower skirt. The bodice is lined with a coarse cotton, the sleeves partially lined with lawn, and there is a facing of plain white fabric around the inside lower edge of the skirt. Overall, the construction is simple, with a basic design—round neck; plain, straight sleeves; no additional bodice shaping apart from the fabric darts. Like the two dresses from NMAAHC discussed in the previous chapter, the arm seams are finished with self-piping, either for additional decoration or to reinforce the seams. The waistband (unlined) seems to have been inserted later, based on the much rougher hand-sewing used to attach it to the

Figure 8.3 Day dress, *ca.* 1860. Exeter, Killerton House, National Trust Collections, NT 1363033.

skirt and bodice and the fact that the fabric stripes run horizontally, not vertically as in the rest of the dress. The dress originally may have been two pieces, a bodice and matching skirt; or if it was a single garment, the waistband could have been added for a taller wearer. In any case, it demonstrates that, modest as this dress was, it was valuable enough to be remodeled as fashion or its owner dictated.

Two-piece dresses, which had grown in popularity beginning in the 1850s (Edwards 2017: 82), were a practical choice for working women. The dress in Figure 8.4 from the Blaise Museum in Bristol, UK, like the previous example, shows signs of careful mending for a garment that was most likely the "best dress" of a woman of limited means. Made of a light blue, plain weave cotton with an optical printed design in purple/brown of circles and spots, the outfit consists of a basque jacket and gathered skirt, all hand sewn. The gathered skirt, unlined except for a six-inch facing at the hem, is neatly sewn into a white muslin waistband and finished at the hem with black woven braid. The jacket construction is more complex, with a fitted white muslin sleeveless underbodice sewn into the side seams and sleeves of the jacket. The underbodice fastens at the front with hooks and eyes, but the more loosely fitted jacket is held closed by a fabric belt. The jacket is drawn in at the waist by the belt, as well as by tiny pleats at the back waist, to create the flared overskirt typical of a basque jacket. The jacket trim includes two lines of black braid that edge the stand-up collar and continue down the front of the jacket, as well as a narrow band of eyelet lace at the jacket hem. The jacket fronts do not meet evenly at the bottom, and the hand sewing is rough in places. The sleeves are heavily gathered at the shoulder and closed with cuffs, also trimmed with black braid.

Figure 8.4 Two-piece day dress, n.d. Bristol, Bristol Museums, Galleries & Archives, TA564.

This outfit was made by a woman who had an eye on fashion trends, as evidenced by the basque jacket, the shape of the sleeves, and the fabric choice. Tears in the skirt are carefully mended. The structure of the jacket is ambitious and perhaps slightly beyond the sewing ability of the maker, based on some of the finishing details and the irregular piecing of the jacket. But looking carefully at this dress and the previous one, in terms of the fabric and design choices as well as construction and evidence of wear, tells a great deal about the women who chose and most likely made these dresses—their fashion aspirations as well as the practical constraints that shaped their wardrobes.

As discussed above, in the first decades of the twentieth century, with the pressing needs of war wounded from the Balkan Wars and World War I, nursing came to be regarded as a socially acceptable occupation for Ottoman women (Segev 2024). Nursing courses were set up to train women for work in military hospitals (figure 8.5), and after the war, longer and more in-depth nurse training programs were established. In this specialized context, self-fashioning was not an option: clean, neat uniforms were an essential part of the job, both for medical reasons and to signal the professionalism of the nurses. Ottoman nurses' uniforms would have been modeled on those familiar from the British and other European nurses who had been working in Istanbul since the Crimean War in the 1850s.

A nurse's uniform in the collection at Killerton House, mentioned above, provides a close example of what the Ottoman nurses may have worn (Figure 8.6). Dated 1910–1920, the one-piece dress is made of a heavy blue and white striped cotton (the Ottoman uniforms in the photograph illustrated here in Figure 8.5 are white). The long sleeves and long skirt provided complete coverage for the nurse, for both hygiene and modesty. The dress buttons up the front from the waist, so would have been easy to take on and off, is fitted at the waist, but would not have required extreme corseting, and the sturdy fabric would have stood up to heavy laundering. It has several pockets of different sizes, intended to accommodate the instruments the nurse may have needed to carry. As a subset of fashion for women, uniforms had a few specific purposes: they were practical, enhancing performance and safety on the job; they signaled a particular affiliation with a profession or work context, creating a sense of belonging with that group; and in public, uniforms were a marker of the

Figure 8.5 Nurses with Dr. Besim Ömer Paşa (Akalin), Beyoğlu hospital, Istanbul, 1913. Courtesy of the Turkish Red Crescent Archive TK 93/24.

Figure 8.6 Nurse's uniform, 1910–1920. Exeter, Killerton House, National Trust Collections, NT 1364840.

economic and social contributions of the wearer. Nurses' uniforms were among the earliest uniforms that Istanbul women wore, but municipal workers, factory workers, and others soon joined them.

Ottoman Working Women

Working women are rarely pictured in the work of nineteenth-century painters in Istanbul. Those who do appear are not modern factory workers or seamstresses but fortune tellers or *bohçacı*, as in Figure 5.12. Photographic evidence of working women is thus an essential source for understanding the dress history of women who are otherwise elusive in the fashion record in this period.

An album produced by the Istanbul-based Swedish photographer Guillaume Berggren (active 1866–1920) provides a valuable visual record of women working in the Cibali Régie tobacco factory (Figure 8.7). The factory began operation in 1884 under French control with proceeds managed by the Ottoman Public Debt Administration. It was nationalized in 1925 and continued operation until 1995. Designed by Alexandre Vallaury to the modern standards of the day, the factory—which produced loose tobacco and cigarettes—employed women right from the start of operations. At times women outnumbered men two to one (Selen and O'Neil); another source reports that women and girls typically constituted around 70 percent of the employees (Z. Atasoy 2022).

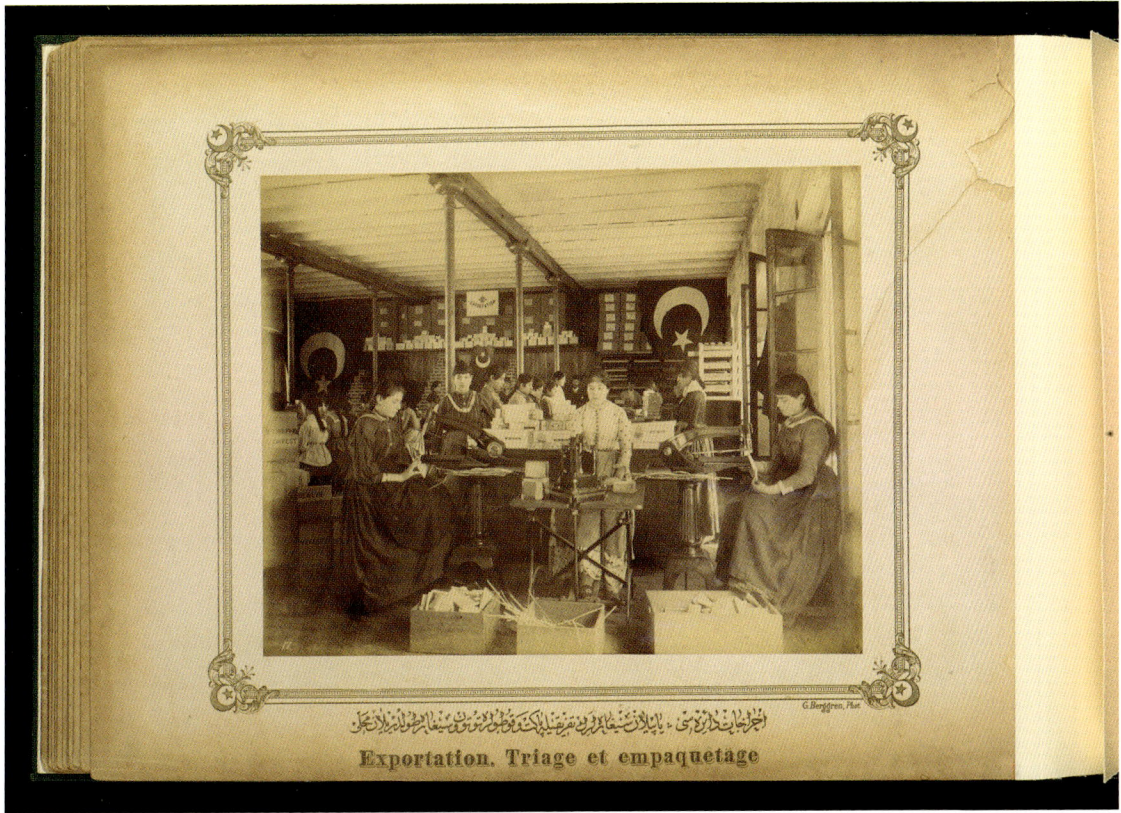

Figure 8.7 Exportation. Triage et empaquetage, in *Constantinople Manufacture Tabac*, Guillaume Berggren, early twentieth century. Los Angeles, Pierre de Gigord collection of photographs of the Ottoman Empire and the Republic of Turkey, Getty Research Institute, 96.R.14 (A15).

The Berggren album most likely dates from the first years of the twentieth century[5] and in its size and format (printed page mounts designed specifically for this album) closely resembles other official and quasi-official albums of the same period.[6] At least two copies of the album exist today, in the Getty Research Institute in Los Angeles and the Rezan Has Museum in Istanbul; others may well exist as it was presumably produced by Berggren in some quantity for distribution by the Régie.

The twenty-seven albumen prints in Berggren's album take the viewer on a methodical tour of the Cibali Régie factory, beginning with a view of the exterior from across the Golden Horne and moving through the steps involved in producing both loose tobacco and cigarettes, from the arrival of the tobacco to the packaging of the tobacco products. The photographs depict a calm, orderly, and clean workplace with modern machinery and busy workers, segregated by gender. Given the extremely tidy state of the workrooms and carefully posed figures of the workers demonstrating their tasks, it is clear that the workers were aware of the photographer, for whose work careful preparations had been made.

The seven photographs documenting women show groups of workers numbering from two to more than one hundred. Women and girls sifted tobacco, rolled cigarettes, filled packages, and did other similar work.[7] They are shown sitting or standing at their tasks, operating small machinery in some cases, and always observed by at least one male supervisor. Despite the constructed nature of the images, the photographs provide close views of the dress of more than two hundred girls and women. Later photographs from the factory show women wearing uniforms (ibid.), but that was not the case in this period. Most likely the workers were directed to appear appropriately and neatly dressed for the photographs, but even so the images give an unparalleled look at what these working women wore. A close look at these seven images reveals that some women appear in more than one, further indication of their staged nature.

Given the fact that the factory was located near Greek and Jewish neighborhoods and that none of the women are veiled in the presence of the male supervisors, it is reasonable to assume that the workers are mostly Greek or Jewish. (Muslim women began working in the factory later.) The clothing worn by the women pictured in Figure 8.7 is representative of what can be seen in the seven photographs: high-necked, long-sleeved dresses buttoning down the front with full skirts. In some cases, an overblouse and full skirt, generally not of matching fabric, are worn instead of a dress. Many of the dresses are trimmed with modest amounts of lace at the neck, yoke, and cuffs, and most workers are wearing aprons. Their hair is braided or worn up, and often covered with a kerchief, most likely to protect it from the ubiquitous tobacco dust of the factory.

Compared to what women factory workers in England and America wore at around the same time, these women are finely dressed, which I see as an indication that they were instructed to wear presentable clothes for the photographs. The light-colored dress with its lace-trimmed bodice worn by the woman standing in the center front of Figure 8.7 is particularly unsuitable for factory work. The clothes in these photographs are similar in style and decoration, if not in fabric, to those discussed above belonging to women in England (Figures 8.3 and 8.4) and would have been the pieces that the Cibali Régie factory workers had made or purchased for their private lives. The photographs of the Cibali Regie factory thus provide invaluable information about the dress of the factory women—not the clothes they would have worn to work, but the clothes for their own self-fashioning.

A dress in the collection of the Metropolitan Museum of Art (Figure 8.8) resembles the dresses worn by some of the women in the Cibali Regie photographs. Combining Ottoman and European dress traditions, the garment shares structural characteristics with the *bindallı* dresses considered in Chapter 4, with its round neck, front opening, *çantalı* gathers at the sides, the use of *peş* to add fullness to the skirt, and long sleeves. However, the dress also has a button closing at the front, unusual horizontal darts in the bodice front and back (most likely an attempt to create a slightly fitted bodice), and the sleeve ends are finished in the European manner, with cuffs and a neatly sewn placket. At least five different fabrics are used in the dress, most of which would have been of local or at least regional manufacture. The body of the dress is made from a vibrantly colored striped warp-faced weave with extra weft cotton motifs added in many of the stripes; sleeves are a red and white striped silk/cotton *çitari* (a sturdy cloth woven in Bursa and elsewhere). The rectangular pieces at the bodice sides and sleeve linings are coarser weave cottons with printed or woven designs, and the dress bodice and skirt are lined with plain muslin, pieced from different sources. Primarily constructed using a sewing machine, it also has some hand piecing and finishing, as well as a few instances of very rough mending done later in the dress's history. Apart from that mending and the replacement of two of the five buttons with slightly larger ones, the dress does not show significant signs of damage, although it appears to have been worn often. This striped dress shows a bold and colorful fashion sensibility despite the fact that the sewing is not particularly skillful. The odd horizontal darts on the back are not at all symmetrical in their placement, and the finishing of the skirt, with two erratic lines of top stitching encircling the hem, is very messy. When worn with an apron the dress would have closely resembled some of the clothing worn by women in the Cibali photograph.

Figure 8.8 Dress, early twentieth century. New York, Metropolitan Museum of Art, Gift of Irene Lewisohn and Alice Lewisohn Crowley, 1939 (C.I.39.91.36). Image copyright © The Metropolitan Museum of Art. Image source: Art Resource, NY.

In addition to the striped dress from the Metropolitan Museum of Art just discussed, I have found two other pieces that, based on fabric, style, and construction details, could well have belonged to Ottoman working women. The first of these is a two-piece outfit now in the collection of the National Museum of Scotland (Figure 8.9). Acquired in Afyon in western Anatolia in 1983 and dated circa 1900, according to Jennifer Scarce, the former curator of Middle Eastern cultures, National Museum of Scotland, the skirt and matching top are an intriguing combination of European and traditional construction techniques. Made of a bright fuchsia silk with silver brocade in a floral pattern, the garments were both machine and hand sewn. The hand sewing is roughly executed, nothing like the meticulous, highly skilled sewing seen on some of the Ottoman garments considered in previous chapters. Both the skirt and the top exhibit creativity in how they are constructed but a certain clumsiness in stitching and the way the fabric has been used. The skirt especially is very irregularly pieced, with selvages visible.

The long, full skirt is gathered into a fabric waistband, closing at the center back with hooks and eyes. Approximately five centimeters of the gathered skirt fabric has been turned inside at the waistband to create more fullness, a construction practice that was often used Euro-American tailoring in this period. (The two dresses discussed in Chapter 7 from the NMAAHC collection (Figure 7.10), as well as the dress in Figure 8.4 from Blaise, were all constructed in this way.) It was not something visible from the outside of the garment, so

Figure 8.9 Two-piece dress, *ca.* 1900. Edinburgh, National Museums of Scotland, 1983.349 a, b. Image © National Museums Scotland.

the person who made this garment would have had access to examples of such tailoring. The skirt, fully lined with muslin and about seventeen centimeters longer in the back, is finished at the lower edge with matching braid (a detail also seen in Figure 8.4) and a facing several centimeters deep of a salmon-colored cotton. Again, this is an intriguing combination of tailoring traditions: edging the skirt hem with braid to protect the fabric is a common practice in Euro-American sewing in this period; the use of a salmon-colored cotton as a facing for the skirt hems of *entaris* can be seen on many examples from earlier decades.

The matching top is also completely lined with muslin and displays an ambitious, complex construction. The muslin interior is boned, closing with hooks and eyes as well as an interior waist tape. A pleated bodice panel folds over the interior closing, fastening off center. Finally, the large, rounded collar folds over from the back and is held in place with two snaps. The bodice is carefully pieced and shaped with the curved seam allowances clipped so that they will lie flat, another tailoring technique invisible from the outside that would only be known to someone who had examined garments made in such a way. The set-in sleeves are very full at the shoulder, tapering toward the wrist, where they end in a diamond shape. The sleeve ends and collar are trimmed with a wide band of cotton lace, made of machine-made tape trim, shaped by hand into elaborate forms.[8] An irregular band of tulle has been tacked inside the collar edge as additional decoration.

This would have been a striking ensemble, and given the color, perhaps originally a wedding dress. Both pieces show signs of wear, an indication that the outfit was worn on many occasions, not just once. With the elaborately pleated and fitted bodice, fashionable sleeve profile, and generous proportions of the skirt, it was designed with an eye to current fashions, yet the construction techniques and irregular piecing suggest a seamstress of rather modest skill, perhaps even a home sewer. At the same time, whoever made these garments was familiar with European tailoring modes and incorporated them here. This single outfit reveals the fashion aspirations of a woman of modest means brought to life through the evolving skills of a local seamstress, working to adapt to the changing modes.

A dress from the Sadberk Hanım Museum displays a similar merging of European and Ottoman construction and decorative modes. The one-piece, full length dress (Figure 8.10) is made of a yellow silk and cotton mix, striped with bands of alternating widths, each comprised of a central repeating floral motif, framed by thin blue and white borders, and in the case of the wider band, a repeating triangular motif in purple. It is a simplified version of the striped *savai* fabrics of earlier times. The silver metallic thread used to decorate the cuffs, center front, and pocket, as well as the narrow braid used for edging the cuffs and pocket, is a more modest version of the elaborate trims used on Ottoman *entaris* and other garments.

The structure of the dress is a hybrid. It displays the round neck, front opening, and straight sleeves of *bindallı* dress construction. At the same time, the sleeves are neatly pleated into cuffs executed in the Euro-American manner, and the skirt of the dress is a separate piece of fabric, joined to the bodice and covered with a waistband. The dress is lined with plain muslin that has a brand stamp (an elaborate letter A) in gold near the hem. The skirt hem is finished with narrow green braid and an interior facing in a teal green cotton at a depth of approximately twelve centimeters. The pointed collar shape and button placket, carried out in black velvet and silver-wrapped thread, evoke a European style, but they are only decorative. The front opening of the dress, which extends below the waistband, closes with hooks and eyes. The construction of the dress is meticulous. The machine stitching used for most of the garment and decoratively at the waistband in a zigzag design in a contrasting color is confident and precise. Hand sewing is neat and regular. An intriguing garment, it seems likely that the dress was made by someone with well-developed sewing skills, in both hand and machine sewing, for a consumer of relatively modest means who desired a dress of familiar style with fashionable touches.

Figure 8.10 Dress, early twentieth century. Büyükdere, Courtesy of the Vehbi Koç Foundation, Sadberk Hanım Museum, 1764-K.288.

Dressing for the Street

Just as women's indoor clothing changed over the long nineteenth century, so did the garments they wore when appearing outdoors, on the street, in public parks, shopping, and going to the bath or to visit friends. Streetwear in Istanbul was "a social skin and a declaration of identity" (Zilfi 2010: 47). It was heavily scrutinized by the government and religious officials, and highly regulated. The sumptuary laws that regulated the clothing of Ottoman subjects had two main goals: to distinguish between Muslims and non-Muslims and to mark social hierarchies. Women of different religious groups were supposed to wear fabric in specific colors, often blue or black for non-Muslims and red or dark green for Muslims. The colors and shapes of shoes were regulated (non-Muslims could not wear yellow shoes of undyed leather, for example), and the use of furs, expensive fabric, and other signs of wealth was also policed (Görünür 2014; Zilfi 2019).

From the early sixteenth century into the twentieth century, Ottoman women out in public in Istanbul wore the *ferace* and *yaşmak*, a voluminous full-length coat and two-piece head covering usually made of a fine white fabric (Eryavuz 2023: 185). Heavier fabric, such as wool or broadcloth, was used for *feraces* worn in winter; lighter fabric would be used in the summer. The manuscript page illustrated in Figure 7.7 shows two examples of late-eighteenth-century outdoor wear, including the long, square collars of the *ferace*, which were a source of ongoing controversy. Women were taken to task for the extravagant use of fabric and conspicuous appearance of their garments. Contemporary documents record instances of outraged officials on the street cutting off collars they deemed too long (Zilfi 2010: 84). Despite the repeated decrees regarding their street wear, women continued to experiment with different *ferace* designs (narrow sleeves, fitted at the waist, floor-length collars), use bright colors instead of the dark colors prescribed by official regulation, and add braided trim, flounces, lace, and other ornaments to their *ferace*. In the 1858 image by Preziosi, *Turkish Women Walking* (Figure 3.19), the two main figures are wearing generously proportioned *ferace* in pastel shades, pink and blue respectively, with collars that reach nearly to the ground. Even the *ferace* of their servant following behind them has a similar collar, although of a drab greenish color.

As Ottoman women in Istanbul began adopting European fashions, their *ferace* also changed. In the snapshot illustrated in Chapter 5 (Figure 5.3) showing two women eating grapes in a garden dated circa 1890–1895, the figure on the left wears a fashionable *ferace*, very much in keeping with the times. Constructed of a light-colored fabric, the *ferace* has a wide, circular collar trimmed in three rows of darker braid with a decorative tie at the front and full sleeves. And in sharp contrast to the very full, loose sleeves of the *ferace* in the Preziosi image, in this example, the sleeves end in cuffs at the wrists, another feature borrowed from European fashion.

A painting by Osman Hamdi done in 1887, a few years earlier than the photograph illustrated in Figure 5.3, presents a panoply of *ferace* styles. Known as *Feraceli Kadınlar* [Ladies with Ferace or Women out Walking], the artist has arranged nine women in two slightly separated groups, promenading in front of the Mosque of Sultan Ahmed (Figure 8.11). The positioning of the women and their different poses shows off the elaborate lace trimmings and pleated flounces of their *ferace*. They are in a range of pastel and bright colors, silk in some cases (based on the way the fabric is reflecting light). The front edges of the *ferace* are no longer straight but cut away to reveal the fashionable dresses beneath. In every case where the dresses are visible, the dress fabric matches the *ferace*, an expensive wardrobe practice. A few women are wearing the bustles that became popular in the mid-1880s, with their *ferace* designed to accommodate the dress structure. But not everyone in the group had embraced that fashion—the figure in pale green shows no sign of having adopted the bustle. In this period, the *yaşmaks* had become particularly transparent, so the face of the wearer was clearly visible through the fabric. Some women draped them loosely enough so that their entire face was exposed. Eight women are carrying parasols, an accessory that became popular earlier in the century.

Figure 8.11 *Feraceli Kadınlar*, Osman Hamdi Bey, 1887. Istanbul, Yapı Kredi Bank Collection.

The ninth woman in the painting, almost exactly in the center of the composition, has a different kind of garment, the *çarşaf* (Figure 8.12). Worn by women in Syria, the *çarşaf* began to be adopted in Istanbul in 1872, and in 1889 the sultan decreed that wearing the *çarşaf* was mandatory (Eryavuz 2023: 187). It was thought that the *çarşaf* was more modest and thus more in keeping with Islamic precepts. Palace women and Ottoman women visiting the palace were allowed to continue wearing the *ferace* and *yaşmak* after men disguised by *çarşaf*s were caught trying to sneak into the palace (ibid.).

The *çarşaf* consists of a long, full skirt gathered at the waist and a cape that is joined at the waist to the skirt. It was held closed beneath the chin or nose of the wearer, and in some cases, a third piece of fabric, *peçe* or veil, was used to cover the face. The first examples from Syria were woven of striped fabric made in Damascus, but soon the *çarşaf* was being made in a variety of fabrics and with different kinds of styling. The example illustrated here is of a striped purple silk, both pieces cut on the bias and using the fabric stripes in a dramatic, eye-catching design. The front edge of the skirt, on the diagonal, is trimmed with wide satin ribbon and nine large ornamental buttons arranged in groups of three. The decorative treatment of the skirt is very similar to a two-piece dress from the Blaise Museum in Bristol, England (TA 1599), made of a navy alpaca wool with an asymmetrical skirt finish that includes four large ornamental buttons, an intriguing example of a decorative trend (the use of ornamental buttons) reaching fashion-forward women in widely disparate regions.

Over time the *çarşaf* took a range of shapes, responding to changes in fashion and women's circumstances. The skirts became narrower, hemlines rose, and capes became shorter and less voluminous. The *çarşaf* worn by "Miss Chocolate" in Figure 7.5 is a good example of a more modest version of the garment. During the tumultuous first two decades of the twentieth century, some women wore only the cape of the *çarşaf*, discarding

Figure 8.12 *Çarşaf* with cape, 1910s. Büyükdere, Courtesy of the Vehbi Koç Foundation, Sadberk Hanım Museum, 2612-K.30 a-c.

the long skirt. Non-Muslim women began wearing coats and hats instead of the *çarşaf*. Nevertheless, a traditional version of the *çarşaf* continued to be worn by women in Istanbul and Anatolia, where it can still be seen on the streets today.

Conclusion

Looking outside the Ottoman example to the dress of working women in Britain demonstrated the similarities in dress practices among these groups of women. In each case, despite the scarcity of surviving garments, it is clear that women of limited means were accomplished seamstresses who took an interest in fashion trends when creating their own garments. Related features of tailoring and finishing indicate a shared knowledge of contemporary garment construction across widely dispersed geographies. The three Ottoman dresses considered here reveal the fashion aspirations of a few nonelite Ottoman women, as well as the hybrid nature of dress style and construction in the late Ottoman period. I am confident that other dresses belonging to nonelite women, perhaps forgotten in museum storage or carefully saved in family cupboards, would help fill out the fashion history sketched here.[9]

The Ottoman women whose dress practices have been examined in the last three chapters, no matter what their economic or social standing, religious or ethnic identification, all lived through times of transformation and uncertainty. In the midst of political upheaval, the city itself was constantly changing, and refugees and foreigners were coming into the city as Armenians and others were fleeing. The pressure to be modern, however that was understood among different groups, was unceasing. The Balkan Wars, World War I, and the occupation of Istanbul by British, French, and Italian forces, all within the space of a decade (1912–1918), changed the lives of Istanbul residents forever. Women were pressed into service to replace men who had been called to the military; supplies, including fabric, were in short supply; and the city was filled with refugees and occupying forces. Their clothing choices reflected these circumstances. With the founding of the Turkish Republic in 1923, women's dress reform became a central tenet of the push to establish a modern state. The Türkiye of a century later looks very different than the Ottoman Empire it succeeded, but is it possible to find traces of Ottoman dress traditions in twenty-first century Türkiye?

EPILOGUE: THE AFTERLIFE OF OTTOMAN DRESS

With the declaration of the Republic of Türkiye in 1923, two tumultuous decades of political instability, war, economic privation, and foreign occupation came to an end, and the fledgling republic began the daunting work of claiming a new identity and building a new, modern state. In the first decades of the republic and in current scholarship about those decades, Turkish women are described as taking center stage in refashioning the new republic, both figuratively and literally.[1] In these early decades, women's clothing was regulated and subject to public debate to an unprecedented extent. Earlier regulations concerning women's dress had been primarily directed at their street garb, not what they wore at home. In the new republic, women were directed to discard their *çarsaf* and *peçe* (veil) and appear publicly in Western-style clothing, thus extending the reach of the new state into women's private wardrobe choices. Images of "modern" Turkish women were widely published in the press and popular periodicals, modeling the new Republican national identity locally and globally.

For the women in urban centers who had already adopted European-style clothing, the new regulations would not have required a significant change in their dress practices, but for many others, the transition would have been challenging. Most likely the changes were gradual, with the familiar traditional clothing worn at home and the "modern" attire worn outside.

And indeed, traditional forms of dress persisted throughout the twentieth century among some Turkish women, especially in rural areas of Anatolia, as the postcard from the 1980s demonstrates (Figure 9.1). But it was not only the traditional dress of rural women that continued to be worn in modern Türkiye: here I consider two examples of the long and perhaps unexpected echoes of elite, urban Ottoman dress in contemporary Türkiye, each with their own resonances with the Ottoman past and contemporary associations.

The Afterlife of Ottoman Dress: *Bindallı* Dresses

The *bindallı* dress, which played such a significant part in the fashion transformation in the mid-nineteenth century as discussed in Chapter 4, continued to be worn for weddings well into the twentieth century. Günay's 1986 book *Historical Costumes of Turkish Women*, a project that collected and photographed examples of traditional dress still being worn, included dozens of examples of wedding outfits from across Turkiye. Many of these outfits included *bindallı* garments. Folklorist Adem Koç's 2010 article described the dress worn then by women at Kutahya weddings, *bindallı* dresses, *şalvar* and *cepken* with metallic thread embroidery, and *tepebaşı entaris*, newly made by dressmakers specializing in traditional garments, or older pieces borrowed or rented for the occasion (Koç 2012: 190–98).

Bindallı outfits, worn in large numbers by women across Anatolia and the Balkans as well as in Syria and Egypt for decades beginning in the middle of the nineteenth century, were saved and passed down, eventually sold or given away. They are among the most numerous examples of women's dress to be found in museum collections in Türkiye as well as in museums outside the country. In the first half of the twentieth century, and perhaps longer, apart from its value as a beautiful, lavishly embroidered garment, the *bindallı* dress became

Figure 9.1 Postcard sent from Anatolia in 1989, with comment by costume historian Patricia Baker that the dress illustrated was commonly seen in Eastern Türkiye. Collection of the author.

an object of nostalgia, evoking customs and family members of the past. The dress-up photograph of Ayhan (Figure 4.2) from Chapter 4 taken in a photographer's studio is a reminder of the sentimental appeal of the dress, as is a photograph of a young woman from an Amasra family dressed as her mother or grandmother might have been in a *bindallı* outfit, headscarf trimmed with oya, and wearing a necklace of gold coins. In the book where the photograph appears, *Cumhuriyet'in Aile Albümleri [Family Albums of the Republic]*, it is presented as an example of the nostalgia of the younger generation for their mother's historical (*tarihsel*) clothes (Sakaoğlu 1998: 51).

In the twentieth century, the *bindallı* dress also took on a new identity as an element of folk costume, worn by folk dancing groups and others (Figure 9.2). Türkiye has a rich dance tradition with distinct regional varieties that has continued to thrive in the Republican period. Regional dance varieties are accompanied by regional costume traditions, including *bindallı* dresses (And 1976). Although not worn initially as a dance costume, in the twentieth century *bindallı* dresses seem to have become more all-purpose garments, signifying tradition and connection with the past. The postcard in Figure 9.2, purchased in the early 1980s and likely dating a few decades earlier, documents the transformation of the *bindallı* dress from a wedding garment to a dance costume.

The *kına gecesi*, or henna night, has long been a component of Turkish wedding celebrations, and in Ottoman times, other religious groups adopted the tradition. Usually taking place the night before the wedding, the

Figure 9.2 *Bindallı* folk dance, mid-twentieth century, postcard. Collection of the author.

kına gecesi was when female friends and relatives of the bride came together to celebrate the bride, say good-bye before she moved to her husband's family, and decorate her hands with henna for good luck.

Bindallı dresses were often worn at this event by the bride as well as close relatives. Although twentieth-century weddings, especially in urban settings, have not always included a *kına gecesi*, the ceremony has become more popular in the past few decades as weddings have become more elaborate. The *bindallı* dress is still described as being the traditional choice for the bride to wear for her *kına gecesi*, but a nineteenth-century guest at a modern ceremony would hardly recognize the bride's outfit as a *bindallı* dress. Although some brides choose to wear a traditional *bindallı* dress, historic garments in some cases (Figure 9.3), often the bride prefers something more modern. A 2017 article in *Daily Sabah* describes current thinking about *kına gecesi* outfits, quoting the bride who was interviewed for the article:

While the traditional "bindallı," a caftan-like red or green costume that is designed especially for henna nights, was typically worn by the bride-to-be, nowadays girls in the upcoming generations prefer to wear at least two costumes in addition to the "bindallı," which has since expanded to include a wide range of colors and styles. Even international and national fashion designers like Alexander McQueen, Ellie Saab, Nur Yerlitaş and Cemil İpekçi are being hired to design these special costumes … "I am only getting married once, so I want everything to be of the highest standard. I want my dress to be similar to a designer's piece."

(Kutlu and Gürbüz-Nurefşan, January 21, 2017)

Figure 9.3 Sadberk Hanım on right with three friends, wearing *bindallı* dresses, 1931. Büyükdere, Vehbi Koç Foundation, Sadberk Hanım Museum.

Sadberk Hanım (standing on the right), Jan. 14th 1931, Kadıköy.

The website of Oleg Cassini, a popular international fashion house specializing in wedding and evening wear that is very successful in Türkiye, has a page described as the most comprehensive guide to the *kına gecesi*. It describes the meaning of the night, the different components, a music play list, and perhaps most importantly, what to buy in preparation for the event, including these suggestions for the bride's outfit:

> The bindalli, the traditional outfit worn by the bride on a henna night, is usually red, green or navy blue and has silver or gold embroidery on it.

> Those who do not prefer traditional clothing can choose from henna evening dress models for their henna night. Depending on the location of the henna night, the concept of the night and the bride's body type, one of the straight, mermaid or princess cut evening dresses can be preferred.

> In both options, the dominant color of the henna night is known to be red. Since red represents love, affection and belonging, brides-to-be prefer red on this special day. https://olegcassini.com.tr/blog/kina-gecesi-nedir-gelenekler-nelerdir-en-kapsamli-rehber.

The gowns illustrated on the site are all red, all modern evening wear with no references to the traditional *bindallı* dress, and no suggestions are provided for sourcing a more traditional kind of dress, hardly surprising because the business of the website is selling the company's dresses. The modern *bindallı* dresses considered to be more traditional, available on many sites online, bear little resemblance to the original garments, apart from a preponderance of red, navy blue, and green and the lavish use of gold-colored ornament. As an evocation of an Ottoman dress tradition, in the modern weddings described in today's press and in shop windows, the *bindallı* dress survives in its association with weddings, particularly the *kına gecesi*, and a remembrance of the colors and gold embroidery used in the original *bindallı* dresses.

The Afterlife of Ottoman Dress: Fashion Tastemakers, the Twenty-First Century Version

In the 1990s, Türkiye's Ottoman past began to play a new role in the country's sense of identity, a trend that materialized in the twenty-first century into the different but overlapping Neo-Ottomanism and Ottomania. Under Recep Tayyip Erdogan's ruling Justice and Development Party (*Adalet ve Kalkınma Partisi*, or AKP) Neo-Ottomanism can be defined as "a political project aimed at reviving the Ottoman past in a variety of domains, including the urban fabric, anniversary celebrations, and foreign policy" (Ergin and Karakaya 2017: 34). Ottomania, on the other hand, describes a fascination with all things Ottoman, in the realm of popular culture—television programs, Ottoman-style hotels, jewelry, Iznik-inspired ceramics, bath products, table linens, and more. Neo-Ottomanism and Ottomania both engage with versions of the Ottoman past, using varying visions of that past to serve contemporary ends; as an important cultural signifier, fashion has played a key role in both. Turkish television, too, has become a space where competing versions of the Ottoman past are presented and debated.

A key series in these debates has been *The Magnificent Century* [*Muhteşem Yüzyıl*], which follows the reign of Sultan Süleyman (r. 1520–1566), known in the West as Süleyman the Magnificent and as Süleyman the Lawgiver in his own realm. The political events of Suleyman's reign are the framework for the narrative, which is centered on the imperial household and the relationships among its various inhabitants. The show ran for four seasons, 2011–2014, 139 episodes, and attracted an audience of five hundred million, being shown in more than seventy countries (Ulusoy and Atalay 2023: 117). One of the most popular Turkish television programs ever produced, *The Magnificent Century* played a large part in the phenomenal growth of the international market for Turkish television. Since then Türkiye has become a top provider of global television content, ahead of Russia, Brazil, Mexico, and the United States (Çevik 2019). Given the show's popularity, the international reach of the program, and its subject—one of the most revered Ottoman sultans—the scrutiny (and criticism) that the show received for its portrayal of Suleyman was not surprising. In 2012 then-Prime Minister Erdogan was quoted in the newspaper *Hürriyet* as follows:

> we don't have ancestors like the ones shown on TV. We don't know such Suleiman the Lawmaker. We don't know such Suleiman the Magnificent. He spent thirty years of his life on horseback. His life was nothing like the one depicted in the show … I object to the screenwriters and directors of that show. We have brought this up with the relevant offices and we are waiting for them to take the necessary steps. This is unacceptable. No one has the right to mess with this nation's values and if they do the nation should respond within the law.

> *(Çevik 2019 :7)*

The show's producers were able to continue with the show, creating content that was consistent with their vision, without falling too far afoul of Neo-Ottomanism's more conservative visions of Ottoman history. With its meticulously designed sets, almost exactly replicating spaces in the Topkapı Palace, stunning costumes, and dramatic, engaging narrative, *The Magnificent Century* was a driving force behind Ottomania.

The Magnificent Century and other Turkish *dizi* (television drama series) are part of a larger genre of costume dramas, television series and movies in which costume, often historic, plays a significant role in conveying the identity of the characters and in the overall popularity of the program. *Downton Abbey*, *Bridgerton*, *The Crown*, and *The Gilded Age*, to name only a few, are all examples of recent television series (and in the case of *Downton Abbey*, movie spin-offs) where costume has a central place in the production. In all these projects, the work of the costume designers and their teams is to shape the viewer's perception of the characters through their dress. A tension always exists between historic truth and viewer appeal—to create an emotional link between viewer and character, the clothes need to be familiar, not obscure or confusing. For *Bridgerton*, a Netflix series set in London between 1813 and 1837 and commissioned for four seasons, the head costume designer, Ellen Mirojnick, describes her engagement with the historical period as "aspirational rather than historically accurate" (Seth 2020). Her team of 238 created an astounding five thousand costumes for the first season in 2020; the fantastical fashions of Bridgerton's characters, only tenuously connected to the historical reality of period dress, are one of the most popular aspects of the series.

In the case of *The Magnificent Century*, the costume designer, Serdar Başbuğ, made very specific choices about how to present the women of the harem, particularly Hürrem, who became the wife of Suleyman. He wanted to create a "stylized, eye-pleasing, modern Ottoman" aesthetic (Ulusoy and Atalay 2023: 123). For example, although women in the sixteenth century would have worn their hair in multiple tiny, long braids, the harem women in the television program have the luxurious, loosely curled hair that is the modern standard of beauty for Turkish women. Similarly, sixteenth-century women would have worn multiple layers of bulky clothing, presenting a robust silhouette quite out of keeping with today's ideal body shapes. The women in *The Magnificent Century* are dressed in close-fitting, low-cut dresses in a range of colors and with elaborate gold embroidery and other ornamentation (Figure 9.4). In one of her interviews about the show's

Figure 9.4 Meryam Uzerli as Hürrem Sultan, with other cast members. *Muhteşem Yüzyıl/The Magnificent Century*.

costume design, Başbuğ said that the costumes of the series "were designed to be talked about and resonated in the public opinion of Turkey the day after each episode was shown" (quoted in ibid.:122).

The designer was successful in that goal—the costumes in the series attracted attention all over the world, not just in Türkiye. The lack of historical accuracy generated complaints about the costumes from the beginning of the series' broadcast (ibid.: 121), to the degree that after the first episodes the low-cut dresses worn by some of the women were modified to be less revealing (Çevik 2019: 233). On the other hand, the popularity of the costumes on the program also led to "Hürrem Sultan" fashion, an international movement based on the costumes, jewelry, and makeup of the show's female characters, particularly Hürrem. An article from the Turkish newspaper *Hurriyet* in 2012 about the new industry created by the impact of *The Magnificent Century* costumes quotes a fashion designer from Izmir, Yavuz Göktetekin, who says that he was unable to keep up with orders for the Hürrem fashions.[2] His clients want to wear them for henna nights instead of the modern *bindallı* dresses worn in recent years, for circumcision ceremonies, and other special events.

Seeing Hürrem fashions in Istanbul bridal shops I wondered who bought them, whether they were replacing the white bridal gowns of previous decades, and how brides and merchants alike saw the relationship of these gowns to Ottoman fashions of the past (Figure 9.5). So, on a gray weekday afternoon in February 2024, a Turkish friend and I visited a street in the Fatih neighborhood of Istanbul that is a center for bridal fashion. We stopped into three places, each with a different business structure. One was a small, high-end designer boutique, one a large showroom for off-the-rack dresses produced in Izmit, and one a mid-level shop with a

Figure 9.5 Gown, February 2024. Fatih bridal shop, Istanbul, photo by the author.

wide selection of dresses made locally and in Izmir. The shops were mostly empty, and the shopkeepers were happy to chat with us.

Our afternoon's visits were not a comprehensive survey, but we did learn quite a bit about the bridal fashion business in Istanbul, which has expanded significantly in recent years. Although brides are interested in buying more than one dress, and want high-fashion looks, the competition among the ever-increasing number of shops makes it difficult for the businesses to be commercially successful. Hürrem fashion gowns are worn by Turkish brides for their *kına gecesi* parties, although they are also purchased by visiting Arab women, who wear them for parties more generally. White wedding dresses in the styles that can be seen in bridal shops in the major cities of Europe and the United States are worn for the actual wedding ceremony.

The responses to our questions about the relationship of current bridal fashion to television programs or the Ottoman past were fascinating. Filiz *hanım*, who had been selling bridal fashions in the mid-level shop for at least a decade, was clear about the fact that wedding dresses in Türkiye had always been white and that the Hürrem fashion dresses being worn for *kına gecesi* were traditional in their appearance. Nothing had changed. The sales staff in the showroom referred us to their management in Izmit, not wanting to express opinions about their stock. The designer in the boutique was the most articulate and thoughtful about the trends she had tracked among her clients. Although she could see a relationship between Turkish television fashion and bridal fashion trends, she found other popular culture forces more significant, particularly what her clients knew of bridal dress trends in fashion cities such as New York, Paris, and London.

Costume designer Başbuğ describes Hürrem fashion as "stylized and modern Ottoman" (Ulusoy and Atalay 2023: 123), but in fact it is difficult to find any traces of actual Ottoman dress in the clothes created as part of Hürrem fashion. And is that even the point? After all, what is the appeal of these fashions? Only minor details of these garments can be traced back to Ottoman women's dress, but for those who see them as "Hürrem fashion" they nonetheless evoke a romanticized version of an Ottoman past as lived by a beautiful, powerful woman. For others, such as Filiz *hanım*, they understand the modern day *bindallı* dress, whatever it's resemblance to the historic garments, as a link to a time-honored wedding tradition going back to their mothers' and grandmothers' days. In either case, these wedding fashions are a dramatic reminder of the power of clothing in performing an identity, even for just a day.

NOTES

Chapter 1

1   It is impossible to mention individually all the important articles on Ottoman women's dress that have informed this work. I have found articles by Nurhan Atasoy, Anastasia Falierou, Lale Görünür, Selin İpek, Draginja Maskareli, Jennifer Scarce, and Hülya Tezcan particularly valuable; see the bibliography for a more complete list.

2   An important exception are the letters written by royal Ottoman women and their female liaisons in the early modern period, a discussion of which is included in Thys-Şenocak 2022 and Barzilai-Lumbroso.

3   Lou Taylor, a key figure in shaping dress history of the past two decades, describes this as the "actuality of clothing," the study of which she asserts is central to dress history, as cited by Charlotte Nicklas and Annebella Pollen, "Dress History Now: Terms, Themes and Tools," in *Dress History. New Directions in Theory and Practice*, ed. Charlotte Nicklas and Annebella Pollen (London: Bloomsbury Academic, 2015), 5.

4   The dress and its matching jacket were collected by Sadberk Koç (d. 1973), the woman after whom the Sadberk Hanım Museum is named and whose collection formed the basis of the museum's holdings when it opened in 1980. By the time she acquired the outfit, most likely from a shop in the bazaar or a dealer, it had already passed from being an actively worn garment, albeit for special occasions or folk celebrations, to an object of historical curiosity or perhaps souvenir. Her purchase of the garment guaranteed it another chapter in its long history: that of museum object, available for study and display.

5   For more on the Ottoman "pictorial turn," see Ersoy 2016 and Ersoy and Türker 2023.

6   Orientalist photos of harem women have been well-studied; for one examination of this material, see Micklewright 2010.

7   Here I am following the categories articulated by Zilfi 2010, chap. 1. She includes a fifth population category: Abode of War (meaning foreign places) versus Abode of Islam, which is less relevant here.

8   Recognizing gender as a social construct and the inadequacy of a binary classification in describing human experience, much more research is needed before it is possible to move beyond a binary gender construct in works such as this.

9   For scholarship on the social history and communal relations of Istanbul in this area, see the pathbreaking 1991 work on Istanbul households by Alan Duben and Cam Behar, the 2010 book *A Social History of Ottoman Istanbul* by Boyar and Fleet, and numerous works by Suraiya Faroqhi, too many to name individually.

10   Detailed research into the shifting makeup and overall numbers of Istanbul's population underlies a substantial amount of work in economic and social history. Here I am relying on Duben and Behar, S. Shaw 1977 and 1979, and Karpat 1985.

11   Detailed information about the locations of census figures, as well as challenges involved with using the data, are provided in each of the sources noted in the previous footnote.

12   For the historiography of work on slavery in the Ottoman Empire, see Faroqhi 2017, Toledano 2007, and Zilfi 2010, chap. 4.

13   In Ehud Toledano's 2007 book, *As if Silent and Absent, Bonds of Enslavement in the Islamic Middle East*, he wrote about Mustafa Olpak (1953–2016), an Afro-Turk who became very interested in the mostly overlooked histories of African slaves in the Ottoman Empire. Olpak published two books, a 2002 family memoir and in 2005, *Kenya-Girit-İstanbul: köle kıyısından insan biyografileri (Kenya-Crete-Istanbul: Human Biographies from the Slave Coast)*. In 2006 he founded a nonprofit organization, Africans' Culture and Solidarity Association, which aims to bring

together Afro-Turks and conduct research on Afro-Turk heritage. It holds an annual festival, the Calf festival, which is related to the festivals Africans held in Istanbul during the Ottoman period. http://afroturkler.com/iletisim/.

14 Key sources on the Ottoman harem include Leslie Peirce's 1993 work, T*he Imperial Harem. Women and Sovereignty in the Ottoman Empire*, and multiple publications by Betül İpşirli Argıt and Madeline Zilfi. For the physical space and functioning of the Topkapi Palace harem, see Gülru Necipoğlu 1992, *Architecture, Ceremonial, and Power: The Topkapi Palace in the Fifteenth and Sixteenth Centuries*, especially chap. 3. For royal women as patrons and consumers, see Thys-Şenocak 2022 and Artan.

Chapter 2

1 There is now an extensive bibliography on women in the Ottoman Empire, too extensive to list here. For my project, the work of Betül İpşirli Argıt, Suraiya Faroqhi, Elizabeth Frierson, Leslie Peirce, and Madeline Zilfi has been particularly important.

2 The most important of these for this project are Banquet of Distinguished Turkish Women, Ladies' Outing at Hünkar Iskeleci along the Bosporus, Turkish Women in the Countryside near Istanbul, Wedding procession on the Bosporus, Armenian wedding; Greek wedding, Lying-in Room of a Distinguished Turkish Woman, all in the Rijksmuseum; and Women drinking coffee, in the Pera Museum. (The titles used here are taken from the respective museum records and do not always match titles used in publications.)

3 *Woman at her Embroidery Frame* is in the Rijksmuseum (SK-A-2042), and *Jewish Woman* is in a private collection. Both are reproduced in Nefedova, p. 120.

4 See Smentek and Compagnon for a discussion of Liotard's place in the artistic community of Pera during his residence there.

5 Suzanne Compagnon's 2023 dissertation, "Clothing and Pictorial Representation in Eighteenth-Century Ottoman Painting: The Levnī and Buhārī Single Figures," makes an important contribution to scholarship on both Bukhari and Levni.

6 Here I am following the chronology laid out in Eldem 2012.

7 See Behdad 2016; Behdad and Gartlan, eds., 2013; Çelik and Edhem, eds., 2015; and Micklewright 2013, 2011, 2010.

8 Using one photograph to stand in for a much larger group of images can be a risky enterprise, but in this case, I am claiming the prerogative of experience.

9 https://projectsave.catalogaccess.com/people/19201.

10 For more on Ali Sami, see Çizgen 1989 and Öztuncay 2003.

11 See also the 2024 book by Richard Ansell, *Servants Abroad: Travel Journals by British Working People*.

12 See Bardakçı 2017; Brookes 2008; Lewis and Micklewright for an introduction to the sources more generally.

13 This is not a conclusive list. Clothing dating from the Ottoman period has also been collected by museums in areas that were once part of the Ottoman empire: the Balkans, Greece, and what were the Arab provinces. There are also examples of Ottoman dress in European and American museums other than those mentioned here.

14 See particularly work by Wendy K. Shaw and Nilay Özlü (full citations in the bibliography).

15 For costume, see Atasoy et al. 2001, Atasoy 2011, 2012, and 2023; Baker et al. 1996; İpek 2009a and 2012; Rogers et al. 1986; and numerous works by Tezcan.

16 See Tezcan 1992; Görünür 2010 and 2014; Görünür. 2023; and Bilgi. 2023.

17 https://uluumay.com/index.

18 https://www.hurriyetdailynews.com/museum-reveals-ottoman-folk-dresses-and-jewelry-22708 (accessed March 5, 2024).

19 https://hansonsauctioneers.co.uk/queen-victorias-boots-and-royal-outfit-sell-for-thousands-and-are-saved-for-the-nation/#:~:text=Queen%20Victoria%20was%20born%20in,enjoy%20for%20years%20to%20come.%E2%80%9D (accessed January 26, 2023).

20 https://www.hrp.org.uk/about-us/conservation-and-collections/royal-ceremonial-dress-collection/ (accessed January 26, 2023).

21 "The London Museum Has Many Treasures," *New York Times*, April 7, 1912. https://timesmachine.nytimes.com/timesmachine/1912/04/07/issue.html (accessed January 26, 2023).

22 https://www.museumoflondon.org.uk/about-us/our-organisation (accessed January 26, 2023).

23 https://www.vam.ac.uk/blog/caring-for-our-collections/the-curator-queen-queen-mary-and-the-va (accessed January 16, 2023).

24 Strasdin ibid.: 138; "Diana Reborn," https://www.vanityfair.com/style/1997/07/princess-diana-reborn (accessed January16,2023).

25 Save Our African American Treasures involved Smithsonian staff, collaborating with local museums and educational institutions, hosting thirteen programs around the United States. At each site, museum staff led workshops about preserving family treasures, collecting family histories, and as Bunch describes it, encouraging people to "bring out your stuff." Smithsonian curators and conservators met with people to talk about what they had brought, and during the conversation the conservator made an archival box to hold the object brought in by the attendee to take home.

26 https://www.ideastream.org//news/national-museum-of-african-american-history-and-culture-celebrates-1-year (accessed April 17, 2023).

27 In the United States these include the Armenian Museum of America in Watertown, Massachusetts, and the Ararat-Eskijian Museum and Research Center in Mission Hills, California, among others.

Chapter 3

1 I found Compagnon's discussion of the performativity of Levni's figures enlightening in thinking about how fabric and costume more broadly are depicted in his work. Compagnon 2023: 135.

2 This work exists in at least three very close copies, one in the Rijksmuseum, one in the Musee d'Art et d'Histoire in Geneva, and this example from the Metropolitan Museum of Art. In addition, Liotard used a similar pose for other portraits, and others of his sitters appeared in these clothes.

3 https://collections.vam.ac.uk/item/O180191/robe-unknown/ (accessed January 23, 2024).

4 SHM 141155-K.813, and Museum of Fine Arts, 44.758

5 Two very similar garments can be seen in the Sadberk Hanım Museum collection (SHM 10331-K.431 and SHM 19334-K.1604). In 10331-K.431, the floral design of the all-over embroidery, executed on a fine white cotton, closely resembles the MMA example, including the graceful ribbon looped throughout the design. The garment's edges are similarly finished with a laid cord design and elaborate floral passementerie, both in colors dyed to match the embroidery. A third garment of this type is on display at the Museum of Turkish and Islamic Art, Env. No. 2617.

Chapter 4

1 Although nearly every provincial museum in Türkiye seems to own at least one example of a *bindallı* garment, the most extensive collections are found in the Sadberk Hanım Museum in Büyükdere, as well as the Ethnography Museum in Ankara. The Metropolitan Museum of Art in New York has a smaller but important collection.

2 See Krody 2000: 40–44 for a full explanation of *dival* work.

3 Plunkett, "Of Hype and Type: The Media Making of Queen Victoria 1837–1845."

4   Lee, "1840—Queen Victoria's Wedding Dress."

5   Brennan, "A Natural History of the Wedding Dress"; Lee, "1840—Queen Victoria's Wedding Dress"; Staniland and Levey, Santina, *Queen Victoria's Wedding Dress and Lace*.

6   1979.346.87a,b; https://www.metmuseum.org/art/collection/search?q=1979.346.87a%2Cb.

7   Personal examination by the author, June 23, 2021.

8   For a fuller discussion, see Duben and Behar 1991 and Zilfi 2009, among others.

9   See https://www.houshamadyan.org/mapottomanempire/vilayetofmamuratulazizharput/kaza-of-agn/local-characteristics/attire.html (accessed March 22, 2024).

10 Public opinion regarding polygyny (the more accurate term in the Ottoman context because women never had more than one husband at the same time) became increasingly negative in the late nineteenth century. The Family Law of 1917 essentially guaranteed women the right to forbid their husbands from taking a second wife, and the practice was outlawed with the passing of the Turkish Civil Code in 1926 (Behar 1991, 478).

11 I am very grateful to the Ararat-Eskijian Museum and Research Center in Mission Hills, California, for kindly allowing me to reproduce this image here.

12 Dautović, "Funerary Photography as a Source for the Dress of Sephardic Jews in Belgrade: From Traditional Costumes to Civil Emancipation," Maskareli, *The Fashion World of the Kalef Family*; and https://fyeaheasterneurope.tumblr.com/post/21200873158/young-jewish-girl-dressed-in-a-characteristically, among others.

13 https://www.theopavlidis.com/ and https://www.theopavlidis.com/AsiaMinor/kermira.pdf.

Chapter 5

1   A full discussion of the book is beyond what I can undertake here; see the excellent article by Marilyn Booth and A. Holly Shissler, "Fatma Aliye's Nisvan-ı Islam: Istanbul, Paris, Beirut, Cairo, 1891–96," in *Ottoman Translations Circulating Translations from Bombay to Paris*, ed. Marilyn Booth and Claire Savina (Edinburgh: Edinburgh University Press, 2023), 327–88.

2   For an overview of the expanded public presence of Ottoman women in this period, see Fleet 2016 and other articles in the same volume, Boyar and Fleet 2016.

3   This photograph is one of a group of fifty-three snapshot-type photos, taken of a family and friends in the period between about 1895 and 1905 (the dating is based on the women's dress). See Micklewright 2010 and 2013.

4   Tezcan 1999, as well as Eryavuz, Falierou, and İpek, among others.

5   Similar practices obtained for American women; see Block 2021.

6   "Laciverdi kadife bu resimi aynı biçesun. Arka etek arşun beş ön etek arşun dört. Açkır (?) nam kumaş bu resimde biçulup dikilecekdir. Arka etek arşun beş ön etek arşun dört" (Tezcan: 86). Translation from Ottoman Turkish to modern Turkish was made by Tezcan; the English translation is mine.

7   Printemps opened in Paris in 1865 and within three years began mail-order sales. According to the store's website, by the beginning of the twentieth century, mail-order business accounted for 25 percent of sales, and eleven million catalogs had been sent out across the globe. https://www.groupe-printemps.com/histoire (accessed February 5, 2024).

8   http://cavafy.onassis.org/object/8fz6-cbck-b5q4/.

9   For an introduction to the growing body of literature on these periodicals, see Başcı 2004, Karaman 2016, and Özgül online edition, 2019. For the *Hanımlara Mahsus Gazete* in particular, see Frierson and Enis.

10 See Burçak 2023 for a full discussion of "The question of the corset."

11 The Gracie stores opened in 1845 in a two-story building next to the Russian Embassy; by 1848, when the Bon Ton ads were running, it had become Le Bazar Parisien. https://www.levantineheritage.com/book18.htm.

12 The mechanics of this international purchasing process are described in Coleman 1989 and Block 2021.

13 Lady Layard's Journal, https://pops.baylor.edu/layard/xml.php?fn=18780614.xml (accessed April 16, 2024).

Chapter 6

1 For comparative examples, see Edwards 2017.

2 *Eid al-Fitr* celebrates the end of the holy month of Ramadan; *Eid al-Adha* marks the willingness of Abraham to sacrifice his son.

3 A *houri* is the pure female companion of paradise in Islam, but in popular usage, also a beautiful maiden.

4 https://www.metmuseum.org/art/collection/search/81112.

5 https://pops.baylor.edu/layard/xml.php?fn=18771206.xml.

Chapter 7

1 Linda Baumgarten's "Clothes for the People: Slave Clothing in Early Virginia," in the *Journal of Early Southern Decorative Arts* 14 (1988): 27–70, was groundbreaking. In the past two decades, scholarship on the dress practices of African American enslaved people has reached a critical mass. There are too many invaluable sources to list here, but I have found the following particularly useful: Martha B. Katz-Hyman and Kym S. Rice, *World of a Slave: Encyclopedia of the Material Life of Slaves in the United States* (Santa Barbara, CA: Greenwood, 2011); Elizabeth Way, ed., *Black Designers in American Fashion* (London: Bloomsbury Visual Arts, 2021), 1–10; Lois K. Alexander, *Blacks in the History of Fashion* (New York: Harlem Institute of Fashion, 1982); and the rich assortment of work by Jonathan Michael Square.

2 I first heard this idea elegantly elucidated by Elaine Nichols, senior curator for culture at NMAAHC, in a talk she gave about the American fashion designer Ann Lowe in 2023.

3 The year 1619 is the date most often cited as the first arrival of enslaved Africans to what became the United States, but the Spanish had brought enslaved Africans to North America in the sixteenth century. See https://guides.loc.gov/slavery-in-america for more information.

4 https://www.loc.gov/rr/geogmap/placesinhistory/archive/2011/20110318_slavery.html (accessed April 6, 2023).

5 Argit says this about other income for enslaved palace women: "Members of the imperial harem, from the top level down, were paid salaries during their stay in the palace. These salaries were one of the sources of their wealth. Additionally, some women were assigned land grants (has). … At the end of the eighteenth century and into the nineteenth, some palace women also had a share from Istanbul customs. Other sources of wealth included bequests and charitable endowments. The position and status of the palace women's husbands also had an impact on their material wealth, as would inheritances transferred from their husbands' estates" (Argit 2020: 168).

6 In his 2021 blog post, Kelbaugh mentions three copies of this image: the one in his collection, now in the National Gallery of Art; a second one whose location is not given; and the third, which is in Special Collections at Louisiana State University (LSU). Each copy has a slightly different caption written on the back. The one in a photograph album at LSU identifies the subject as "Contraband Camp, formerly used as a Female Seminary." Purchased by a Union soldier in the spring of 1863, the album was intended to document the presence of the Union Army and the impact of the war on Baton Rouge. A second copy of the image, in the National Gallery of Art, identifies the site as the Bullard Plantation. Ross Kelbaugh, "Free at Last," *Military Images Digital* (blog), August 31, 2021, https://www.militaryimagesmagazine-digital.com/2021/08/31/free-at-last/ (accessed March 27, 2023). Although the National Gallery copy has been dated 1864, an 1863 date seems more likely given the information in the LSU Special Collections.

7   On the subject of Civil War contraband camps, see Chandra Manning. "Contraband Camps and the African American Refugee Experience during the Civil War," in *Oxford Research Encyclopedia of American History*, 2017. https://doi.org/10.1093/acrefore/9780199329175.013.203.

8   https://www.historicnorthampton.org/chaotic-freedom-3.html (accessed March 27, 2023).

9   These two statements present an unequivocal example of the impact of author attitude and research on the interpretation of the same image and are a reminder of the importance of considering the source of any description of a photograph or other visual document.

10 For more about the slave trade from Africa to Istanbul, see Ehud Toledano, *The Ottoman Slave Trade and Its Suppression*; and Eva Troutt Powell, *Tell This in My Memory, Stories of Enslavement from Egypt, Sudan, and the Ottoman Empire*.

11 Grace Ellison was an English feminist and journalist who made multiple trips to Istanbul, producing a wide range of written material (memoirs, newspaper articles, biography) about what she encountered and coediting the work of two Turkish women, Hadidje Zennour and Noury eel-Nissa (writing under the pseudonyms Zeyneb and Malek Hanoum). Heffernan and Lewis 2007.

12 The two best-known illustrated copies of the Zenanname are in the British Library, Or.7094, and the Istanbul University Library, T.5502.

13 Costume albums have received a great deal of scholarly attention, a full account of which is outside the bounds of this work. For a detailed investigation of this genre, see Gwendolyn Collaço's unpublished dissertation, *The Image as Commodity: The Commercial Market for Single-Folio Paintings in Ottoman Istanbul, 17th–18th Centuries*, Harvard University, 2020.

14 Preziosi (1816–1882) was born in Malta but spent most of his adult life in Istanbul, where he married a Greek woman and established a popular studio. He painted and sketched the people and places of Istanbul; many of his original works became the basis for albums of his works that were printed and sold widely. See Llewellyn and Newton 1985 and Micklewright 1990.

15 I am grateful to Elaine Nichols, supervisory museum curator at NMAAHC; Mary Elliott, NMAAHC curator; Candace Oubre, NMAAHC collections manager; and Laura Mina, NMAAHC textile conservator, for sharing their time and expertise as I explored the NMAAHC holdings and history.

16 For more about how enslaved African American women acquired their clothing, see multiple entries in Katz-Hyman and Rice, *World of a Slave: Encyclopedia of the Material Life of Slaves in the United States*; and Way, *Black Designers in American Fashion*.

17 I thank Laura Mina for these suggestions. Conversation May 1, 2023.

18 See Lewis 2021 for an extended discussion of the significance of gifts of textiles and clothing in the Ottoman context.

Chapter 8

1   Estimates of the numbers of girls enrolled in Istanbul *rüşdiyyes* varies widely according to the sources quoted; these numbers are on the low side compared to some quoted elsewhere.

2   Paul Fesch, *Constantinople aux derniers jours d'Abdul-Hamid* (Paris: M. Riveriere, 1907).

3   I am grateful to Emily Gallagher Sharma for graciously sending me her MA thesis, *Locating & Critically Analysing Victorian and Edwardian (1850–1910) Working-Class Dress in England's Museums*, which eventually led me to two key collections of historic dress, at Killerton House and Blaise Museum. I thank the curators at those sites, Shelley Tobin and Catherine Littlejohns, for their invaluable help in locating relevant garments and sharing their insights about their collections with me.

4   Charles Baugniet (1814–1886) was a successful portrait painter, born and trained in Belgium. With his career well established, Baugniet moved to London in 1843, dividing his time between London, Paris, and Brussels. *The Seamstress* is in the Victoria and Albert Museum, London, 1564-1869.

5   The copy in the Getty Research Institute has been given a date of 1885, but the factory did not begin producing cigarettes until 1900, work that is illustrated in a number of the album's photographs, so a date shortly after 1900 seems more likely.

6   See Micklewright 2013 and Çelik and Eldem 2015 for more on the use of albums by the court and other organizations in Istanbul during this period to document specific events or accomplishments.

7   See Balsoy 2009 on the gendered nature of work in the Cibali Régie factory.

8   Personal communication, Elena Kanagy-Loux, September 1, 2023.

9   As I was writing this chapter, a posting of a dress very similar to the Edinburgh example came across my Instagram feed. Corresponding with the American owner of the post, I learned that her Turkish mother-in-law had given her a number of dresses saved by the family that dated to the early twentieth century.

Epilogue: The Afterlife of Ottoman Dress

1   Mary Lou O'Neil, "You Are What You Wear: Clothing/Appearance Laws and the Construction of the Public Citizen in Turkey," *Fashion Theory* 14, no. 1 (March 1, 2010); and Hale Yilmaz, *Becoming Turkish: Nationalist Reforms and Cultural Negotiations in Early Republican Turkey 1923–1945* (Syracuse, NY: Syracuse University Press, 2013), among others.

2   https://www.milliyet.com.tr/gundem/hurrem-modasi-1607470.

BIBLIOGRAPHY

Abel, Matthew. "The Curator Queen: Queen Mary and the V&A." *V&A Blog* (blog), March 2, 2020. https://www.vam. ac.uk/blog/caring-for-our-collections/the-curator-queen-queen-mary-and-the-va.

Aça, Mustafa. "Balıkesir Yöresinde Güncellenmeye Çalışılan Geleneksel Bir Gelinlik: Balıkesir Pullusu / A Traditional Bridal Gown Which Is Tried to Be Updated in Balikesir Locality: Balikesir Pullusu." In *Motif Vakfı Uluslararası Sosyal Bilimler Semposyumu Bildiriler Kıtabı*, 217–25. İstanbul: Motif Vakfı Yayınları, 2018.

Adıvar, Halide Edib. *Memoirs of Halidé Edib*. New York: Century Company, 1926.

Ağca, Sevgi. "Organizational Structure of Topkapı Harem." In *Topkapı Palace: The Imperial Harem: House of the Sultan*, 12–17. Istanbul: Topkapı Palace Museum, 2012.

Alexander, Lois K. *Blacks in the History of Fashion*. New York: Harlem Institute of Fashion, 1982.

Allom, Thomas. *Character and Costume in Turkey and Italy. Designed and Drawn from Nature. With Descriptive Letter-Press by Emily Reeve*. London: Fisher, Son & Co., 1839.

Altin, Ersin. "Rationalizing Everyday Life in Late Nineteenth Century Istanbul *c*. 1900." PhD diss., New Jersey Institute of Technology, Newark, 2014.

Altin, Rüstem Ertuğ. "Dressing the Nation the Girls' Institutes and the Politics of Fashion in Turkey." Turkish Cultural Foundation. Accessed March 24, 2021. http://www.turkishculture.org/textile-arts/clothing/dressing-the-nation-the-girls-institutes-and-the-politics-of-fashion-in-turkey-1092.htm?type=1.

Amies, Marion. "The Victorian Governess and Colonial Ideals of Womanhood." *Victorian Studies* 31, no. 4 (1988): 537–65.

Argıt, Betül İpşirli. "An Evaluation of the Tulip Period and the Period of Selim III in the Light of Clothing Regulations." *Osmanlı Araştırmaları/The Journal of Ottoman Studies* 24 (2004): 11–28.

Argıt, Betül İpşirli. "Clothing Habits, Regulations and Non-Muslims in the Ottoman Empire." *Akademik Araştırmalar Dergisi* 24 (2005): 79–96.

Argıt, Betül İpşirli. "Visual Materials as Source for the History of Ottoman Women." In *Women's Memory: The Problem of Sources*, edited by F. Ture and B. Talay, 29–39. Cambridge: Cambridge Scholars Publishing, 2011.

Argıt, Betül İpşirli. "Women in the Early Modern Ottoman World: A Bibliographical Essay." *Akademik Araştırmalar Dergisi* 60 (2014): 1–28.

Argıt, Betül İpşirli. "Clothing and Fashion in Istanbul (1453–1923)." *History of Istanbul*, 4 (2019): 1–50. https://istanbultarihi.ist/485-clothing-and-fashion-in-Istanbul-14531923.

Argıt, Betül İpşirli. *Life after the Harem: Female Palace Slaves, Patronage and the Imperial Ottoman Court*. Cambridge: Cambridge University Press, 2020a.

Argıt, Betül İpşirli. "Manumitted Female Palace Slaves and Their Material World." In *Slaves and Slave Agency in the Ottoman Empire*, edited by Stephen Conermann and Gul Sen, 189–209. Göttingen: Vandenhoeck & Ruprecht, 2020b.

Arlı, Alim. "Istanbul's Long Century: On a Global and National Scale." *History of Istanbul* 1 (2019). https://istanbultarihi.ist/384-istanbuls-long-century-on-a-global-and-national-scale.

Arnold, Rebecca, Katherine Faulkner, Katerina Pantelides, and Eugenie Shinkle. "Letter from the Editors." *Fashion Theory* 21, no. 2 (2017): 129–30.

Arnold, Rebecca. "The Kodak Ensemble: Fashion, Images and Materiality in 1920s America." *Fashion Theory*, 23 (2019): 1–27.

Artaç, Berna Yıldırım, and Emine Koca. "A Period Analysis on Values Shaped by Culture: Turkish and Armenian Women's Clothing." *European Scientific Journal* 14, no. 32 (2018): 131–53.

artam. "Portrait of Mihri Hanım in the Painting and Sculpture Museum," February 16, 2024. https://artam.com/makaleler/sergiler/mihri-hanimin-portresi-resim-heykel-muzesinde.

Artan, Tülay, and İrvin Cemil Schick. "Ottomanizing Pornotopia: Changing Visual Codes in Eighteenth-Century Ottoman Erotic Miniatures." In *Eros and Sexuality in Islamic Art*, edited by F. Leoni and Mika Natif, 157–207. London: Ashgate, 2013.

Atasoy, Nurhan. *Harem*. Istanbul: Bilkent Kültür Girişimi Publications, 2011.

Atasoy, Nurhan. *Portraits and Caftans of the Ottoman Sultans*. Istanbul: Assouline, 2012.

Atasoy, Nurhan. *Kaftan*. Istanbul: Masa, 2023.

Atasoy, Nurhan, Walter B. Denny, Louise W. Mackie, and Hülya Tezcan. *İpek. Imperial Ottoman Silks and Velvets*. London: Azimuth Editions, 2001.

Atasoy, Zehra Betül. "Ever-Present Tobacco Dust: Women's Labor Conditions at the Cibali Tobacco Factory." Billet. *TRAFO – Blog for Transregional Research* (blog), July 19, 2022. https://trafo.hypotheses.org/39612.

Auerbach, Jeffrey A. "What They Read: Mid-Nineteenth Century English Women's Magazines and the Emergence of a Consumer Culture." *Victorian Periodicals Review* 30, no. 2 (1997): 121–40.

Avcıoğlu, Nebahat. "Immigrant Narratives: The Ottoman Sultans' Portraits in Elisabeth Leitner's Family Photo Album, circa 1862–72." *Muqarnas* 35, no. 1 (2018): 193–228.

Aydınlık, Badegül Eren, and Seyfi Kenan. "Between Men, Time and the State: Education of Girls during the Late Ottoman Empire (1859–1908)." *Paedagogica Historica* 57, no. 4 (2021): 400–18.

Baker, Christopher, William Hauptman, and MaryAnne Stevens. *Jean-Etienne Liotard 1702–1789*. London: Royal Academy of the Arts, 2015.

Baker, Patricia. *Islamic Textiles*. London: British Museum Press, 1995.

Baker, Patricia, Hülya Tezcan, and Jennifer Wearden. *Silks for the Sultans: Ottoman Imperial Garments from Topkapı Palace*. Istanbul: Ertuğ & Kocabıyık, 1996.

Bali, Rifat N. "A Short History of Young Women's Christian Association (YWCA) Activities in Turkey." In *A Bridge between Cultures. Studies on Ottoman and Republican Turkey in Memory of Ali Ihsan Bagis*, edited by Sinan Kuneralp, 193–250. Piscataway, NJ: Gorgias Press, 2010.

Balsoy, Gülhan. "Gendering Ottoman Labor History: The Cibali Régie Factory in the Early Twentieth Century." *International Review of Social History* 54, (2009): 45–68.

Balta, Evangelia, and Ayşe Kavak. "Publisher of the Newspaper Konstantinoupolis for Half a Century. Following the Trail of Dimitris Nikolaidis in the Ottoman Archives." In *Press and Mass Communication in the Middle East Festschrift for Martin Strohmeier*, edited by Börte Sagaster, Theoharis Stavrides, and Birgitt Hoffmann, 33–64. Bamberg, Germany: University of Bamberg Press, 2017.

Banks-Walker, Hannah. "How Costume Drama Is Dominating Our Screens and Influencing Our Wardrobes." *Harper's Bazaar*, May 16, 2023. https://www.harpersbazaar.com/uk/fashion/a43850585/costume-drama-fashion-trend/.

Bardakçı, Murat. *Neslihah, The Last Ottoman Princess*. Cairo: American University in Cairo Press, 2017.

Bartlett, Willian, and Julia Pardoe. *The Beauties of the Bosphorus. Illustrated in a Series of Views of Constantinople and Its Environs from Original Drawings by William H. Bartlett*. London: George Virtue, 1838.

Barzilai-Lumbroso, Ruth. "Turkish Men and the History of Ottoman Women: Studying the History of the Ottoman Dynasty's Private Sphere through Women's Writings." *Journal of Middle East Women's Studies* 5, no. 2 (2009): 53–82.

Basch, Sophie. "What Did Istanbul Travelers Read? (Que Lisaient Les Voyageurs à Constantinople? Istanbul Gezginleri Ne Okuyordu?)." In *Journey to the Center of the East 1850–1950, 100 Years of Travelers in İstanbul from Pierre de Gigord Collection*, edited by Catherine Pinguet and Ekrem Işın, 55–66. Istanbul: Istanbul Research Center, 2015.

Bastermajian, Harry. "Emergence of the Global Armenian in Nineteenth-Century Istanbul." PhD diss., University of Chicago, 2017.

Başcı, Pelin. "Love, Marriage, and Motherhood: Changing Expectations of Women in Late Ottoman Istanbul." *Journal of Turkish Studies* 4, no. 3 (2003): 145–77.

Başcı, Pelin. "Advertising Modernity in Women's World: Women's Lifestyle and Leisure in Late-Ottoman Istanbul." *HAWWA Journal of Women of the Middle East and the Islamic World* 2, no. 1 (2004): 34–63.

Başcı, Pelin. "Advertising 'The New Woman': Fashion, Beauty, and Health in Women's World." *International Journal of Turkish Studies* 11, nos. 1 and 2 (2005): 61–79.

Başcı, Pelin. "Visual Materials as Source for the History of Ottoman Women." In *Women's Memory: The Problem of Sources*, edited by F. Ture and B. Talay, 29–39. Cambridge: Cambridge Scholars Publishing, 2011.

Başcı, Pelin. "Women in the Early Modern Ottoman World: A Bibliographical Essay." *Akademik Araştırmalar Dergisi* 60 (2014): 1–28.

Batuman, Elif. "Ottomania." *New Yorker*, February 9, 2014. https://www.newyorker.com/magazine/2014/02/17/ottomania.

Batur, Afife. "Galata and Pera 1, A Short History, Urban Development Architecture and Today." *ARI The Bulletin of the İstanbul Technical University* 55, no. 1 (2002): 1–10.

Baumgarten, Linda. "Clothes for the People: Slave Clothing in Early Virginia." *Journal of Early Southern Decorative Arts* 14, no. 2 (1988): 27–70.

Behar, Cem. "Polygyny in Istanbul, 1885–1926." *Middle Eastern Studies* 27, no. 3 (1991): 477–86.

Behdad, Ali. *Camera Orientalis: Reflections on Photography of the Middle East*. Chicago: University of Chicago Press, 2016.

Behdad, Ali, and Luke Gartlan, eds. *Photography's Orientalism: New Essays on Colonial Representation*. Los Angeles: Getty Research Institute, 2013.

Berberoğlu, Alev. "Dynamics of an Artistic Duo: Reciprocal Influences between Elisa and Fausto Zonaro." *Journal of the Ottoman and Turkish Studies Association* 8, no. 2 (2021): 261–70.

Berberoğlu, Alev. "Unwritten Histories of Photography: Elisa Zonaro, An Italian Photographer in Ottoman Istanbul." PhD diss., Koç University, Istanbul, 2023.

Berberoğlu, Alev. "A Portrait of the Artist as a Young Woman: Müfide Kadri's Photograph." *Keshif* 2, no. 2 (September 30, 2024): 10–19.

Berker, Nurhayat. *İşlemeler*. Istanbul: Yapı ve Kredi Bankası, 1981.

Bide, Bethan. "Signs of Wear: Encountering Memory in the Worn Materiality of a Museum Fashion Collection." *Fashion Theory* 21, no. 4 (2017): 449–76.

Bilgi, Hülya. *Çatma ve Kemha. Ottoman Silk Textiles*. Istanbul: Vehbi Koç Vakfı, Sadberk Hanım Muzesi, 2007.

Bilgi, Hülya, ed. *Elegance from Past to Future, Women's Costume from the Late Ottoman Empire to the Early Republican Era*. Istanbul: Vehbi Koç Vakfı, 2023.

Block, Elizabeth L. *Dressing Up: The Women Who Influenced French Fashion*. Cambridge, MA: MIT Press, 2021.

Booth, Marilyn, ed. *Harem Histories. Envisioning Places and Living Spaces*. Durham, NC: Duke University Press, 2010.

Booth, Marilyn, and A. Holly Shissler. "Fatma Aliye's Nisvan-ı Islam: Istanbul, Paris, Beirut, Cairo, 1891–96." In *Ottoman Translations Circulating Translations from Bombay to Paris*, edited by Marilyn Booth and Claire Savina, 327–88. Edinburgh: Edinburgh University Press, 2023.

Boppe, Auguste. *Les Peintures Du Bosphore Au XVIIIe Siecle*. Paris: Librarie Hachette et Cie., 1911.

Bosscha Erdbrink, G. R. *Jean Baptiste Vanmour'un Tabloari 1671–1737, Amsterdam'daki Devlet Müzesi Kolleksiyonlarindan/Les Peintures "Turques" de Jean-Baptiste Vanmour, 1671–1737 Conservées Au Rijksmuseum à Amsterdam*. Leiden: Brill, 1978.

Boyar, Ebru. "The Press and the Palace: The Two-Way Relationship between Abdülhamid II and the Press, 1876–1908." *Bulletin of the School of Oriental and African Studies, University of London* 69, no. 3 (2006): 417–32.

Boyar, Ebru, and Kate Fleet. *A Social History of Ottoman Istanbul*. Cambridge: Cambridge University Press, 2010.

Boyar, Ebru, and Kate Fleet, eds. *Ottoman Women in Public Space*. Leiden: Brill, 2016.

Bozkurt, Fatih. "Istanbul Families during the Ottoman Period." *History of Istanbul* 4 (2019). https://istanbultarihi.ist/469-istanbul-families-during-the-ottoman-period.

Bölük, Gülderen. *İstanbul'un 100 Fotoğrafçısı*. İstanbul: istanbul Büyüşehir Belediyesi Kültür A. Şç Yayınları, 2009.

Brassey, Annie. *Sunshine and Storm in the East, Or Cruises to Cyprus and Constantinople*. London: Longmans, Green and Company, 1880.

Brennan, Summer. "A Natural History of the Wedding Dress." JSTOR Daily, September 27, 2017. https://daily.jstor.org/a-natural-history-of-the-wedding-dress/.

Breward, Christopher. "Cultures, Identities, Histories: Fashioning a Cultural Approach to Dress." *Fashion Theory* 2, no. 4 (1998): 301–13.

Breward, Christopher. "Fashion Cities." In *Berg Encyclopedia of World Dress and Fashion, Volume 10 Global Perspectives*, edited by Joanne B. Eicher and Phyllis G. Tortora, 226–29. London: Berg, 2010.

Brindesi, Jean. *Elbicei Atika, Museé de Ancienes Costumes de Constantinople*. Paris: Lemercier, 1855.

Brookes, Douglas Scott. *The Concubine, the Princess, and the Teacher: Voices from the Ottoman Harem*. Austin: University of Texas Press, 2008.

Brummett, Palmira. *Image and Imperialism in the Ottoman Revolutionary Press*. Binghamton: State University of New York Press, 2000.

Buck, Anne M. *The Gallery of English Costume, Picture Book Number Four, Women's Costume, 1835–1870*. Manchester: Art Galleries Committee of the Corporation of Manchester, 1951.

Buck, Anne M. *The Gallery of English Costume, Picture Book Number Five, Women's Costume, 1870–1900*. Manchester: Art Galleries Committee of the Corporation of Manchester, 1953.

Buck, Anne M. *The Gallery of English Costume, Picture Book Number Six, Women's Costume, 1900–1930*. Manchester: Art Galleries Committee of the Corporation of Manchester, 1956.

Budak, Ali. "The French Revolution's Gift to the Ottomans: The Newspaper." *International Journal of Humanities and Social Science* 2, no. 19 (2012): 157–69.

Budde, Gunilla. "Traveling Teachers in Europe: Gouvernanten, Governesses, and Gouvernantes." *European History Online (EGO)*, 2018. http://www.ieg-ego.eu/buddeg-2011-enURN:urn:nbn:de:0159-2018082808.

Bull, Duncan. "Princess, Countess, Lover or Wife? Liotard's 'Lady on a Sofa.'" *Burlington Magazine* 150, no. 1266 (2008): 592–602.

Bunch, Lonnie G. *A Fool's Errand. Creating the National Museum of African American History and Culture in the Age of Bush, Obama and Trump*. Washington, DC: Smithsonian Books, 2019.

Burçak, Berrak. "'The Question of the Corset': Fashion, Health and Identity in Late Ottoman History." *British Journal of Middle Eastern Studies* 50, no. 2 (2023): 219–39.

Calafato, Özge Baykan. *Making the Modern Turkish Citizen. Vernacular Photography in the Early Republican Era*. London: Bloomsbury, 2022.

Calefato, Patrizia. "Fashion and Worldliness: Language and Imagery of the Clothed Body." *Fashion Theory* 1, no. 1 (1997): 69–90.

Çapar İleri, S., and A. Atilla Mat. "Women in 19th Century Istanbul: Considering Lady Emelia Bithynia Maceroni Hornby's Travelogue Constantinople during the Crimean War (1866)." *RumeliDE Dil ve Edebiyat Araştırmaları Dergisi*, 15 (2024): 920–32.

Carney, Josh. "Re-Creating History and Recreating Publics: The Success and Failure of Recent Ottoman Costume Dramas in Turkish Media." *European Journal of Turkish Studies* 19 (2014): 1–25.

Carney, Josh. "ResurReaction: Competing Visions of Turkey's (Proto) Ottoman Past in Magnificent Century and Resurrection Ertuğrul." *Middle East Critique* 28, no. 2 (2019): 101–20.

Casaretto, Fabrizio. *Aile Arşivinden Sébah/Joaıllıer Fotoğrafanesi The Sébah/Joaıllıer Photography Studio from the Family Archive*. İstanbul: Türkiye İş Bankası Kültür Yayınları, 2023.

Cephanecigil, Gül. "Istanbul Museums in the Ottoman Era." *History of Istanbul*, 7 (2019). https://istanbultarihi.ist/643-istanbul-museums-in-the-ottoman-era.

Chaffin, Tom. "The Southern Mathew Brady." *New York Times*, February 11, 2011, sec. Opinion. https://archive.nytimes.com/opinionator.blogs.nytimes.com/2011/02/11/the-southern-matthew-brady/.

Chapman, Wilson. "How 'The Gilded Age' Costume Designer Kasia Walicka-Maimone Captured a Changing Era of Fashion." *Variety* (blog), January 31, 2022. https://variety.com/2022/artisans/news/gilded-age-costume-design-kasia-walicka-maimone-1235164476/.

Cheang, Sarah, Erica De Greef, and Yoko Takagi. "Introduction." In *Rethinking Fashion Globalization*, edited by Sarah Cheang, Erica De Greef, and Yoko Takagi, 1–19. London: Bloomsbury Visual Arts, 2021.

Cheang, Sarah, Erica De Greef, and Yoko Takagi, eds. *Rethinking Fashion Globalization*. London: Bloomsbury Visual Arts, 2021.

Cohen, Julia Phillips. "Between Civic and Islamic Ottomanism: Jewish Imperial Citizenship in the Hamidian Era." *International Journal of Middle East Studies* 44, no. 2 (2012): 237–55.

Coleman, Elizabeth A. *The Opulent Era: Fashions of Worth, Doucet and Pingat*. London: Thames and Hudson, 1989.

Collaço, Gwendolyn. "Dressing a City's Demeanour: Ottoman Costume Albums and the Portrayal of Urban Identity in the Early Seventeenth Century." *Textile History* 48, no. 2 (2017): 248–67.

Collaço, Gwendolyn. "Albums of Conspicuous Consumption: A Composite Mirror of an 18th-Century Collector's World." *Journal 18* (Fall 2018). http://www.journal18.org/3089.

Collaço, Gwendolyn. "Between Brush, Stone, and Copper: The Harvard Fulgenzi Album Mediating Print Techniques and Crosscurrents of the Press." In *Prints and Impressions from Ottoman Smyrna*, edited by Gwendolyn Collaço, 9–20. Bonn : Max Weber Stiftung, Orient-Institut Istanbul, 2019.

Collaço, Gwendolyn. "The Image as Commodity: The Commercial Market for Single-Folio Paintings in Ottoman Istanbul, 17th–18th Centuries." PhD diss., Cambridge, MA, Harvard University, 2020.

Compagnon, Suzanne Alice. "Clothing and Pictorial Representation in Eighteenth-Century Ottoman Painting: The Levnī and Buhārī Single Figures." PhD diss., University of Vienna, Vienna, 2023.

Comte Fleury, Maurice. *Memoirs of the Empress Eugenie*. London: Appleton, 1920.

Connolly, Marguerite. "The Disappearance of the Domestic Sewing Machine, 1890–1925." *Winterthur Portfolio* 34, no. 1 (1999): 31–48.

Crane, Diana. "Clothing Behavior as Non-Verbal Resistance: Marginal Women and Alternative Dress in the Nineteenth Century." *Fashion Theory* 3, no. 2 (1999): 241–68.

Craven, Elizabeth Lady. *A Journey through the Crimea to Constantinople. In a Series of Letters from the Right Honourable Elizabeth Lady Craven, to His Serene Highness the Margrave of Brandenburg, Anspach, and Bareith.* London: G. G. J. and J. Robinson, 1789.

Criss, N. B. *Istanbul under Allied Occupation, 1918–1923.* Leiden: Brill, 1999.

Croutier, Alev Lytle. *Harem. The World behind the Veil.* New York: Abbeville Press, 1989.

Çelik, Zeynep. *The Remaking of Istanbul. Portrait of an Ottoman City in the Nineteenth Century.* Seattle: University of Washington Press, 1986.

Çelik, Zeynep, and Edhem Eldem, eds. *Camera Ottomana: Photography and Modernity in the Ottoman Empire, 1840–1914.* Istanbul: Koç University Press, 2015.

Çevik, Senem. "Turkish Historical Television Series: Public Broadcasting of Neo-Ottoman Illusions." *Southeast European and Black Sea Studies* 19 (2019): 1–17.

Çizakça, Murat. "A Short History of the Bursa Silk Industry (1500–1900)." *Journal of the Economic and Social History of the Orient* 23, no. 1/2 (1980): 142–52.

Çizgen, Engin. *Photographer/Fotoğrafçı Ali Sami.* Istanbul, Haşet Kıtabevi: 1989.

Dağoğlu, Özlem Gülin. "Mihri Rasim and the Founding of the Women's Academy Inas Sanayi-i Nefise Mektebi: A Double-Edged New Social Reality." *Journal of the Ottoman and Turkish Studies Association* 6, no. 2 (2019): 33–54.

Dautović, Vuk. "Funerary Photography as a Source for the Dress of Sephardic Jews in Belgrade: From Traditional Costumes to Civil Emancipation." Paper presented at the 17th World Congress of Jewish Studies, Jerusalem, 2017.

Davidian, Vazken Khatchig. "Imagining Ottoman Armenia: Realism and Allegory in Garabed Nichanian's Provincial Wedding in Moush and Late Ottoman Art Criticism." *Études Arméniennes Contemporaines*, 6 (2015): 155–225.

Davidson, Hilary. "The Embodied Turn: Making and Remaking Dress as an Academic Practice." *Fashion Theory* 23, no. 3 (2019): 329–62.

Davis, Fanny. *The Ottoman Lady. A Social History from 1817 to 1918.* New York: Greenwood Press, 1986.

Dawson, Barbara. *White Work Embroidery.* London: B. T. Batsford, 1987.

Delibaş, Selma. "Embroidery." In *Traditional Turkish Arts. Weaving, Carpets and Kilims, Embroidery, Cloth,* edited by Nazan Ölçen, 47–59. Ankara: Ministry of Culture and Tourism, General Directorate of Fine Arts, 1987.

Denny, Margaret. "Framing the Victorians, Photography, Fashion, and Identity." In *The Places and Spaces of Fashion, 1800–2007,* edited by J. Potvin, 34–51. London: Routledge, 2008.

Derviş Pelin, Bulent Tanju and Uğur Tanyeli, eds. *Becoming Istanbul, An Encyclopedia.* Istanbul: Salt, 2015.

Dodson, Howard. "Introduction." In *The Legacy of Arthur A. Schomburg, A Celebration of the Past, A Vision for the Future,* edited by Howard Dodson, 7–15. New York: New York Public Library, 1986.

Dölen, Emre. "Industrial Organizations." In *History of Istanbul. Volume 6 Industrial Organizations in Istanbul: Textile, Paper, Glass.* Istanbul: Türkiye Diyanet Foundation Center for Islamic Studies (İSAM) and İstanbul Metropolitan Municipality Kültür ve Sanat Ürünleri A.Ş., 2019. https://istanbultarihi.ist/569-industrial-organizations-in-istanbul-textile-paper-glass.

Dölen, Emre. "Textile Factories." In *History of Istanbul. Volume 6 Industrial Organizations in Istanbul: Textile, Paper, Glass.* Istanbul: Türkiye Diyanet Foundation Center for Islamic Studies (İSAM) and İstanbul Metropolitan Municipality Kültür ve Sanat Ürünleri A.Ş., 2019. https://istanbultarihi.ist/569-industrial-organizations-in-istanbul-textile-paper-glass.

Drampyan, Khazhak. "Attire." Houshamadyan, 2018. https://www.houshamadyan.org/mapottomanempire/vilayetofmamuratulazizharput/kaza-of-agn/local-characteristics/attire.html.

Duben, Alan, and Cem Behar. *Istanbul Households; Marriage. Family and Fertility, 1880–1940.* Cambridge: Cambridge University Press, 1991.

Dunn, Sophie. "'No Objection to Go Abroad': Servants' Travel Advertisements in The Morning Post, London, 1815." *Journal for Eighteenth-Century Studies* 45, no. 4 (2022): 487–506.

Durakbaşı, Ayşe, and Dilek Cindoğlu. "Encounters at the Counter: Gender and the Shopping Experience." In *Fragments of Culture: The Everyday of Modern Turkey,* edited by Deniz Kandiyoti and Ayşe Saktanber, 73–90. New Brunswick, NJ: Rutgers University Press, 2002.

Dyer, Serena. *Material Lives: Women Makers and Consumer Culture in the 18th Century.* London: Bloomsbury, 2021.

East, Charles. *Baton Rouge, A Civil War Album.* Baton Rouge, LA: Self-published, 1977.

Eder, Jens, and Charlotte Klonk. *Image Operations: Visual Media and Political Conflict.* Manchester: Manchester University Press, 2016.

Edwards, Elizabeth. "Little Theatres of Self: Thinking about the Social." In *We Are the People. Postcards from the Collection of Tom Phillips*, edited by James Fenton, 26–37. London: National Portrait Gallery, 2004.

Edwards, Lydia. *How to Read a Dress. A Guide to Changing Fashion from the 16th to the 20th Century.* London: Bloomsbury Visual Arts, 2017.

Edwards, Penny. "Restyling Colonial Cambodia (1860–1954): French Dressing, Indigenous Custom and National Costume." *Fashion Theory* 5, no. 4 (2001): 389–416.

Eicher, Joanne B., ed. *Berg Encyclopedia of World Dress and Fashion: Global Perspectives,* Vol. 10. Oxford: Berg, 2011.

Ekinci, Ekrem Buğra. "The Bitter Story of the Ottoman Dynasty's Exile." *Daily Sabah*, March 13, 2015. https://www.dailysabah.com/feature/2015/03/13/the-bitter-story-of-the-ottoman-dynastys-exile.

Ekinci, Ekrem Buğra. "The Abdullah Brothers: Pioneers of Photography in the Late Ottoman Period," May 16, 2016. https://www.ekrembugraekinci.com/article/?ID=698&the-abdullah-brothers:-pioneers-of-photography-in-the-late-ottoman-period.

Eldem, Edhem. *French Trade in Istanbul in the Eighteenth Century.* Leiden: Brill, 1999.

Eldem, Edhem. *Pride and Privilege: A History of Ottoman Orders, Medals and Decorations.* Istanbul: Osmanlı Bankası Arşiv ve Araştırma Merkezi, 2004.

Eldem, Edhem. "Ottoman Galata and Pera Between Myth and Reality." In *From 'Milieu de Memoire' to 'Lieu Du Memoire': The Cultural Memory of Istanbul in the 20th Century*, edited by Ulrike Tischler, 18–36. Karl-Franzens University of Graz: M. Meidenbauer, 2006.

Eldem, Edhem. "Making Sense of Osman Hamdi Bey and His Paintings." *Muqarnas* 29 (2012): 339–83.

Eldem, Edhem. "The Search for an Ottoman Vernacular Photography." In *The Indigenous Lens? Early Photography in the near and Middle East*, edited by Markus Ritter and Staci G. Scheiwiller, 29–56. Berlin: Walter de Gruyter GmbH, 2017.

Ellis, Marianne. "Metal Thread Embroidery from Ottoman Turkey." *Embroidery* 43, no. 1 (1992): 37–39.

Ellis, Marianne. *Ottoman Embroidery.* London: V&A Publications, 2001.

Ellison, Grace. *An English Woman in a Turkish Harem.* London: Methuen, 1915.

Enis, Ayşe Zeren. *Everyday Lives of Ottoman Muslim Women: Hanımlara Mahsus Gazete.* Istanbul: Libra Yayınları, 2013.

Entwistle, Joanne. "Fashion and Its Social Agendas: Class, Gender and Identity in Clothing by Diana Crane." *Fashion Theory* 6, no. 3 (2002): 331–33.

Entwistle, Joanne, and Agnès Rocamora. "The Field of Fashion Materialized: A Study of London Fashion Week." *Sociology* 40, no. 4 (2006): 735–51.

Entwistle, Joanne, and Elizabeth Wilson, eds. *Body Dressing: Dress, Body, Culture.* London: Bloomsbury, 2001.

Erdem, Hakan. *Slavery in the Ottoman Empire and Its Demise, 1800–1909.* Oxford: Macmillan Press, Ltd, 1996.

Ergin, Murat, and Yağmur Karakaya. "Between Neo-Ottomanism and Ottomania: Navigating State-Led and Popular Cultural Representations of the Past." *New Perspectives on Turkey* 56 (2017): 33–59.

Ersoy, Ahmet A. "A Sartorial Tribute to Late Tanzimat Ottomanism: The Elbise-i 'Osmaniyye Album." *Muqarnas* 20 (2003): 187–207.

Ersoy, Ahmet A. "The Popular Costumes of Turkey in 1873." In *National Romanticism: The Formation of National Movements: Discourses of Collective Identity in Central and Southeast Europe 1770–1945, Volume II*, edited by Balázs Trencsényi and Michal Kopeček, 174–80. Budapest: Central European University Press, 2007.

Ersoy, Ahmet A. "Ottomans and the Kodak Galaxy: Archiving Everyday Life and Historical Space in Ottoman Illustrated Journals." *History of Photography* 40, no. 3 (2016): 330–57.

Ersoy, Ahmet A., and Matthew C. Potter. "History as You Go: Mobility, Photography, and the Visibility of the Past in Late Ottoman Print Space." In *Representing the Past in the Art of the Long Nineteenth Century*, edited by Matthew C. Potter, 240–62. New York: Routledge, 2022.

Ersoy, Ahmet A., and Türker, Deniz. "The Hamidian Visual Archive, 1878–1909: A User's Manual." In *Crafting History: Essays on the Ottoman World and Beyond in Honor of Cemal Kafadar*, edited by Rachel Goshgarian, Ilham Khuri-Makdisi, and Ali Yaycioğlu, 319–42. Brookline, MA: Academic Studies Press, 2023.

Eryavuz, Şebnam. "Elegance from Past to Future from the Sadberk Hanım Museum, Rahni Koç Museum and İnönü Foundation Collections." In *Elegance from Past to Future, Women's Costume from the Late Ottoman Empire to the Early Republican Era*, edited by Hülya Bilgi: 107–361. Istanbul: Vehbi Koç Vakfı, 2023.

Exertzoglou, Haris. "The Cultural Uses of Consumption: Negotiating Class, Gender, and Nation in the Ottoman Urban Centers during the 19th Century." *International Journal of Middle East Studies* 35, no. 1 (February 2003): 77–101.

Fair, Laura. "Remaking Fashion in the Paris of the Indian Ocean: Dress, Performance, and the Cultural Construction of a Cosmopolitan Zanzibari Identity." In *Fashioning Africa: Power and the Politics of Dress*, edited by Jean Allman, 13–30. Bloomington: Indiana University Press, 2004.

Falierou, Anastasia. "From the Ottoman Empire to the Turkish Republic: Ottoman Turkish Clothing between Tradition and Modernity." In *Traditional Attire to Modern Dress: Modes of Identification, Modes of Recognition in the Balkans (XVIth–XXth Centuries)*, edited by Constanta Vintilă-Ghiţulescu, 175–92. Cambridge: Cambridge Scholars Publisher, 2011.

Falierou, Anastasia. "European Fashion, Consumption Patterns, and Intercommunal Relations in the 19th-Century Ottoman Istanbul." In *Women, Consumption, and the Circulation of Ideas in South-Eastern Europe, 17th–19th Centuries*, edited by Constanţa Vintilă-Ghiţulescu, 150–68. Leiden: Brill, 2017.

Faroqhi, Suraiya. *Subjects of the Sultans. Culture and Everyday Life in the Ottoman Empire from the Middle Ages until the Beginning of the Twentieth Century*. London: I. B. Tauris, 2000.

Faroqhi, Suraiya. *Artisans of Empire. Crafts and Craftspeople under the Ottomans*. London: I. B. Tauris, 2009.

Faroqhi, Suraiya. "Surviving in Difficult Times, The Cotton and Silk Trades in Bursa around 1800." In *Bread from the Lion's Mouth: Artisans Struggling for a Livelihood in Ottoman Cities*, edited by Suraiya Faroqhi, 136–56. Brooklyn, NY: Berghahn Books, 2015.

Faroqhi, Suraiya. *A Cultural History of the Ottomans: The Imperial Elite and Its Artefacts*. London: I. B. Tauris, 2016.

Faroqhi, Suraiya. *Slavery in the Ottoman World: A Literature Survey*. Otto Spies Memorial Lecture, Vol. 4. Berlin: Verlag, 2017.

Faroqhi, Suraiya, and Christoph K. Neumann, eds. *Ottoman Costumes from Textile to Identity*. Istanbul: EREN, 2004.

Farr, Cheryl Ann. "Metallic Yarns: A Technological and Cultural Perspective for the Development of a Morphological Classification System." *Ars Textrina* 22 (1994): 65–85.

Fehlmann, Marc. "Orientalism." In *Jean-Etienne Liotard 1702–1789*, edited by Christopher Baker, William Hauptman, and Mary-Anne Stevens, 62–87. London: Royal Academy of the Arts, 2015.

Findley, Carter Vaughn. *Turkey, Islam, Nationalism and Modernity, A History, 1789–2007*. London: Yale University Press, 2010.

Fisher-Onar, Nora, Susan C. Pearce, and E. Fuat Keyman, eds. *Istanbul: Living with Difference in a Global City*. New Brunswick, NJ: Rutgers University Press, 2019.

Fleet, Kate. "The Powerful Public Presence of the Ottoman Female Consumer." In *Ottoman Women in Public Space*, edited by Ebru Boyar and Kate Fleet, 91–128. Leiden: Brill, 2016.

Fortna, Benjamin C. "Bonbons and Bayonets: Mixed Messages of Childhood in the Late Ottoman Empire and the Early Turkish Republic." In *Childhood in the Late Ottoman Empire and After*, edited by Benjamin C. Fortna, 173–88. Leiden: Brill, 2016.

Foster, Helen Bradley, and Donald Clay Johnson. *Wedding Dress across Cultures*. Oxford: Berg, 2003.

Foster, Vanda. *A Visual History of Costume, The Nineteenth Century*. London: B. T. Batsford, 1984.

Fraser, Elisabeth. "The Color of the Orient: On Ottoman Costume Albums, European Print Culture, and Cross-Cultural Exchange." In *Visual Typologies from the Early Modern to the Contemporary: Local Practices and Global Contexts*, edited by Tara Zanardi and Lynda Klich, 45–59. New York: Routledge, 2018.

Friedman, Vanessa. "The Incredible Whiteness of the Museum Fashion Collection." *New York Times*, September 29, 2020. https://www.nytimes.com/2020/09/29/style/museums-fashion-racism.html.

Frierson, Elizabeth B. "'Is There Any Future for Us in Trying to Be Ladylike?' The Ethnic Politics of Late-Ottoman Dress and Manufacture." Unpublished paper, Princeton University, 1995.

Frierson, Elizabeth B. "Cheap and Easy: The Creation of Consumer Culture in Late Ottoman Society." In *Consumption Studies and the History of the Ottoman Empire, 1550–1922, An Introduction*, edited by Donald Quataert, 243–60. Albany: State University of New York Press, 2000.

Friese, S. "The Wedding Dress: From Use Value to Sacred Object." In *Through the Wardrobe: Women's Relationships with Their Clothes*, edited by A. Guy, E. Green, and M. Banim, 53–70. Oxford: Berg, 2001.

Fukai, Akiko, Tamami Suoh, Miki Iwagami, Reiko Koga, and Rii Nie. *Fashion. A History from the 18th to the 20th Century. The Collection of the Kyoto Costume Institute*. New York: Barnes and Noble, 2006.

Gallagher, Emily. "Locating and Critically Analysing Victorian and Edwardian Dress (1850–1910) Working-Class Dress in England's Museums." MA thesis, London, University of the Arts, 2020.

Gallagher, Emily. "Victorians Re-Dressed." Unseen Histories. October 2021. https://www.unseenhistories.com/victorians-redressed.

Gamm, Niki. "Weddings: A Lavish Affairs under the Ottomans." *Hürriyet Daily News*, June 10, 2012. https://www.hurriyetdailynews.com/weddings-a-lavish-affairs-under-the-ottomans-22725#:~:text=A%20large%20banquet%20would%20be,the%20bride%20to%20her%20room.

Garnett, Lucy M. J. *The Women of Turkey and their Folklore*. London: David Nutt, 1890.

Gates, Henry Louis Jr. "Frederick Douglass' Camera Obscura: Representing the Antislave 'Clothes and in Their Own Form.'" *Critical Inquiry* 42, no. 1 (2015): 31–60.

Gayed, Andrew, and Siobhan Angus. "Visual Pedagogies: Decolonizing and Decentering the History of Photography." *Studies in Art Education* 59, no. 3 (2018): 228–42.

Geczy, Adam. *Fashion and Orientalism. Dress. Textiles and Culture from the 17th to the 21st Century*. London: Bloomsbury, 2013.

Geczy, Adam. *Transorientalism in Art, Fashion, and Film, Inventions of Identity*. London: Bloomsbury: 2019.

Georgini, Sara. "An Indian Chintz Gown: Slavery and Fashion." *The Junto* (blog), September 12, 2018. https://earlyamericanists.com/2018/09/12/an-indian-chintz-gown-slavery-and-fashion/.

Germaner, Semra, and Zeynep İnankur. *Orientalism and Turkey*. Istanbul: Turkish Cultural Foundation, 1989.

Gernsheim, Alison. *Victorian and Edwardian Fashion. A Photographic Survey*. New York: Dover, 1963.

Gierlichs, Joachim. "Europeans in Turkish Dress." In *Fashioning the Self in Transcultural Settings: The Uses and Significance of Dress in Self-Narratives*, edited by Claudia Ulbrich and Richard Wittman, 151–86. Würzburg: Ergon Verlag Würzburg, 2015.

Go, Kaycee. "Downton Abbey: 6 Things That Were Historically Accurate about the Costumes (& 4 That Weren't)." *ScreenRant*, November 4, 2019. https://screenrant.com/downton-abbey-historically-accurate-costumes/.

Goffman, Carolyn. "The American College for Girls." *History of Istanbul*, Vol. 8, 2015. https://istanbultarihi.ist/664-the-american-college-for-girls.

Goldthorpe, Caroline. *From Queen to Empress. Victorian Dress 1837–1877*. New York: Metropolitan Museum of Art, 1988.

Gopin, Seth, and Eveline Sint Nicolaas. *Jean Baptiste Vanmour Peintre de La Sublime Porte, 1671–1737*. Valenciennes: Musée des Beaux Arts de Valenciennes, 2009.

Gormally, Mary Frances. "The House of Worth: Portrait of an Archive." *Fashion Theory* 21, no. 1 (2017): 109–26.

Görünür, Lale. *Osmanlı İmparatorluğu'nun Son Döneminden Kadın Giysileri, Sadberk Hanım Müzesi Koleksiyonu/Women's Costume of the Late Ottoman Era from the Sadberk Hanım Museum*. Istanbul: Vehbi Koç Vakfı, 2010.

Görünür, Lale. *Pabuç Sadberk Hanım Müzesi Koleksiyondan/Shoes From the Sadberk Hanım Museum Collection*. Istanbul: Vehbi Koç Vakfı, 2014.

Görünür, Lale, ed. *Adorable & Precocious—Children's Costumes in the Sadberk Hanım Museum Collection/Büyümüş de Küçülmüş—Sadberk Hanım Müzesi Koleksiyonu'ndan Çocuk Kıyafetleri*. Istanbul. Vehbi Koç Vakfı, Sadberk Hanım Muzesi, 2023.

Gratien, Chris, and Seçil Yılmaz. "Red Crescent Archives (Turkey)." *Hazine* (blog), November 13, 2013. https://hazine.info/turkish-red-crescent-kizilay-archives-ankara/.

Graves, Margaret S., and Alex Dika Seggerman, eds. *Making Modernity in the Islamic Mediterranean*. Bloomington: Indiana University Press, 2022.

Graves, R. E., and Anne Pimlott Baker. *Bartlett, William Henry (1809–1854), Topographical Artist*. Oxford University Press, 2004.

Green, Katie. "Victorian Governesses: A Look at Education and Professionalization." MA diss., University of Toledo, Toledo, OH, 2009.

Grey, Hon. Mrs. William. *Journal of a Visit to Egypt, Constantinople, The Crimea, Greece, Etc*. London: Smith, Elder & Co., 1869.

Gün, Doğan. "Jewish Women in Ottoman Education and the Activities of the Alliance Israelite Universelle: The Case of Istanbul (1839–1916)." *Avrasya Uluslararası Araştırmalar Dergisi* 12, no. 39 (2024): 173–93.

Günay, Umay. *Historical Costumes of Turkish Women*. Istanbul: Midde East Video Corp., 1986.

Gürbüz, Şeyma Nazlı, and Nurefşan Kutlu. "The Perfect Henna Night: Transformation of a Traditional Turkish Wedding Ritual." *Daily Sabah*, January 21, 2017. https://www.dailysabah.com/feature/2017/01/21/the-perfect-henna-night-transformation-of-a-traditional-turkish-wedding.

Gürtuna, Sevgi. *Osmanlı Kadın Giyisi*. Ankara: Kültür Bakanlığı, 1999.

Haim Gerber. "Ottoman Historiography: Challenges of the Twenty-First Century." *Journal of the American Oriental Society* 138, no. 2 (2018): 369–84.

Halliday, W.R. "A Greek Marriage in Cappadocia." *Folklore* 23, no. 1 (1912): 81–88.

Hamadeh, Shirine. *The City's Pleasures. Istanbul in the Eighteenth Century*. Seattle: University of Washington Press, 2008.

Hamadeh, Shirine and Çiğdem Kafescioğlu. "Yerlerin Tarihi: Reşat Ekrem Koçu ve İstanbul Ansiklopedisi." In *Başka Kayda Rastlanmadı*, edited by Bülent Tanju, Cansu Yapıcı, Ezgi Yurteri, Gülce Özkara, and Masum Yıldız, 91–107. İstanbul: Salt e-Yayın, 2023.

Hannoush, Michele. "Practices of Photography: Circulation and Mobility in the Nineteenth-Century Mediterranean." *History of Photography* 40, no. 1 (2016): 3–27.

Harrison, Martin. *Appearances: Fashion Photography since 1945*. New York: Rizzoli, 1991.

Hart, Kimberly. "Marriage Practices: Turkey." In *Encyclopedia of Women & Islamic Cultures*, edited by Suad Joseph. Leiden: Brill, 2009. https://doi.org/10.1163/1872-5309_ewic_EWICCOM_0183h.

Hartmann, Elke. "Family Portraits: Visual Sources for a Social History of the Late Ottoman Empire." In *Ways of Knowing Muslim Cultures and Societies. Studies in Honour of Gudrun Krämer*, edited by Bettina Gräf, Birgit Krawietz, Amir-Moazami Schirin, Ulrike Freitag, and Konrad Hirschler, 111–31. Leiden: Brill, 2018.

Haworth-Booth, Mark. *Camille Silvy. Photographer of Modern Life*. London: National Portrait Gallery, 2010.

Hedlund, Ragnar. "'A Dream to Dream Again' – Accounts of Travels to Constantinople in the Late 19th and Early 20th Centuries." In *Topoi, Topographies and Travellers: Papers of a conference at the Swedish Institute for Classical Studies in Rome*, edited by Stefano Fogelberg Rota and Anna Blennow, 177–93. Rome: Swedish Institute in Rome, 2019.

Heffernan, Teresa, and Reina Lewis. "Feminist Dialogues across Cultures: An English Woman in a Turkish Harem and the Turkish Harem in an English Woman." In Grace Ellison, *An Englishwoman in a Turkish Harem*, vi–xxix. Piscataway, NJ: Gorgias Press, 2007.

Higonnet, Anne. *Liberty, Equality, Fashion. The Women Who Styled the French Revolution*. New York: Norton, 2024.

Hill, Marian. "The Importance of Accuracy: A Look at Costume Design in Period Dramas." *Medium* (blog), January 21, 2020. https://medium.com/she-her/the-importance-of-accuracy-a-look-at-costume-design-in-period-dramas-41f090c5a765.

Hirshler, Erica. *Sargent and Fashion*. London: Tate Britain, 2023.

Hornby, Emelia B. M. *Constantinople during the Crimean War*. London: Richard Bentley, 1863.

Horuz, Semra. "Touring Europe, Envisioning Homeland: Istanbul in Two Nineteenth-Century Ottoman Travelogues." *YILLIK: Annual of Istanbul Studies* 3 (2021): 69–91.

Horyn, Cathy. "Diana Reborn." *Vanity Fair*, July 1, 1997. https://www.vanityfair.com/style/1997/07/princess-diana-reborn.

Hughes, Kathryn. "The Figure of the Governess." *Discovering Literature: Romantics and Victorians* (blog), May 15, 2014. https://www.bl.uk/romantics-and-victorians/articles/the-figure-of-the-governess.

Inal, Onur. "Women's Fashions in Transition: Ottoman Borderlands and the Anglo-Ottoman Exchange of Costumes." *Journal of World History* 22, no. 2 (2011): 243–72.

Inankur, Zeynep, Reina Lewis, and Mary Roberts, eds. *The Poetics and Politics of Place. Ottoman Istanbul and British Orientalism*. Istanbul: Pera Museum, 2011.

Isom-Verhaaren, Christine, and Kent F. Schull. "Introduction: Dealing with Identity in the Ottoman Empire." In *Living in the Ottoman Realm, Empire and Identity, 13th to 20th Centuries*, edited by Christine Isom-Verhaaren and Kent F. Schull, 1–16. Bloomington: Indiana University Press, 2016.

İleri, Nurçin. "Objects of Nature and Scientific Knowledge on the Move: The Robert College Natural History Museum in Istanbul." *European Journal of Turkish Studies*, 32 (2021): 96–128.

İpek, Selin. "Fashion in Court Women's Attire of the Eighteenth and Nineteenth Centuries in the Light of Written and Visual Sources kept in the Topkapi Palace Museum." PhD diss., Mimar Sinan Fine Arts University, Istanbul, 2009a.

İpek, Selin. "Haremin Bayramlık Elbiseleri: Dikişçi Matmazel Kokona'nın Defteri." *Acta Turcica* 1 (2009b): 64–78. https://actaturcica.wordpress.com/wp-content/uploads/2019/12/64_78.pdf.

İpek, Selin. "Ottoman Fabrics during the 18th and 19th Centuries." *Textile Society of America Symposium Proceedings* (2012): 1–8.

İpek, Selin. "European Influences on Eighteenth-Century Ottoman Imperial Fashion." In *Ottoman Empire and European Theatre Vol. I The Age of Mozart and Selim III (1756–1808)*, edited by Michael Hüttler and Hans Ernst Weidinger, 695–719. Vienna: Hollitzer Verlag, 2013.

İrepoğlu, Gül. "Vanmour and Levni: Two Faces of the Mirror." In *An Eyewitness of the Tulip Era*, edited by Eveline Sint Nicolaas, Duncan Bull, Günsel Renda, and Gül İrepoğlu, 73–101. Istanbul: Koç University Press, 2003.

Jansen, M. Angela. "Fashion and the Phantasmagoria of Modernity: An Introduction to Decolonial Fashion Discourse." *Fashion Theory* 24, no. 6 (2020): 815–36.

Jasienski, Adam. "A Savage Magnificence: Ottomanizing Fashion and the Politics of Display in Early Modern East-Central Europe." *Muqarnas* 31, no. 1 (2014): 173–205.

Jeffares, Neil. "The Dictionary of Pastellists before 1800." *Pastels & Pastellists*. Accessed March 22, 2021. http://www.pastellists.com/.

Jenkins, Hester Donaldson. *Behind Turkish Lattices. The Story of a Turkish Woman's Life*. London: Chatto & Windus, 1911.

Jirousek, Charlotte A. "The Transition to Mass Fashion System Dress in the Later Ottoman Empire." In *Consumption Studies and the History of the Ottoman Empire, 1550–1922, An Introduction*, edited by Donald Quataert, 201–41. Albany: State University of New York Press, 2000.

Jirousek, Charlotte A., and Sara Catterall. *Ottoman Dress and Design in the West. A Visual History of Cultural Exchange*. Bloomington: Indiana University Press, 2019.

Johnston, Lucy. *19th-Century Fashion in Detail*. London: Thames and Hudson, 2016.

Johnstone, Pauline. *Turkish Embroidery*. London: Victoria and Albert Museum, 1985.

Juhasz, Esther, ed. *Sephardi Jews in the Ottoman Empire, Aspects of Material Culture*. Jerusalem: Israel Museum, 1990.

Juhasz, Esther. *The Jewish Wardrobe. From the Collection of the Israel Museum, Jerusalem*. Jerusalem: Israel Museum, 2012.

Kaiser, Susan. *The Social Psychology of Clothing: Symbolic Appearances in Context*. New York: Fairchild Publications, 1998.

Karaca, Nilay. "The Making of Gülhane Park: From Royal Gardens to Public Spaces in Late Ottoman Istanbul." In *Spectacle, Entertainment, and Recreation in Late Ottoman and Early Turkish Republican Cities*, edited by Nilay Karaca and Seda Kula. Bristol: Intellect, 2023.

Karaman, Tuğba. "Recasting Late Ottoman Women: Nation, Press and Islam (1876–1914)." Phd diss., University of Manchester, 2016.

Karamürsel, Ceyda. "Ottoman Slavery as a Tool for Historical Analysis: A Review of Recent Literature." *New Perspectives on Turkey* 50 (2014): 193–203.

Karamürsel, Ceyda. "Shiny Things and Sovereign Legalities: Expropriation of Dynastic Property in the Late Ottoman Empire and Early Turkish Republic." *International Journal of Middle East Studies* 51 (2019): 445–63.

Karamürsel, Ceyda. "Relics of an Unwanted Past: Slavery, Polygamy, and the Harem at the End of the Ottoman Empire." *Gender and History* (2023).

Karpat, Kemal H. *Ottoman Population, 1830–1914. Demographic and Social Characteristics*. Madison: University of Wisconsin Press, 1985.

Katz-Hyman, Martha B., and Kym S. Rice. *World of a Slave: Encyclopedia of the Material Life of Slaves in the United States*. Santa Barbara, CA: Greenwood, 2011.

Kaya, Gülsen Sevinç. *150 Yılın Sessiz Tanıkları; Dolmabahçe Sarayı Fotoğraf Albümleri*. Istanbul: TBMM Milli Saraylar, 2006.

Kaya, Gülsen Sevinç. *Milli Saraylar Tablo Koleksiyonu/National Palaces Painting Collection*. Istanbul: Directorate of National Palaces Administration, 2019.

Kelbaugh, Ross. "Free at Last." *Military Images Digital* (blog), August 31, 2021. https://www.militaryimagesmagazine-digital.com/2021/08/31/free-at-last/.

Keydar, Çağlar. "Imperial, National and Global Istanbul. Three Istanbul 'Moments' from the Nineteenth to Twenty-First Centuries." In *Istanbul: Living with Difference in a Global City*, edited by Nora Fisher-Onar, Susan C. Pearce, and E. Fuat Keyman, 25–37. New Brunswick, NJ: Rutgers University Press, 2019.

Kıbrıs, Barış, ed. *Istanbul: The City of Dreams*. Istanbul: Pera Museum, 2008.

Kılıç Çelikten, Havva. "Sultan Abdülmecid'in Kızı Behice Sultan'ın Hayatı (1848–1876)." MA diss., İstanbul 29 Mayıs Üniversitesi, İstanbul, 2022.

Kietzman, Mary Jo. "Montagu's Turkish Embassy Letters and Cultural Dislocation." *Studies in English Literature, 1500–1900* 38, no. 3 (1998): 537–51.

King, Steven, and Christiana Payne. "The Dress of the Poor." *Textile History* 33, no. 1 (2002): 1–8.

Knowles, Katie. "The Fabric of Fast Fashion: Enslaved Wearers and Makers as Designers in the American Fashion System." In *Black Designers in American Fashion*, edited by Elizabeth Way, 13–28. London: Bloomsbury Visual Arts, 2021.

Kocher, A. Lawrence, and Howard Dearstyne. *Shadows in Silver, A Record of Virginia, 1850–1900 in Contemporary Photographs Taken by George and Huestis Cook with Additions from the Cook Collection*. New York: Charles Scribner's Sons, 1953.

Koç, Adem. "The Significance and Compatibility of the Traditional Clothing-Finery Culture of Women in Kutahya in Terms of Sustainability." *Milli Folklor. Uluslararası Kültür Araştırmaları Dergesi* 93 (2012): 184–99.

Koç, Hüsniye. "Hanımlara Mahsus Gazete'deki Hikâyeler ve Temaşa Fikri." *Istanbul University Faculty of Letters Journal of Turkish Language and Literature* 59, no. 2 (2019): 333–61.

Koçak, Neslıhan. "Turkish Weddings: Traditions, History, Celebrating Life." *Daily Sabah*, June 18, 2023. https://www.dailysabah.com/life/turkish-weddings-traditions-history-celebrating-life/news.

Koçu, Reşad Ekrem. *Türk Giyim Kuşam ve Süslenme Sözlüğü*. Istanbul: Doğan Kitap, 1967.

Kodal, Tuğba. "Türk Resim Sanatında Düğün Konolu Resimlerin Ortak Birliktelikleri" *Idil* 7, no. 48 (2018): 939–50.

Koning, Georgette, and Els Verhaak. *New for Now, The Origin of Fashion Magazines*. Amsterdam: Rijksmuseum, 2015.

Köse, Yavuz. "Vertical Bazaars of Modernity: Western Department Stores and Their Staff in Istanbul (1889–1921)." *International Review of Social History* 54, Supplement (2009): 91–114.

Köseoğlu, Talha. "Osmanlı Modernitesinin Bir Panoraması: 19. Yüzyılda Tüketim Örüntüleri." *Karamanoğlu Mehmetbey Üniversitesi (KMÜ) Sosyal ve Ekonomik Araştırmalar Dergisi* 24, no. 43 (2022): 1005–17.

Krody, Sumru Belger. *Flowers of Silk and Gold. Four Centuries of Ottoman Embroidery*. Washington, DC: Merrell, 2000.

Krody, Sumru Belger. "Brides and Grooms: Embroidery of the Epirus Region." In *Textile Society of America Symposium Proceedings*: 425–32. 2006.

Krody, Sumru Belger, and Gillian Vogelsang-Eastwood. "The Tradition of the Bridal Trousseau." In *Berg Encyclopedia of World Dress and Fashion: Central and Southwest Asia*, 430–34. Oxford: Berg, 2010.

Kupferschmidt, Uri M. "The Social History of the Sewing Machine in the Middle East." *Die Welt Des Islams* 44, no. 2 (2004): 195–213.

Kupferschmidt, Uri M. *The Orosdi-Back Saga, European Department Stores and Middle Eastern Consumers*. Istanbul: Ottoman Bank Archive and Research Center, 2007.

Kurkdjian, Sophie. "Paris as the Capital of Fashion, 1858–1939: An Inquiry." *Fashion Theory* 24, no. 3 (2020): 371–91.

Kürkman, Garo. *Armenian Painters in the Ottoman Empire, 1600–1923*. Istanbul: Matüsalem Publications, 2004.

Lambert, Miles. *Fashion in Photographs, 1860–1180*. London: B. T. Batsford, 1991.

Landweber, Julia Anne. "Venedikli Serseriler ve Öfkeli Fransızlar: Galata'da Yaşayan Avrupalıların Milliyetçi ve Kozmopolit Reflfleksleri." *Osmanlı Araştırmaları*, 2014: 197–220.

Lansdell, Avril. *Wedding Fashions 1860–1980*. Aylesbury, Bucks: Shire Publications, 1983.

Lansdell, Avril. *Fashion a La Carte 1860–1900*. Haverfordwest: Shire Publications, 1985.

Law, Ernest. *The London Museum at Kensington Palace, Being an Historical Guide to The Palace and Its Contents, and Likewise to the Orangery Museum Annexe and Gardens*. London: Hugh Rees Ltd., 1912.

Lee, Summer. "1840—Queen Victoria's Wedding Dress." Fashion History Timeline. Accessed November 12, 2020. https://fashionhistory.fitnyc.edu/1840-queen-victorias-wedding-dress/.

Levitt, Sarah. *Fashion in Photography, 1980–1900*. London: B. T. Batsford, 1991.

Lewis, Reina. *Gendering Orientalism, Race, Femininity and Representation*. London: Routledge, 1996.

Lewis, Reina. *Rethinking Orientalism. Women, Travel and the Ottoman Harem*. New Brunswick, NJ: Rutgers University Press, 2004.

Lewis, Reina. "Veils and Sales: Muslims and the Spaces of Postcolonial Fashion Retail." *Fashion Theory* 11, no. 4 (2007): 423–41.

Lewis, Reina. "Patronage, Taste, and Power: Slave, Manumitted and Free Subjects in the Fashioning of MIddle Eastern Modernity." In *Fashioning the Modern Middle East. Gender, Body and Nation*, edited by Reina Lewis and Yasmine Taan. London: Bloomsbury Visual Arts, 2021, 71–89.

Lewis, Reina, and Nancy Micklewright. *Gender, Modernity and Liberty: Middle Eastern and Western Feminisms, a Critical Sourcebook*. London: I. B. Tauris, 2006.

Lewis, Reina, and Yasmine Taan, eds. *Fashioning the Modern Middle East, Gender, Body and Nation*. London: Bloomsbury Visual Arts, 2021.

Lewisohn, Irene. *Folk Costumes of Europe and Asia from the Collection of Irene Lewisohn*. Worcester, MA: Worcester Art Museum, 1937.

Linkman, Audrey. *The Victorians, Photographic Portraits*. London: Tauris Parke Books, 1993.

Llewellyn, Briony, and Charles Newton. *The People and Places of Constantinople. Watercolors by Amadeo Count Preziosi 1816–1882*. London: Victoria and Albert Museum, 1985.

Loche, Renee, and Marcel Roethlisberger. *L'opera Completa Di Liotard*. Milan: Rizzoli, 1978.

Lott, Emmeline. *The Governess in Egypt. Harem Life in Egypt and Constantinople*. London: R. Bentley, 1865.

Mackie, Louise W. *Symbols of Power. Luxury Textiles from Islamic Lands, 7–21st Century*. New Haven, CT: Yale University Press, 2015.

Major, John S. "Fashioning London: Clothing and the Modern Metropolis by Christopher Breward." *Fashion Theory* 9, no. 1 (2005): 117–20.

Manning, Chandra. "Contraband Camps and the African American Refugee Experience during the Civil War." *Oxford Research Encyclopedia of American History*, 2017. https://doi.org/10.1093/acrefore/9780199329175.013.203.

Manocherian, Justine. "Bridgerton's Season 3 Costumes Include Carrie Bradshaw's Favorite Shoe." *InStyle*. Accessed October 16, 2024. https://www.instyle.com/bridgerton-season-3-costume-fashion-details-8650314.

Martin, Ann Smart. "Makers, Buyers, and Users, Consumerism as a Material Culture Framework." *Winterthur Portfolio* 28, no. 2/3 (1993): 141–57.

Maskareli, Draginja. "Wedding Dresses in Serbia in the Second Half of the 19th and the Beginning of the 20th Century from the Collection of the Museum of Applied Art in Belgrade [in Serbian]." *Journal (Belgrade Museum of Applied Arts)* 7 (2011): 31–40.

Maskareli, Draginja. *Fashion in Modern Serbia*. Belgrade: Museum of Applied Arts, 2019.

Maskareli, Draginja. "Fashion in Modern Serbia: Tradition, Innovation, and Interpretation." In *Innovation and Fashion: Proceedings of the ICOM Costume Committee Annual Meeting*, edited by Elise Breukers. Utrecht, The Netherlands: International Council of Museums, 2020.

Maskareli, Draginja. *The Fashion World of the Kalef Family*. Belgrade: Museum of Applied Arts, 2022.

Maskareli, Draginja, and Dušan Otašević. "Bindallı Dress of Poleksija Stanković from Mušutište." In *Serbian Artistic Heritage in Kosovo and Metohija. Identity, Significance, Vulnerability*, edited by Dušan Otašević: 513. Belgrade: Serbian Academy of Sciences and Arts, 2017.

Mavi Boncuk Cornucopia of Ottomania and Turcomania. "Empress Eugénie/Memories of İstanbul," June 3, 2004. http://maviboncuk.blogspot.com/2004/06/empress-eugnie-memories-of-istanbul.html.

McBride, Theresa M. "A Woman's World: Department Stores and the Evolution of Women's Employment, 1870–1920." *French Historical Studies* 10, no. 4 (1978): 664–83.

McKendry, Virginia. "The 'Illustrated London News' and the Invention of Tradition." *Victorian Periodicals Review* 27, no. 1 (1994): 1–24.

Metinsoy, Elif Mahir. *Ottoman Women during World War I: Everyday Experiences, Politics, and Conflict*. Cambridge: Cambridge University Press, 2017.

Metinsoy, Elif Mahir. "Women's Changing Lives and the Evolution of Fashion from the Ottoman Empire to the Turkish Republic." In *Elegance from Past to Future, Women's Costume from the Late Ottoman Empire to the Early Republican Era*, edited by Hülya Bilgi: 41–73. Istanbul: Vehbi Koç Vakfı, Sadberk Hanım Muzesi, 2023.

Micklewright, Nancy. "Looking at the Past: Nineteenth Century Images of Constantinople as Historic Documents." *Expedition Magazine* 32, no. 1 (1990): 24–32.

Micklewright, Nancy. *A Victorian Traveler in the Middle East: The Photography and Travel Writing of Annie Lady Brassey*. Burlington, VT: Ashgate, 2003.

Micklewright, Nancy. "Harem/House/Set: Domestic Interiors in Photography from the Late Ottoman World." In *Harem Histories. Envisioning Places and Living Spaces*, edited by Marilyn Booth, 239–60. Durham, NC: Duke University Press, 2010.

Micklewright, Nancy. "Orientalism and Photography." In *The Poetics and Politics of Place. Ottoman Istanbul and British Orientalism*, edited by Zeynep Inankur, Reina Lewis, and Mary Roberts, 99–114. Istanbul: Pera Museum, 2011.

Micklewright, Nancy. "Alternative Histories of Photography in the Middle East." In *Photography's Orientalism: New Essays on Colonial Representation*, edited by Ali Behdad and Luke Gartlan, 75–92. Los Angeles: Getty Research Institute, 2013.

Micklewright, Nancy. "Clothes Make the Man." *Ars Orientalis* 47 (2017): 6–17.

Micklewright, Nancy. "Fashion and the Camera: Istanbul in the Late Ottoman Empire." In *Fashioning the Modern Middle East, Gender, Body and Nation*, edited by Reina Lewis and Yasmine Taan, 19–44. London: Bloomsbury Visual Arts, 2021.

Miles, Tiya. "Packed Sacks and Pieced Quilts: Sampling Slavery's Vast Materials." *Winterthur Portfolio* 54, no. 4 (2020): 205–22.

Miles, Tiya. *All That She Carried: The Journey of Ashley's Sack, a Black Family Keepsake*. New York: Random House, 2022.

Miller, Michael B. *The Bon Marche: Bourgeois Culture and the Department Store, 1869–1920*. Princeton, NJ: Princeton University Press, 1981.

Mitsi, Efterpi. "Private Rituals and Public Selves: The Turkish Bath in Women's Travel Writing." In *Inside Out, Women Negotiating, Subverting, Appropriating Public and Private Space*, edited by Teresa Gomez Reus and Aranzazu Usandizaga, 47–63. Leiden: Brill, 2008.

Montagu, Mary Wortley. *Letters of the Right Honourable Lady Mary Wortley Montagu; Written during Her Travels in Europe, Asia and Africa to Persons of Distinction, Men of Letters, &c. in Different Parts of Europe*. London: Thomas Martin, 1790.

Moors, Annelies, and Emma Tarlo. "Introduction." *Fashion Theory* 11, nos. 2–3 (2007): 133–41.

Morrow, Lisa. "Turkish Wedding Traditions." *Insideoutinistanbul* (blog), March 4, 2014. https://www.insideoutinistanbul.com/turkish-weddings-2/.

Müller, Mrs. Max. *Letters from Constantinople*. London: Longmans, Green and Company, 1897.

Murphy, Devla. *Embassy to Constantinople. The Travels of Lady Mary Wortley Montagu*. London: Century Hutchinson, 1988.

Najmabadi, Afsaneh. "The Photography, the Dress and the Conjugalization of the Family." In *Fashioning the Modern Middle East, Gender Body and Nation*, edited by Reina Lewis and Yasmine Taan, 175–93. London: Bloomsbury Visual Arts, 2021.

Neave, Dorina L. *Twenty-Six Years on the Bosphorus*. London: Grayson & Grayson, 1933.

Necipoğlu, Gülru. *Architecture, Ceremonial, and Power: The Topkapi Palace in the Fifteenth and Sixteenth Centuries*. Cambridge, MA: MIT Press, 1992.

Nefedova, Olga. *A Journey into the World of the Ottomans: The Art of Jean-Baptiste Vanmour (1671–1737)*. Milan: Skira, 2009.

Nelson, Steven. "Decolonization." *October* 174 (2020): 89.

Nicklas, Charlotte, and Annebella Pollen, eds. *Dress History. New Directions in Theory and Practice*. London: Bloomsbury Academic, 2015.

Nicklas, Charlotte, and Annebella Pollen. "Dress History Now: Terms, Themes and Tools." In *Dress History. New Directions in Theory and Practice*, edited by Charlotte Nicklas and Annebella Pollen, 1–14. London: Bloomsbury Academic, 2015.

Nolan, Erin Hyde. "You Are What You Wear: Ottoman Costume Portraits in the Elbise-i Osmaniyye." *Ars Orientalis* 47 (2017): 178–209.

Nordtorp-Madson, Michelle. "Wedding Costume." In *The Berg Companion to Fashion*, edited by Valerie Steele 720–23. Oxford: Bloomsbury Academic, 2010.

Oğuz, Mustafa. "Hürrem modası." *Milliyet*, October 6, 2012. https://www.milliyet.com.tr/gundem/hurrem-modasi-1607470.

Okumuşö Evun. "Gelinlik." *100 SENE 100 NESNE* (blog), May 1, 2022. https://100sene100nesne.com/gelinlik/.

olegcassini.com.tr. "Kına Gecesi Nedir? Gelenekler Nelerdir? En Kapsamlı Rehber," August 9, 2023. https://olegcassini.com.tr/blog/kina-gecesi-nedir-gelenekler-nelerdir-en-kapsamli-rehber.

O'Neil, Mary Lou. "You Are What You Wear: Clothing/Appearance Laws and the Construction of the Public Citizen in Turkey." *Fashion Theory* 14, no. 1 (2010): 65–81.

Os, Nicole A. N. M. Van. "Ottoman Women's Organizations: Sources of the Past, Sources for the Future." *Islam and Christian–Muslim Relations* 11, no. 3 (2000): 369–83.

Os, Nicole A. N. M. Van. "Women's Mobilization for War (Ottoman Empire/Middle East)." 1914–1918-Online (WW1) Encyclopedia, July 16, 2018. https://encyclopedia.1914-1918-online.net/article/womens-mobilization-for-war-ottoman-empire-middle-east/.

Osman, Hamdi Bey, and Marie de Launay. *Les Costumes Populaires de La Turquie En 1873*. Istanbul: Levant Times & Shipping Gazette, 1873.

Osmanoğlu, Ayşe. *Babam Sultan Abdülhamid (Hatıralarım)*. Istanbul: Selçuk Press, 1994.

Osmanoğlu, Ayşe. *The Gilded Cage on the Bosphorus*. London: Hanedan Press, 2020.

Osmanoğlu, Ayşe. *A Farewell to Imperial Istanbul. The Ottomans, Story of a Family*. London: Hanedan Press, 2024.

Ovadya, Silvyo. *Osmanlı'da Yahudi Kıyafetleri/Jewish Costumes in the Ottoman Empire*. Istanbul: Gözlem Sanat Gallerisi, 2000.

"Overlooked No More: Mihri Rassim, Feminist Artist in the Ottoman Empire." *New York Times*. September 12, 2019, sec. Obituaries. https://www.nytimes.com/2019/09/12/obituaries/mihri-rassim-overlooked.html.

Öndin, Nilüfer. *Halil Paşa (1852–1939)*. Istanbul: Hayalperest Yayınevi, 2022.

Öz, Tahsin. *Turkish Textiles and Velvets: XIV–XVI Centuries*. Ankara: Turkish Press, Broadcasting and Tourist Department, n.d.

Özdamar, Esen Gokce. "The Transformation of Tobacco Factories and Depots in İstanbul Waterfront." *Changing Societies & Personalities* 6 (2022): 397–430.

"'Özel Koleksiyonlardan Özel Eserler' sergisi!" *Habertürk*, April 16, 2018. https://www.haberturk.com/ozel-koleksiyonlardan-ozel-eserler-sergisi-1921263.

Özen, Saadet. "The Visual Making of the Harem." *Art in Translation* 9, no. sup. 1 (2017): 51–58.

Özgül, M. Kayahan. "The Effects of Periodicals on Istanbul Culture." *History of Istanbul*, 7(2019). Accessed May 7, 2024. https://istanbultarihi.ist/613-the-effects-of-periodicals-on-istanbul-culture.

Özlü, Nilay. "Single p(a)Lace, Multiple Narratives. The Topkapı Palace in Western Travel Accounts from the Eighteenth to the Twentieth Century." In *The City in the Muslim World Depictions by Western Travel Writers*, edited by Mohammad Gharipour and Nilay Özlü, 168–88. London: Routledge, 2015.

Özlü, Nilay. "From Imperial Palace to Museum: The Topkapı Palace during the Long Nineteenth Century/İmparatorluk Sarayından Müzeye: Uzun On Dokuzuncu Yüzyılda Topkapı Sarayı," PhD diss., Boğaziçi University, Istanbul, 2018.

Özlü, Nilay. "'Barbarous Magnificence in Glass Cases': The Imperial Treasury and Ottoman Self-Display at the Topkapı Palace." *Muqarnas* 39, no. 1 (2022): 153–92.

Öztuncay, Bahattin. *The Photographers of Constantinople: Text & Photographs*. Istanbul: Aygaz, 2003.

Öztuncay, Bahattin. *Hanedan ve Kamera, Osmanlı Sarayından Portreler/Dynasty and Camera. Portraits from the Ottoman Court*. İstanbul: Aygaz, 2010.

Öztuncay, Bahattin. "The Origins and Development of Photography in Istanbul." In *Camera Ottomana. Photography and Modernity in the Ottoman Empire 1840–1914*, edited by Zeynep Çelik and Edhem Eldem, 66–105. Istanbul: Koç University Press, 2015.

Özyiğit, Halil. "1928 Yılında Halil Paşa İle Hayatı ve Sanatı Üzerine Yapılan Bir Söyleşi." In *Sanat Göstergeler/Artistic Indicators*, edited by Kıymet Giray, 99–112. Ankara: Ankara Universitesi Basımevi, 2013.

Paine, Carolyn. *Tent and Harem. Notes of an Oriental Trip*. New York: Appleton, 1859.

Pardoe, Julia. *The City of the Sultan, and, Domestic Manners of the Turks in 1836*. London: Henry Colburn, 1837.

Pardoe, Julia. *The Beauties of the Bosphorus*. London: George Virtue, 1838.

Peers, Juliette. "Empress Eugénie and the Arts; Impressionism, Fashion, and Modernity." *Fashion Theory* 17, no. 4 (2013): 513–26.

Peirce, Leslie. *The Imperial Harem. Women and Sovereignty in the Ottoman Empire*. Oxford: Oxford University Press, 1993.

Peirce, Leslie. *A Spectrum of Freedom. Captives and Slaves in the Ottoman Empire*. Budapest: Central European University Press, 2021.

Pera Museum. "Witness of His Time: Fausto Zonaro," September 17, 2021. https://www.peramuzesi.org.tr/blog/zamaninin-tanigi-fausto-zonaro/1568.

Perry, Lara. "The Carte de Visite in the 1860s and the Serial Dynamic of Photographic Likeness." *Art History* 35, no. 4 (2012): 728–49.

Phillips, Amanda. "Little Known Ottoman-Period Cotton and Linen Textiles in Oxford's Ashmolean Museum." In *Proceedings from the 13th International Congress of Turkish Art, Budapest*, edited by Geza David and Ibolya Gerelyes, 593–607. Budapest: Hungarian National Museum: 2009.

Phillips, Amanda. "The Historiography of Ottoman Velvets." *Journal of Art Historiography* 6 (2012): 1–26.

Phillips, Amanda. "A Material Culture: Ottoman Velvets and Their Owners, 1600–1750." *Muqarnas* 31, no. 1 (2014): 151–72.

Phillips, Amanda. *Everyday Luxuries. Art and Objects in Ottoman Constantinople, 1600–1800*. Dortmund, Germany: Verlag Kettler, 2016.

Bibliography

Phillips, Amanda. "The Localisation of the Global: Ottoman Silk Textiles and Markets, 1500–1790." In *Threads of Global Desire: Silk in the Pre-Modern World*, edited by Dagmar Schafer, Giorgio Riello, and Luca Molà, 103–23. Woodbridge, UK: Boydell Press, 2018.

Phillips, Amanda. *Sea Change. Ottoman Textiles between the Mediterranean and the Indian Ocean*. Oakland: University of California Press, 2021.

Piper, Brian, John Edwin Mason, Carla Williams, and Russell Lord. *Called to the Camera, Black American Studio Photographers*. New Orleans: New Orleans Museum of Art, 2023.

Plunkett, John. "Of Hype and Type: The Media Making of Queen Victoria 1837–1845." *Critical Survey* 13, no. 2 (2001): 7–25.

Plunkett, John. "Celebrity and Community: The Poetics of the Carte-de-Visite." *Journal of Victorian Culture* 8, no. 1 (2003): 55–79.

Quataert, Donald. *Manufacturing and Technology Transfer in the Ottoman Empire 1800–1914*. Istanbul: Isis Press, 1992.

Quataert, Donald. "Clothing Laws, State and Society in the Ottoman Empire, 1720–1829." *International Journal of Middle East Studies* 29 (1997): 403–25.

Quataert, Donald, ed. *Consumption Studies and the History of the Ottoman Empire, 1550–1922, An Introduction*. Albany: State University of New York Press, 2000a.

Quataert, Donald. *The Ottoman Empire, 1700–1922*. Cambridge: Cambridge University Press, 2000b.

Renard, Alexis, and Frederic Hitzel. *Turkophilia Revealed/Ottoman Art in Private Collections*. Paris: Sotheby's: 2011.

Renda, Günsel. *A History of Turkish Painting*. Seattle: University of Washington Press, 1988.

Renda, Günsel, ed. *Woman in Anatolia. 9000 Years of the Anatolian Woman*. Istanbul: Ministry of Culture, 1993.

Renda, Günsel, and Zeynep İnankur. *Portraits from the Empire*. Istanbul: Pera Museum, 2005.

Ribeiro, Aileen. "The Beauty of the Particular: Dress in Liotard's Images of Women." In *Jean-Etienne Liotard 1702–1789*, edited by Christopher Baker, William Hauptman, and Mary-Anne Stevens, 34–41. London: Royal Academy of the Arts, 2015.

Ritter, Markus, and Staci G. Scheiwiller. *The Indigenous Lens?: Early Photography in the Near and Middle East*. Berlin: Walter de Gruyter GmbH, 2017.

Roberts, Mary. *Intimate Outsiders. The Harem in Ottoman Art and Travel Literature*. Durham, NC: Duke University Press, 2007.

Roberts, Mary. *Istanbul Exchanges. Ottomans, Orientalists, and Nineteenth Century Visual Culture*. Oakland: University of California Press, 2015.

Rocamora, Agnès. "The Datafication and Quantification of Fashion: The Case of Fashion Influencers." *Fashion Theory* 26, no. 7 (2022): 1109–33.

Roeber, Catharine Dann, Jennifer Van Horn, and Jonathan Michael Square. "Editor's Introduction." *Winterthur Portfolio* 55, no. 1 (2021): 1–8.

Rogers, J. M., Hülya Tezcan, and Selma Delibaş. *The Topkapi Saray Museum Costumes, Embroideries and Other Textiles*. Boston: Little, Brown, 1986.

Rolley, Katrina, and Catherine Aish. *Fashion in Photography, 1900–1920*. London: B. T. Batsford, 1992.

Rothman, E. Natalie. "Visualizing a Space of Encounter: Intimacy, Alterity, and Trans-Imperial Perspective in an Ottoman-Venetian Miniature Album." *Osmanlı Araştırmaları/Journal of Ottoman Studies* XL (2012): 39–80.

Rothstein, Natalie. *From East to West: Textiles from G. P. and J. Baker*. London: Victoria and Albert Museum, 1984.

Roxburgh, David J. "November 1869: The Suez Canal Inauguration." In *Making Modernity: Art and Architecture in the Nineteenth-Century Islamic Mediterranean*, edited by Margaret S. Graves and Alex Dika Seggerman, 234–55. Bloomington: Indiana University Press, 2022.

Russell, William Howard. *A Diary in the East: During the Tour of the Prince and Princess of Wales*. London: Routledge, 1869.

Rüstem, Ünver. "Dressing the Part: Ottoman Self-Representation in the Age of Orientalism." Presented at The Objects of Orientalism, The Clark, April 29, 2016. https://www.academia.edu/29741669/Dressing_the_Part_Ottoman_Self_ Representation_in_the_Age_of_Orientalism.

Rüstem, Ünver. "The Spectacle of Legitimacy: The Dome-Closing Ceremony of the Sultan Ahmed Mosque." *Muqarnas* 33, no. 1 (2016): 253–344.

Ryzova, Lucie. "The Image sans Orientalism Local Histories of Photography in the Middle East." *Middle East Journal of Culture and Communication* 8 (2015): 159–71.

Sakaoğlu, Necdet. "Edhemağalar Ailesi, Amasra'da Beş Kuşaklık Bir Konak." In *Cumhuriyet'in Aile Albümleri*, edited by Oya Baydar and Feride Çiçekoğlu, 38–59. Istanbul: Tarih Vakfı Yayınları, 1998.

Salt. "Mihri: Nomadic Painter of Modern Times/SALT," March 2019. https://saltonline.org/tr/1956/mihri-modern-zamanlarin-gocebe-ressami.

Sandıkcı, Özlem, and Güliz Ger. "Constructing and Representing the Islamic Consumer in Turkey." *Fashion Theory* 11, nos. 2–3 (2007): 189–210.

Saz Hanımefendi, Leyla. *The Imperial Harem of the Sultans Daily Life at the Cirağan Palace during the 19th Century*. Istanbul: PEVA Publications, 1994.

Scarce, Jennifer. "Turkish Fashion in Transition." *Costume* 14 (1980): 144–67.

Scarce, Jennifer. *Women's Costume of the Near and Middle East*. London: Unwin Hyman, 1987.

Scarce, Jennifer. "Principles of Ottoman Turkish Costume." *Costume* 22 (1988): 13–31.

Schick, Leslie Meral. "The Place of Dress in Pre-Modern Costume Albums." In *Ottoman Costumes from Textile to Identity*, edited by Suraiya Faroqhi and Christoph K. Neumann, 93–101. Istanbul: Eren, 2004.

Schick, İrvin Cemil. "Erotica, Ottoman." In *The Encyclopaedia of Islam*, Vol. 3. Leiden: Brill (2018): 28–38.

Schick, İrvin Cemil, and Gizem Tongo. "Turquerie." *Pera Museum Blog*. Accessed April 15, 2020. https://www.academia.edu/42652665/Turquerie.

Schick, İrvin Cemil. "Between the Abstraction of Miniatures and the Literalism of Photography: Amateur Erotica in Early Twentieth-Century Turkey." *Anthropology of the Contemporary Middle East and Central Eurasia* 5 & 6 (2021): 1–26.

Scott, Joan W., and Louise A. Tilly. "Women's Work and the Family in Nineteenth-Century Europe." *Comparative Studies in Society and History* 17, no. 1 (1975): 36–64.

Segev, Ronen. "The Late Ottoman Era and Its Legacy for Nursing in Turkey." *Turkish Studies* 25, no. 2 (2024): 352–65.

Selen, Eser, and Mary Lou O'Neil. "'I Am Here': Women Workers' Experiences at the Former Cibali Tekel Tobacco and Cigarette Factory in Istanbul." *Gender, Place & Culture* 24, no. 8 (2017): 1165–84.

Seth, Radhika. "The 'Bridgerton' Bonnet-Ban and Every Intricate Detail Behind Its Gaudy, Decadent Costumes." *British Vogue*, December 24, 2020. https://www.vogue.co.uk/arts-and-lifestyle/article/bridgerton-costume-designer.

Severa, Joan. *Dressed for the Photographer. Ordinary Americans and Fashion, 1840–1900*. Kent, Ohio: Kent State University Press, 1995.

Shaarawi, Huda. *Harem Years. The Memoirs of an Egyptian Feminist*. New York: Feminist Press at the City University of New York, 1986.

Shaw, Stanford J. "The Population of Istanbul in the Nineteenth Century." *International Journal of Middle East Studies* 10, no. 2 (1979): 265–77.

Shaw, Stanford J., and Ezel Kural Shaw. *History of the Ottoman Empire and Modern Turkey. Vol. II Reform, Revolution and Republic. The Rise of Modern Turkey, 1808 1975*. Cambridge: Cambridge University Press, 1977.

Shaw, Wendy. "Museums and Narratives of Display from the Late Ottoman Empire to the Turkish Republic." *Muqarnas* 24 (2007): 253–79.

Shaw, Wendy. "National Museums in the Republic of Turkey: Palimpsests within a Centralized State," in *Building National Museums in Europe 1750–2010*, edited by Peter Aronsson and Gabriella Elgenius (Bologna: Linköping University Electronic Press, 2011a), 925–51.

Shaw, Wendy. *Ottoman Painting, Reflections of Western Art from the Ottoman Empire to the Turkish Republic*. London: I. B. Tauris, 2011b.

Sheppard, Francis. *The Treasure of London's Past, An Historical Account of the Museum of London and Its Predecessors, The Guildhall Museum and the London Museum*. London: HMSO, 1991.

Shinkle, Eugenie. "The Feminine Awkward: Graceless Bodies and the Performance of Femininity in Fashion Photographs." *Fashion Theory* 21, no. 2 (2017): 201–17.

Sint Nicolaas, Eveline, Duncan Bull, and Günsel Renda. *The Ambassador, the Sultan and the Artist. An Audience in Istanbul*. Amsterdam: Rijksmuseum, 2003.

Sint Nicolaas, Eveline, Duncan Bull, Günsel Renda, and Gül İrepoğlu. *Jean-Baptiste Vanmour. An Eyewitness of the Tulip Era*. Amsterdam: Rijksmuseum, 2003.

Slade, Toby, and M. Angela Jansen. "Letter from the Editors: Decoloniality and Fashion." *Fashion Theory* 24, no. 6 (2020): 809–14.

Smallwood, Valerie. "Women's Education in Turkey (1860–1950) and Its Impact upon Journalism and Women's Journals." PhD diss., School of Oriental and African Studies, University of London, 2002.

Smentek, Kristel. "Looking East: Jean-Étienne Liotard, the Turkish Painter." *Ars Orientalis* 39 (2010): 84–112.

Sokol, Laurie. "Irene Lewisohn." Jewish Women's Archive. Accessed March 23, 2021. https://jwa.org/encyclopedia/article/lewisohn-irene.

Special Correspondence. "The London Museum Has Many Treasures; New Institution Opened by the King Starts with Unique Collections." *New York Times*, April 7, 1912. https://www.nytimes.com/1912/04/07/archives/the-london-museum-has-many-treasures-new-institution-opened-by-the.html.

Square, Jonathan Michael. "Slavery's Warp, Liberty's Weft: A Look at the Work of Eighteenth and Nineteenth-Century Enslaved Fashion Makers and Their Legacies." In *Black Designers in American Fashion*, edited by Elizabeth Way, 29–46. London: Bloomsbury Visual Arts, 2021.

Square, Jonathan Michael. "The Two Harriets." *Ms. Magazine* (blog), March 1, 2022. https://msmagazine.com/2022/03/01/harriet-tubman-black-women-history-art-clothes-fashion-photography/.

Staniland, Kay, and Santina Levey. *Queen Victoria's Wedding Dress and Lace*. London: Museum of London, 1983.

Steele, Valerie. "A Museum of Fashion Is More Than a Clothes-Bag." *Fashion Theory* 2, no. 4 (1998): 327–35.

Steele, Valerie. "Museum Quality: The Rise of the Fashion Exhibition." *Fashion Theory* 12, no. 1 (2008): 7–30.

Steele, Valerie, ed. *The Berg Companion to Fashion*. London: Bloomsbury, 2010.

Stein, Sarah Abrevaya. *Making Jews Modern: The Yiddish and Ladino Press in the Russian and Ottoman Empires*. Bloomington: Indiana University Press, 2004.

Stewart, Kristen E. "Dressing Up: The Rise of Fannie Criss." In *Black Designers in American Fashion*, edited by Elizabeth Way, 71–90. London: Bloomsbury Visual Arts, 2021.

Strasdin, Kate. *Inside the Royal Wardrobe. A Dress History of Queen Alexandra*. London: Bloomsbury Academic, 2017.

Styles, John. "Dress in History: Reflections on a Contested Terrain." *Fashion Theory* 2, no. 4 (1998): 383–92.

Şahin, Emine. "İkdam Gazetesi'ndeki Efemera Örnekleri Bağlamında Osmanlı'daki Gündelik Yaşamda Modernitenin İzleri (Evidence of Modernity in Ottoman Daily Life in the Context of Examples of Ephemera in İkdam Newspaper)." In *Geçici Belgelerin Kalıcı Etkisi: I. Uluslararası Efemera Çalışmaları Sempozyumu (Permanent Impact of Transient Documents: 1st International Ephemera Studies Symposium Proceedings)*, 357–74. Ankara: VEKAM Vehbi Koç Ankara Araştırmaları Merkezi, 2020.

Tarlo, Emma. "Islamic Cosmopolitanism: The Sartorial Biographies of Three Muslim Women in London." *Fashion Theory* 11, nos. 2–3 (2007): 143–72.

Taylor, Lou. "Doing the Laundry? A Reassessment of Object-Based Dress History." *Fashion Theory* 2, no. 4 (1998): 337–58.

Taylor, Roderick. *Ottoman Embroidery*. Wesel, Germany: Uta Hülsey, 1993.

Terndrup, Alison P. "Cross-Cultural Spaces in an Anonymously Painted Portrait of the Ottoman Sultan Mahmud II." MA thesis, University of South Florida, Tampa, 2015.

Tezcan, Hülya. *19.Yy Sonuna Ait Bir Terzi Defteri. A Late 19th Century Tailor's Order Book*. Istanbul: Sadberk Hanım Museum, 1992.

Tezcan, Hülya. *Atlaslar Atlası, Pamuklu, Yün, ve İpek Kumaş Koleksiyonu. Cotton, Woolen and Silk: Fabrics Collection*. İstanbul: Yapı Kredi, 1993.

Tezcan, Hülya. "Batılılaşma Döneminde Saray Kadının Modası." *P: Sanat, Kültür, Antika* 12, Winter 98/99 (1999): 82–87.

Tezcan, Hülya. "Fashion at the Ottoman Court." *P Art, Culture, Antiques* 3 (2000a): 2–49.

Tezcan, Hülya. "Ottoman Fabric Weaving and Women's Fashion in the Eighteenth Century." *P Art, Culture, Antiques* 3, no. 18–29 (2000b): 18–29.

Tezcan, Hülya. "Furs and Skins Owned by the Sultans." In *Ottoman Costumes. From Textile to Identity*, edited by Suraiya Faroqhi and Christoph K. Neumann. Istanbul: Eren, 2004, 63–80.

Tezcan, Hülya. *Osmanlı Sarayının Çocuklarıç Şehzadeler ve Hanım Sultanların Yaşamları ve Giysileri*. Istanbul: Aygaz, 2006.

Tezcan, Hülya. *Bursa'nın İpeklisi/Silk of Bursa*. Bursa: Bursa Büyükşehir Belediyesi Kitaplağı, 2016.

Thorpe, Vanessa. "Rewriting History: How Imperfect Costume Dramas Make the Past Relevant." *The Observer*, June 27, 2021, sec. Television & radio. https://www.theguardian.com/tv-and-radio/2021/jun/27/rewriting-history-how-imperfect-costume-dramas-make-the-past-relevant.

Thys-Şenocak, Lucienne. "Women in the City." In *A Companion to Early Modern Istanbul*, edited by Shirine Hamadeh and Çiğdem Kefescioğlu, 86–113. Leiden: Brill, 2022.

Tilaver, Yıldırım. *Amadeo Preziosi Exhibition for the Love of Istanbul, 1842–1882*. Istanbul: Sultanbeyli Belediyesi, 2011.

Toledano, Ehud. *The Ottoman Slave Trade and Its Suppression*. Princeton, NJ: Princeton University Press, 1982.

Toledano, Ehud. *As If Silent and Absent. Bonds of Enslavement in the Islamic Middle East*. New Haven, CT: Yale University Press, 2007.

Tortora, Phyllis G. "History and Development of Fashion." In *Berg Encyclopedia of World Dress and Fashion, Volume 10 Global Perspectives*, edited by Joanne B. Eicher and Phyllis G. Tortora, 159–70. London: Berg, 2010.

Troutt Powell, Eve M. *Tell This in My Memory: Stories of Enslavement from Egypt, Sudan, and the Ottoman Empire*. Redwood City, CA: Stanford University Press, 2012.

Tugay, Emine Fuat. *Three Centuries, Family Chronicles of Turkey and Egypt*. Leiden: Oxford University Press, 1963.

Tuğlacı, Pars. *Osmanlı Saray Kadınları*. Istanbul: Cem Yayınevi, 1985.

Uca, M. Merve. "Inveniam Viam Aut Faciam: Sadberk Koç as a Rigorous Collector." Presented at the Artefacts and Identities Conference, Orient Institut, Istanbul, November 9, 2022.

Ulu, Cafer, and Kemal Ozden. "Minority Press and Control in the Ottoman State and the Republic of Turkey: The Example of the Armenian Press" *Journal of Global Social Sciences* 4, no. 13 (2023): 25–45.

Uluçay, M. Çağatay. *Padişahların Kadınları ve Kızları*. Ankara: Türk Tarih Kurumu Basımevi, 1980.

Ulusoy, Nilay, and Deniz Gürgen Atalay. "The Glamour of the Muhteşem Yuzyil: The Fashionable Ottoman Court in the Twenty-First Century." *Clothing Cultures* 9, nos. 1 & 2 (2023): 117–35.

Unal, R. Arzu. "Notes on Sartorial Representations of the Middle East." In *Hand Book of Middle East Women*, edited by Suad Joseph and Zeina Zaatari, 610–22. London and New York: Routledge, 2023.

Vaka Brown, Demetra. *Haremlik. Some Pages from the Life of Turkish Women*. Boston: Houghton Mifflin, 1910.

Venable, Malcom. "Dressing the Ton: What the 'Bridgerton' Costume Designers Want You to Know about the Season 3 Looks." *Shondaland*, June 17, 2024. https://www.shondaland.com/shondaland-series/shondaland-bridgerton-behind-the-scenes/a61109598/bridgerton-costume-designers-on-season-three-costumes/.

Vintilă-Ghiţulescu, Constanta, ed. *From Traditional Attire to Modern Dress: Modes of Identification, Modes of Recognition in the Balkans*. Cambridge: Cambridge Scholars Publishing, 2011.

Vintilă-Ghiţulescu, Constanta, ed. *Women, Consumption, and the Circulation of Ideas in South-Eastern Europe, 17th–19th Centuries*. Leiden: Brill, 2018.

Walker, Cameron. "Selling Style I: The History of Fashion Marketing Through the 19th Century." *Wilson College of Textiles* (blog), May 24, 2019. https://textiles.ncsu.edu/news/2019/05/selling-style-i-the-history-of-fashion-marketing-through-the-19th-century/.

Walker, Mary Adelaide. *Eastern Life and Scenery with Excursions in Asia Minor, Mytilene, Crete, and Roumania*. Leiden: Chapman and Hall, 1886.

Walkley, Christina, and Vanda Foster. *Crinolines and Crimping Irons. Victorian Clothes: How They Were Cleaned and Cared For*. London: Peter Owen Limited, 1978.

Walsh, Robert, and Thomas Allom. *Constantinople and the Scenery of the Seven Churches of Asia Minor*. London: Fisher, Son & Co., 1838.

Watson, Oliver. "The Case of the Ottoman Table." *David Collection Journal*, 3 (2010): 3–33.

Way, Elizabeth. "Introduction." In *Black Designers in American Fashion*, edited by Elizabeth Way, 1–10. London: Bloomsbury Visual Arts, 2021.

Way, Elizabeth. "A Matrilineal Thread: Nineteenth- and Early Twentieth-Century Black New York Dressmakers." In *Black Designers in American Fashion*, edited by Elizabeth Way, 46–67. London: Bloomsbury Visual Arts, 2021.

White, Charles. *Three Years in Constantinople; or Domestic Manners of the Turks in 1844*. London: Henry Colburn, 1845.

White, Shane, and Graham White. *Stylin'. African American Culture from Its Beginnings to the Zoot Suit*. Ithaca, NY: Cornell University Press, 1998.

Whitley, Zoe. "Mallarmé on Fashion: A Translation of the Fashion Magazine *La Dernière Mode*, with Commentary by P. N. Furbank and A. M. Cain." *Fashion Theory* 9, no. 4 (2005): 495–502.

Wigh, Leif. *Fotografiska Vyer Från Bosporen Och Konstantinopel/Photographic Views of the Bosphorus and Constantinople*. Stockholm: Fotografiska Museet, 1984.

Wilcox, Claire. "'Who Gives a Frock?' Valerie D. Mendes, Jean Muir and the Building of the National Collection at the Victoria and Albert Museum." *Fashion Theory* 22, no. 4–5 (2018): 435–55.

Williams, Val. "A Heady Relationship: Fashion Photography and the Museum, 1979 to the Present." *Fashion Theory* 12, no. 2 (2008): 197–218.

Wilson, Mabel O. *Begin with the Past. Building the National Museum of African American History and Culture*. Washington, DC: Smithsonian Books, 2016.

Wilson, Mark, ed. *Thomas Allom's Constantinople and the Scenery of the Seven Churches of Asia Minor*. Piscataway, NJ: Gorgias Press, 2006.

Yagou, Artemis. "Novel and Desirable Technology: Pocket Watches for the Ottoman Market (Late 18th–Early 19th c.)." *Icon* 24 (2019): 78–107.

Yalçınkaya, Fisun. "Özel Eserlerin Buluşması." *Milliyet Sanat,* April 9, 2018. http://www.milliyetsanat.com/haberler/plastik-sanatlar/ozel-eserlerin-bulusmasi/9898.

Yalçınkaya, M. Alper. "Muslims' Contributions to Science and Ottoman Identity." In *Living in the Ottoman Realm, Empire and Identity, 13th to 20th Centuries*, edited by Christine Isom-Verhaaren and Kent F. Schull, 272–83. Bloomington: Indiana University Press, 2016.

Yaman, Zeynep Yasa. *Kadınlar Resimler Öyküler, Modernleşme Sürecindekı Türk Resimde "Kadın" Imgesinin Dönüşümü/ Women Paintings Stories, Transformation of the Image of "Woman" in Turkish Painting in the Modernization Era*. Istanbul: Pera Museum, 2006.

Yanatma, Servet. "The International News Agencies in the Ottoman Empire (1854–1908)." PhD diss., Middle East Technical University, Ankara, 2015.

Yilmaz, Hale. *Becoming Turkish: Nationalist Reforms and Cultural Negotiations in Early Republican Turkey 1923–1945*. Syracuse, NY: Syracuse University Press, 2013.

Young, Arlene. "'The Rise of the Victorian Working Lady: The New-Style Nurse and the Typewriter, 1840–1900." *BRANCH: Britain, Representation and Nineteenth-Century History*, March 2015. https://branchcollective.org/?ps_articles=arlene-young-the-rise-of-the-victorian-working-lady-the-new-style-nurse-and-the-typewriter-1840-1900.

Young, Arlene. *From Spinster to Career Woman: Middle-Class Women and Work in Victorian England*. Montreal: McGill-Queen's University Press, 2019.

Zarinebaf-Shahr, Fariba. "The Role of Women in the Urban Economy of Istanbul, 1700–1850." *International Labor and Working-Class History* 60 (Fall 2001): 141–52.

Zeig, Emma Winter. "Chaotic Freedom 3." *Historic Northampton*, 2022. https://www.historicnorthampton.org/chaotic-freedom-3.html.

Zeyneb Hanoum. *A Turkish Woman's European Impressions*. Edited by Grace Ellison. Philadelphia: Lippincott, 1913.

Zilfi, Madeline C. "Whose Laws? Gendering the Ottoman Sumptuary Regime." In *Ottoman Costumes from Textile to Identity*, edited by Suraiya Faroqhi and Christoph K. Neumann, 125–41. Istanbul: EREN, 2004.

Zilfi, Madeline C. "Marriage Practices: Ottoman Empire." In *Encyclopedia of Women & Islamic Cultures*. Brill, 2009. https://referenceworks.brillonline.com/entries/encyclopedia-of-women-and-islamic-cultures/marriage-practices-ottoman-empire-EWICCOM_0183f?s.num=0&s.f.s2_parent=s.f.book.encyclopedia-of-women-and-islamic-cultures&s.q=marriage+practices+Ottoman.

Zilfi, Madeline C. *Women and Slavery in the Late Ottoman Empire, The Design of Difference*. Cambridge: Cambridge University Press, 2010.

Zilfi, Madeline C. "Women, Minorities and the Changing Politics of Dress in the Ottoman Empire, 1650–1830." In *The Right to Dress: Sumptuary Laws in a Global Perspective, c. 1200–1800*, edited by Giorgio Riello and Ulinka Rublack, 393–415. Cambridge: Cambridge University Press, 2019.

Zilfi, Madeline C. "Review of Life after the Harem: Female Palace Slaves, Patronage, and the Imperial Ottoman Court by Betül İpşirli Argıt." *American Historical Review* 127, no. 1 (2022): 566–67.

Zürcher, Erik J. *The Young Turk Legacy and Nation Building, From the Ottoman Empire to Ataturk's Legacy*. London: I. B. Tauris, 2010.

INDEX

Index